THE BOOK LOVER'S TOUR OF TEXAS

THE BOOK LOVER'S TOUR OF TEXAS

JESSIE GUNN STEPHENS

TAYLOR TRADE PUBLISHING
Dallas ✳ Lanham ✳ Boulder ✳ New York ✳ Toronto ✳ Oxford

Copyright © 2004 by Jessie Gunn Stephens

First Taylor Trade Publishing edition 2004

This Taylor Trade Publishing paperback edition of *The Book Lover's Tour of Texas* is an original publication. It is published by arrangement with the author.

All rights reserved.

No part of this book may be reproduced in any form or by any electronic or mechanical means, including information storage and retrieval systems, without written permission from the publisher, except by a reviewer who may quote passages in a review.

Published by Taylor Trade Publishing
An imprint of
The Rowman & Littlefield Publishing Group, Inc.
4501 Forbes Boulevard, Suite 200
Lanham, MD 20706

Distributed by NATIONAL BOOK NETWORK

Library of Congress Cataloging-in-Publication Data

Stephens, Jessie Gunn.
  The book lover's tour of Texas / Jessie Gunn Stephens.— 1st Taylor Trade Pub. ed.
    p. cm.
  Includes bibliographical references and index.
  ISBN 1-58979-144-4 (alk. paper)
  1. Literary landmarks—Texas. 2. American literature—Texas—History and criticism. 3. Authors, American—Homes and haunts—Texas. 4. Texas—Description and travel. 5. Texas—Intellectual life. 6. Texas—In literature. I. Title.
  PS144.T4S74 2004
  810.9'9764—dc22

                                2004004846

∞™The paper used in this publication meets the minimum requirements of American National Standard for Information Sciences—Permanence of Paper for Printed Library Materials, ANSI/NISO Z39.48-1992.

Manufactured in the United States of America.

My thanks go to editor Janet Harris, who envisioned a book about Texas books and inspired me to tackle the project . . . and then wouldn't let me get away with anything.

✭ ✭ ✭

✴ CONTENTS ✴

Foreword by Kent Biffle   ix
Introduction   xi

1 The Book Lover Tours the Panhandle's Western Plains *1*

2 The Book Lover Tours the Southern Plains *15*

3 The Book Lover Tours
       the Big Bend and Trans-Pecos *37*

4 The Book Lover Tours
       North Central Texas and the Metroplex *61*

5 The Book Lover Tours
       Central Texas and the Hill Country *95*

6 The Book Lover Tours
       San Antonio, the Brush Country, and the Rio Grande Valley . . . *121*

7 The Book Lover Tours Houston and the Gulf Coast *143*

8 The Book Lover Tours East Texas *173*

Photo Credits   187
Index   189

✳FOREWORD✳

Truth in advertising requires me to state that this book doesn't really describe a tour. It's more of a romp.

Jessie Gunn Stephens romps over the literary landscape of Texas. First, dancing across the Texas Panhandle in seven-league cowboy boots, she pauses amid the buffalo grass to pay respects to J. Evetts Haley's biographical masterpiece *Charles Goodnight: Cowman and Plainsman*, surely the best of breed.

She gambols on to encompass such fiction artists as novelist Jane Roberts Wood of Dallas, whose portrayal of the Panhandle's treeless terrain is realistic enough to put a bit of virtual grit in a reader's teeth. Author Wood's masterwork is her trilogy: *The Train to Estelline*, *A Place Called Sweet Shrub*, and *Dance a Little Longer*. Mrs. Wood demonstrates a secret of success by making a virtue of narrative understatement.

To capture the color and flavor of the grandly diverse regions of Texas, Stephens consistently introduces us to those mystery writers who best invest their plots with details of their immediate surroundings. A good example is Panhandle celebrity D. R. Meredith, who opens her *Murder by Reference* in the Panhandle-Plains Historical Museum in the Randall County university campus town of Canyon, "when someone bashes in the curator's head and leaves the corpse perched atop the skull of a triceratops on display, 'like a bull rider in some surrealistic rodeo.'"

Stephens neatly sidesteps any slanderous accusation that she may be a stuffy literary highbrow by welcoming into her campfire's glowing circle authors often consigned to the shadows: the critically battered, although popularly adored, romance writers. In the Panhandle section of her book, she introduces us to Jodi Thomas (*To Tame a Texan's Heart*) and Ronda Thompson (*Prickly Pear*).

Stephens categorizes Thomas's books as "westerns for women." Of romancer Thompson's *Prickly Pear*, Stephens writes: "Expect fireworks when blonde firebrand meets virile stranger. In cowboy boots." She delineates Ms. Thompson's *Call of the Moon* as a "contemporary paranormal romance [that] features secret tribal worlds and deadly clashes with werewolves, but all is secondary to the romance."

Authors Meredith, Thomas, and Thompson have the sand of Amarillo in their boots. So does gambler Amarillo Slim Preston, who has sadly, if factually, titled his new book *Amarillo Slim in a World Full of Fat People*.

Bounding from one bibliophilic landmark to the next, our pathfinder makes side trips to such centers of civilization as Turkey, a Hall County village where fiddler Bob Wills once owned a mailbox in which was found, along with his resin bills no doubt, letters from a faded love or two. Somehow, Stephens found a book to justify a happy-footed Book Lover's mileage to Turkey for Bob Wills Day, an annual dance-all-night street festival. She writes, "Wills's daughter Rosetta tells the story of this Texas original's life and her relationship with him in her biography, *The King of Western Swing: Bob Wills Remembered*."

Peregrinating Jessie Gunn Stephens has much to report on the Texas Panhandle, but please remember it's only the beginning of her page-turning journey through a big state. Texas has generously provided her with a half dozen additional literary regions. As she travels, she delves into the literary secrets of distinctive cities and precincts. The book's designed to fit into a motorist's glove compartment.

So, crank up the car for the big tour. Or do as I did—find an easy chair and a bag of popcorn.

—Kent Biffle, Texana Columnist, *Dallas Morning News*

✶INTRODUCTION✶

On the Road with the Texas Book Lover

This is not a book about literature. *The Book Lover's Tour of Texas* is a book about traveling through Texas and reading about what you're seeing, or about what happened in history in the place you're passing through, or about which novelists have chosen to set their works in the very city you're visiting.

Wherever you go when you tour Texas, you will step upon land described somewhere in some book by some Texan. *The Book Lover's Tour of Texas* helps you find that book. If you want to read a mystery set in the Hill Country while you're there, or a western based on real-life events in the Panhandle, or a nature guide to help you identify the birds you'll see along the Gulf Coast, tuck this resource in your luggage and keep it handy. A true Book Lover will use it over and over.

All This, and a Travel Guide, Too

The Book Lover's Tour of Texas performs another service, too. It operates like a standard travel guide to lead you to must-see attractions in each area of the state, particularly those most closely related to history and natural history. With its help you will be able to find the grave of Katherine Anne Porter, the house where Robert E. Howard lived, a bookstore where you might catch a glimpse of a famous author, and a museum dedicated exclusively to memorabilia associated with *Gone with the Wind*, both the novel and the movie. The standard attractions are covered, too. No one should miss the Johnson Space Center, for instance, or the state's selection of gigantic water parks.

> ### A QUICK TASTE OF TEXAS
>
> If you can read only a few books about Texas, you can't go wrong with these classics:
>
> *The Birds of Texas* by John L. Tveten
>
> *Lone Star Literature: From the Red River to the Rio Grande*, edited by Don Graham, foreword by Larry McMurtry
>
> *Lone Star: A History of Texas and the Texans* by T. R. Fehrenbach
>
> *Lonesome Dove* by Larry McMurtry
>
> *Roadside History of Texas* by Leon Metz (if you can have only one)
>
> *Texas Almanac, 2004*, by the Dallas Morning News
>
> *Wildflowers of Texas* by Geyata Ajilvsgi

But there are lots of guidebooks out there to tell you about those exciting places. Only *The Book Lover's Tour of Texas* takes you into the literary heart of the state. Welcome, Book Lover, and enjoy your trip.

Specialty Libraries: Using Special Collections and Research Libraries

Among the literary treasures Texas harbors is a colossal amount of primary historic material: papers of prominent citizens, oral histories, diaries, government archives, and maps, drawings, and photographs. Collections of such material, as well as rare books and original artworks, films and music, biography and genealogy, find homes in libraries around the state. All are open to the public for research for education, publication or genealogy at least part of the time, but you will want to be well prepared before you approach them.

Call ahead or peek at a web site to determine an institution's current days and hours of operation. Some of these libraries are associated with universities, and their hours are subject to frequent change. Many require an appointment. Some will want to know the nature of your research project. Be prepared to do all your work on-site, because almost never will you be allowed to take material out of the research room. Ask if you should bring pencils and paper, and find out the rules about ink pens and photocopying. By contacting the library and learning about their rules and practices, you can be prepared to make the most of your visit.

1

The Book Lover Tours the Panhandle's Western Plains

Amarillo, Canyon, Dalhart, Estelline, Lubbock, Palo Duro Canyon, Turkey

Say the word "Texas" almost anywhere around the globe and you'll conjure the image of a lanky, squinty-eyed fellow in jeans, boots and hat, instantly recognizable as the iconic "cowboy." Chances are, he lives around here somewhere. Chances are, too, that he or his forebears will figure prominently in most of the books you pick up about this area.

The history of the Plains is cows and geography, Indians and oil. And water. Cattle first brought prosperity to the Panhandle Plains and later etched an unshakable image of Texas into the minds of millions of people who would never visit here. The writers who settle around here find their inspiration in the arid beauties of the landscape and in the region's history—the brutalities of Indian battles, what it was like to cut tongues out of dead buffalo and collect them to sell for thirty cents apiece, why you don't want to herd panicked cows through a prairie fire in a high wind.

Stories from this region, fiction and nonfiction alike, tell dramatic tales, often set outside of cities and out of doors, where the endless plains and skies heighten the mythic feel of the telling. They speak of a peculiar characteristic of the people—toughness. Call it resilience or guts or stubborn stupidity; it's whatever made people first say that there is something in the harsh beauties of this land worth holding onto and whatever makes them say it today.

Cities play a role in the Panhandle's identity, too, especially in preserving and celebrating the region's colorful history. A Ranching Heritage Center in Lubbock, the American Quarter Horse Heritage Center in Amarillo, the world's largest collection of horns from longhorn steers in Big Spring, and the dependable county museums in almost every county seat work together to proclaim this region's identity to the world.

Charles Goodnight and the Ranching Heritage

Charles Goodnight would today be instantly recognized all around the world as one of those iconic cowboys. In 1875, he scrounged up a couple of thousand head of longhorns and established the first cattle ranch in West Texas. And he did it inside the high, steep walls of the second largest canyon on the continent, Palo Duro. Over the next fifty years he would put his stamp on more than a million acres of these plains and canyonlands.

In telling his story, biographer J. Evetts Haley recounts the development of the Panhandle Plains from an area dominated by Comanches and buffalo into the center for ranching and farming it had become by the time Goodnight died in 1929.

The 1936 biography, called *Charles Goodnight: Cowman and Plainsman*, relies not only on scholarship but also on interviews with the cattleman that the author recorded when his subject was in his nineties. The book is so complete and remains today so readable that no real challenger has risen to dislodge it as the authority on this great adventurer's life. Kept in print by the University of Oklahoma Press, it is the saga of one of the most remarkable men in Texas history, who was "born and bound," in Haley's words, "to be a pioneer."

Goodnight's life was literally the stuff of legend, made up of the kinds of exploits that later attained the stature of myth in print and film. When you see John Wayne pushing a herd across the Red River, or Burt Lancaster protecting settlers from slaughter by Indians, or Kevin Costner communing with the wolves, you're glimpsing the life this man really lived.

And this book captures it all. You'll find the gunfights here, the running battles with the Indians and Comancheros, the rustlers, outlaws and rangers, the horse thieves, drovers and cattle barons, and the legendary trail-leading steers like Old Blue. Most of all, you'll find the tough, smart men and women who settled this last frontier and brought the cattle industry to it.

At the time he drove his scrawny herd of longhorns into Palo Duro Canyon, Goodnight was thirty-nine years old, not yet halfway through his ninety-three years on the planet. He had been trailing cows from Palo Pinto County through Kansas and into Colorado since before the Civil War. When war came, he scouted for the rangers defending the western frontier against Indians and took part in the battle to recapture Cynthia Ann Parker, who had been captured as a child by Comanches.

His adventures with the rangers gained him intimate knowledge of the Panhandle Plains, and as soon as the war ended, he set out with his friend Oliver Loving to blaze a trail from Fort Belknap to Fort Sumner in New Mexico by way of the Pecos River. Cattle drovers get the credit these days for having opened such trails, but the trails themselves were determined by the immutable fact that cows, like armies, travel on their bellies. Not only water but grazing land must be available along the entire way. The path Loving and Goodnight marked off was so efficient that it received heavy use from many other outfits, despite the constant threat of Indian attacks along parts of the way. One such attack ended the life of Oliver Loving in 1867.

By 1870, Goodnight was a prosperous rancher, with extensive property including farmlands in southeastern Colorado. An economic downturn in 1873 sent him back to the poorhouse, where he had started. Undaunted, he gathered up what cattle he had left and drove them to Palo Duro Canyon in Texas, where he set up a ranch and then borrowed money to buy Durham bulls and start improving his cattle's bloodlines. Five years later, Goodnight had control of one and a third million acres and a hundred thousand head of cattle.

Charles Goodnight was the first to organize and use a chuck wagon and the first to use barbed wire fences in the Panhandle. He introduced Hereford bulls to Texas breeders. He made friends with the great Comanche chief Quanah Parker. Later in his life, he worked hard at preserving the remnants of the nation's buffalo herds and developing agriculture on the Plains. He died in 1929 and is buried in the community cemetery near the Panhandle village that bears his name.

Other histories of the Panhandle abound. The evocatively named *6000 Miles of Fence* by Cordia Sloan Duke and Joe B. Frantz is one of the most colorful.

That amount of fencing may seem excessive to the modern observer. But it was needed to enclose the more than three million acres of the XIT Ranch, once the largest cattle operation in the world under one fence. As a young ranch wife, Sloan realized just after the turn of the twentieth century that she was witnessing the end of a unique period. The time when the XIT had run 150,000 head of cattle over fifty-five hundred square miles was over. Sloan set out to capture, through encouraging cowboys to jot down their memories, "what it was like to have been a hand on a vanished ranch in a vanished era." In the 1960s, with help from university professor Frantz, she pulled together the contributions she had collected into a story of the cowboy life as told by those who had lived it.

The cowboys recount lurid tales of rustlers damaging calves' eyes to make them easier to control, of strangers shot on sight for suspicion of stealing, of snake whiskey and cigarette smoke and red-light girls. But they tell, too, of barbecues and fireworks and parties where "no one was killed and no one was hurt, so they all went to the dance platform and began the square dances." Replete with black and white photographs of cows, horses, windmills and cowboys, this wonderful book offers a deeply authentic taste of ranching life at the end of the nineteenth century.

Taking the professional historian's broader viewpoint, Walter Prescott Webb wrote extensively about the West from his position at the University of Texas. The fact that *The Great Frontier*, first published in 1951, was reissued in 2003 tells you something about how compelling the story is and how masterfully Webb tells it. He was the kind of scholar who heads up state historical societies and ends up in encyclopedias years after his death. Many still consider his theories, which include economic and social aspects of frontier life, indispensable to a complete understanding of West Texas and its role in the development of the nation.

A different take on the subject is provided in Frederick W. Rathjen's *Texas Panhandle Frontier*. A native of the area and history professor at West Texas A&M University, Rathjen brings a distinctive regional outlook to the subject. First published in 1973, the book was revised and reissued in 1998.

To bring the subject of ranching firmly into the twenty-first century, you will want to see *Contemporary Ranches of Texas*, written by Lawrence Clayton and full of stirring photos by master photographer Wyman Meinzer. The sixteen ranches spotlighted here are located not only in the Panhandle but in South Texas and the Trans-Pecos, too, giving readers a well-rounded understanding of how modern outfits are run in different parts of the state.

As for Fiction

The Panhandle's most famous fictional ranch hand is a floppy-eared canine called Hank the Cowdog. He is the wildly popular creation of West Texan John R. Erickson, who had to start his own publishing company to launch the now-famous dog into the hearts of millions of young readers all over the country. His first printing of two thousand copies sold out in six weeks, he started getting

"Dear Hank" letters from schoolchildren, and he knew he was on to something. Some four and a half million copies of more than forty Hank the Cowdog adventures later, Erickson and his illustrator Gerald L. Holmes keep the stories coming. They're all on CDs these days, and audio tapes, too.

Hank serves as Head of Ranch Security and mixes it up with characters like Pete the Barncat and Sinister the Bobcat, Rambo the Great Dane, Slim the Cowboy, Wallace and Junior the Buzzards, and Rip and Snort the Coyotes. His adventures sport titles like *The Case of the Halloween Ghost* and *The Case of the Midnight Rustler*, with a reading level for ages of around seven through twelve. Truth is, though, that adults often laugh as loudly at Hank's smart-alecky antics as the young'uns do.

Accounts of the wars with the Indians over this land include at least two exceptional novels. *Dying Thunder: The Fight at Adobe Walls and the Battle of Palo Duro Canyon, 1874–1875*, by Terry C. Johnston gives a riproaring account of how some thirty settlers fought off a five-day siege by Comanches at Adobe Walls, spurring the U.S. Army into action that led to the bloody battle in the Canyon. This is the seventh book in Johnston's award-winning Plainsman series. It's the sort of historically authentic fictionalization that can lead a reader eagerly on to the next volume.

Henry Chappell's *The Callings* rises from a different literary tradition, as concerned with moral issues as with action. Torture, cannibalism, racism and other brutalities remind us that much of what we think of as "the West" today was carved out of the experiences of people who knew suffering and deprivation in a harsh land.

The Train to Estelline by Jane Roberts Wood is a low-key evocation of pre–World War I West Texas, as seen through the eyes and reported through the letters of Lucinda Richards, who arrives in Estelline in 1911 at the age of seventeen to teach school. Out in its third edition in 2000, this is a novel for the generations, the kind of book that women save to give to their daughters when the time is right. It tells of an independent young woman's introduction to responsibility, love, citizenship, danger and betrayal. There is death here, by accident and by murder, by sickness and hunger. But there is beauty, too, and birth, family affection, humor, grace, and above all growth.

This novel is the first in a trilogy, but it can stand alone, despite an ending that some readers will find less than satisfying. If you prefer to have all the strands knitted together before you leave characters behind, you will be pleased to know that the story of Lucy's life continues in two more volumes, *A Place Called Sweet*

Jane Roberts Wood

Shrub and *Dance a Little Longer*. Wood never wears on the reader. All of her characters are colorful, even riveting, and Lucy continues to mature and grow and never loses her ability to laugh at herself.

Folks in these parts also enjoy the works of local author Gerald McCathern. His popular westerns include *Horns*, *Dry Bones* and *Devil's Rope*. A modern-day mystery-thriller, *Quarantine* pits old-time cowboy know-how against the evils of organized crime. Two million cows get quarantined for a disease that may have been caused by a terrorist attack, and everyone from CIA agents to Texas Rangers gets into the action.

Romance writers Jodi Thomas and Ronda Thompson live and write in Amarillo, as does the self-proclaimed "greatest gambler who ever lived," Amarillo Slim Preston. Thomas serves as Writer-in-Residence at West Texas A&M University in Canyon. She likes to set her romances in West Texas, with titles like *Beneath the Texas Sky* and *To Wed in Texas*. She writes about essentially good people, most of them with finely-tuned senses of humor, caught up in plots that forge far beyond the simple frontier romance. You might almost call her historicals "westerns for women." Frequently recognized as a leader in her field—*To Tame a Texan's Heart* and *The Tender Texan* both won Romance Writers of America's Best Historical Series Award—she keeps her fans happy by turning out warm stories with well developed characters.

Ronda Thompson's *Prickly Pear* is a steamy western romance of the "Texas was not big enough for the two of them" variety set in the Panhandle during the 1800s. Expect fireworks when blond firebrand meets virile stranger. In cowboy boots. *Call of the Moon* enters a different realm. A contemporary paranormal romance, it features secret tribal worlds and deadly clashes with werewolves, but all is secondary to the romance.

Crime novelist D. R. Meredith calls Amarillo home, too. Author of more than fifteen mystery novels set in the area, Meredith has built a fan following for her relatively low-violence, highly-plotted, sympathetically-peopled stories. In *Murder Past Due*, some book club members take a tour of famous Amarillo murder sites and end up as targets for a killer. *Murder by Reference* starts off in the famous Panhandle-Plains Historical Museum in Canyon when someone bashes in the curator's head and leaves the corpse perched atop the skull of a triceratops on display, "like a bull rider in some surrealistic rodeo."

A Gambler from Amarillo

Amarillo Slim Preston writes about himself and the modern gaming life in a colorful memoir called *Amarillo Slim in a World Full of Fat People*. Whether he's beating Willie Nelson at dominoes or Minnesota Fats at pocket pool, Slim is the master of snookery and wants you to know it. This is a fun-to-read book about a one-of-a-kind character who plays with the big boys and often wins, but don't expect to learn any poker secrets here. Slim's much too savvy to start giving away tricks of his lifelong and remunerative trade.

Natural History of the Western Plains

The people who inhabit these plains today descended from what must have been the toughest stock ever to wander into this state. They settled down in holes dug into the ground, because there was no timber with which to build cabins; learned to face and defeat the blue norther, the rattlesnake, the drought and the Comanche; and built towns and then cities and then universities with libraries.

With few great exceptions, and they are great, you can sum the geography up in one word—flat. Some parts of the Southern Plains can be described as gently rolling, but if you spend much time in the Western Plains, you're going to become very well acquainted with the horizon. The Caprock, an escarpment that marks a change from the lower plains to the upper plains, leads the traveler atop what is in actuality a giant mesa, or tableland, a geographic feature that stretches over thirty-two thousand square miles. And they don't call this kind of structure a mesa (Spanish for "table") for nothing. It is flat.

Below that mesa lies one of the wonders of the Southwest. Palo Duro, a spectacular canyon carved through colorful rock, plunges hundreds of feet into a rugged wilderness. Today, camping, horseback riding, biking and hiking opportunities draw people into two different state parks within the canyon.

To underscore your visit, have a look at a striking work about the great canyon cutting across this land, Duane Guy's *The Story of Palo Duro Canyon*. A collection

TREATS FOR BOOK LOVERS

Panhandle-Plains Historical Museum Research Center

2503 4th Avenue
Canyon 79016
806-651-2244

Open Monday through Friday, 9–12 and 1–5.

Charles Goodnight, Georgia O'Keeffe, and History of the Southwest

Library: Seventeen thousand volumes on Texas and the Southwest; historic maps, periodicals; microfilm records of Spanish explorer Coronado.

Special Collections Holdings: books, manuscripts, photographs, oral interviews, and manufacturers' trade literature.

Subjects: Early artists of Texas and the Southwest; records from the XIT and other ranches; the papers of Charles Goodnight; history of buffalo hunters and early settlers; development of the petroleum industry; history of regional agriculture; photographs showing Indians from several tribes and documenting the development of watermilling and irrigation; film footage of the JA Ranch; oral records among the earliest taken in Texas on the subjects of the frontier, the Dust Bowl, early education in the region, and Georgia O'Keeffe at West Texas State Normal College, 1916–1918; advertising literature featuring farming and oil and gas production.

Southwest Collection/Special Collections Library

Texas Tech University
18th Street and Boston Avenue
Lubbock 79409
806-742-9070

Hours vary according to university schedule. Call for information.

History, Fine Books, and Vietnam

Holdings in the University Archives: Manuscripts, books, microfilm, microfiche, videos, recordings, photographs.

Subjects: local history, county records and newspapers; Indian records; oral histories ranging in subject from agriculture and medicine to tent shows and religion; literary records and personal correspondence, and more.

Rare Books Collection

Holdings: Thirty-eight thousand manuscripts, early printed books and maps; fine bindings and limited editions; signed copies and authors' personal writings.

Subjects: nineteenth- and twentieth-century British and American literature, especially Joseph Conrad, John Donne, Walt Whitman, James Dickey and others; manuscripts of varying significance by historic figures, including Thomas Jefferson and Isaac Newton.

The Archive of the Vietnam Conflict (806-742-9010)

Holdings: books, manuscripts, microfilm.
Subjects: Vietnam, Laos, Cambodia.

of seven essays, it answers the questions visitors almost always find themselves asking about geology, archeology, paleontology, the local flora, and the human structures in the canyon.

You will sometimes hear the High Plains called the "llano estacado," or "staked plains." No one knows for certain why early Spanish explorers attached such a seemingly odd name to the area, but one attractive theory has to do with the geology of the cliff that forms part of the eastern boundary of the High Plains, called the Caprock Escarpment. In places, this landmark rises out of the earth like a shoulder-to-shoulder row of skinny red buildings and is visible for many miles. Both the early Spanish and the nineteenth-century Americans who explored this area used words like "palisades" and "stockade" as metaphors to describe what they saw.

Caprock Canyonlands: Journeys into the Heart of the Southern Plains by Dan Flores uses narrative and photographs to explore many of the environmental, historical and social issues that make these western badlands so intriguing today.

Texas is so friendly to wildflowers that they bloom even on the highest and driest plains. *Wildflowers of the Llano Estacado* by Francis L. Rose and Russell W. Strandtmann helps you identify them with 141 color photos.

Ranching Attractions in the Panhandle's Western Plains

AMARILLO

The town called Amarillo developed from a collection of buffalo-hide huts into the commercial center of the Panhandle. What you will drive into here is the heart of cowboy land, but it is also a modern city with a lot on its mind. Its population has grown from 482 in 1890 to about 175,000 today. It has a thriving two-year college and four public libraries that circulate more than two million books a year. It offers 2,323 acres of park land, thirty-two miles of jogging trails, forty-six tennis courts, sixty-five soccer fields, and two golf courses. Details are available from **Amarillo Visitor Information Center (806-374-VISIT)**, Entrance #2 at the Amarillo Civic Center, 401 S. Buchanan.

Amarillo boasts an art museum and a zoo, but don't miss the **American Quarter Horse Heritage Center (806-376-5181)**, where is celebrated every aspect, historical and modern, of this uniquely American horse. If you've just come into town from crossing the canyon country, the Caprock or the High Plains, you can see at once why the people who settled here needed a horse that was tough, canny, alert and, unlike the mustang, gentle. The West was built by men and women on the backs of such animals. The Center houses a research library, invaluable to anyone studying the history of the horse in the United States. Fine art, live demonstrations, and other exhibits honor the Quarter Horse.

If you're in town on an auction day and you'd rather look at beef cattle than rodeo horses, drop by the **Amarillo Livestock Auction** (806-373-7464) at 100 S. Manhattan. You can stroll through the facility any day and eat at the Stockyard Café, but sales are held only one day a week, so call for a current schedule. Folks move hundreds of thousands of head through here every year. The sounds, the smells, the rules of the auction, just getting that close to cows and mounts may give you a whole new appreciation for what it's like to live and work with animals, the way many of our forebears did.

If you yearn for the true cowboy experience, you may want to arrange to have **breakfast or supper out on the range** in the midst of a bunch of real cowboys swinging ropes and hefting branding irons. You will need reservations, of course, so check with the Amarillo Visitor Information Center or look at the web site of one of the companies offering this experience at www.cowboymorning.com.

Other attractions in Amarillo include **Don Harrington Discovery Center** (806-355-9547), a fifty-acre park with a planetarium, a botanical garden and a monument to the element helium, which is more abundant in this area than anywhere else in the world.

CANYON

The **Panhandle-Plains Historical Museum** (806-651-2244) on the campus of West Texas A&M University delves into the past far beyond the coming of Anglo settlers to these parts. Humans have inhabited the Panhandle for at least twelve thousand years, and this large museum, with 103,841 square feet of exhibition space, bears witness to their activities with displays devoted to archaeology, paleontology, art and history. A **special library** collecting documents important to the history of the Panhandle and the Southwest is open to researchers.

DALHART

More about the ranching industry can be found in Dalhart, about eighty miles to the north. The **XIT Historical Museum** (806-244-5390) at 108 E. Fifth Street commemorates a period when the largest ranch in the world under one fence flourished here. On the first Thursday, Friday and Saturday of August each year, the **XIT Rodeo and Reunion** features both amateur and professional events, plus a parade and street festival (806-249-5646).

Lubbock
A city of almost two hundred thousand today, Lubbock grew from its early role as the hub of cattle empires into a farming community and then into a transportation and distribution center for the High Plains. Wherever you drive near Lubbock, cotton fields surround you, yielding three million bales a year. Factories turn cottonseed into animal feed or oil, feedlots fatten beef cattle, and Texas Tech University draws education seekers from all over the state. You will find the city's Convention and Visitors Bureau (800-692-4035 or 806-747-5232) at 1301 Broadway.

Like other modern cities, Lubbock supports the historical and fine arts with galleries and museums. Wineries with tasting rooms lend it an even more sophisticated air. A **Ranching Heritage Center** (806-742-0498) recreates homes, schools and work buildings of different eras in the history of ranching. The **American Wind Power Center** (806-747-8734) showcases the role of the windmill in the settling of the west. But there are surprising caches of literary treasure here, too.

Cowboy poets abound here, especially during the annual **National Cowboy Symposium and Celebration** (806-795-2455), usually held just after Labor Day. People who write, people who publish, and people who read poetry, novels, histories, and other books gather with musicians, artists and storytellers. Many of them will be competing for the American Cowboy Culture Awards, including kudos for Best Western Writing and Best Cowboy Poetry.

Natural History Attractions of the Panhandle's Western Plains

Today, wide, straight, flat roads make travel seem easy all over these plains. Indeed, on the main highways, you're rarely more than an hour away from the next hamburger, cold drink and tank of gas. But many empty miles separate the settlements once you leave the major highways. A good habit to cultivate when you travel in these parts is to keep an eye on the gas gauge. Another is to tuck some drinking water in among the gear littering your back seat.

One of the state's most **scenic trails** is etched by State Highway 207 between Claude and State Highway 86 just west of Silverton. Another will lead you east from Silverton on State Highway 86 to Quitaque (kitty-kway) and then north on FM 1065 to rugged **Caprock Canyons State Park and Trailway** (800-792-1112).

You can access **Palo Duro Canyon State Park** (806-488-2227) by taking State Highway 217 twelve miles east of Canyon. Musical and other events are staged at the **Outdoor Epic Theater** (806-655-2181) during the warmer months.

Other natural attractions include **Buffalo Lake National Wildlife Refuge** south of Umbarger on FM 168, with both walking and auto trails for birdwatching; **Lake Meredith** near Dumas, offering water sports; the **Croton Breaks** canyon region outside Dickens; and **Muleshoe National Wildlife Refuge**, south of Muleshoe on State Highway 214.

One Last Word

Many of the features of this land that tourists find most attractive have some connection with Charles Goodnight or the heritage of ranching. Others have their own unique appeal.

> *"No matter where I go I know people are going to laugh when I tell them I'm from Turkey, Texas."* —Gary Johnson, citizen

If you take State Highway 82 west out of Estelline, the village of Turkey rises on the horizon and, if it's spring, a hint of fiddles and guitars tinges the air. Turkey's population is miniscule except during the annual Bob Wills Day street festival held the last Saturday in April. Then the town swells with thousands of fans who come for a parade, barbecue, dance and concert in memory of country music great Bob Wills, who founded his Texas Playboys band here in the 1930s and introduced the world to Western Swing.

The **Bob Wills Museum** at Sixth and Lyles Streets is a collection of memorabilia of interest to the music fan, and a recently-formed heritage foundation has begun restoring historic buildings in the area. If you're interested in accommodations or eateries, call 806-423-1033 or look at the town's web site at www.turkeytexas.com.

Wills's daughter Rosetta tells the story of this Texas original's life and of her relationship with him in her biography, *The King of Western Swing: Bob Wills Remembered*.

The Reading Tour

Carlson, Paul H. *The Cowboy Way: An Exploration of History and Culture*. Lubbock: Texas Tech University Press, 2000.

———. *Empire Builder in the Texas Panhandle: William Henry Bush*. Lubbock: Texas Tech University Press, 1996.

Chappell, Henry. *The Callings*. Lubbock: Texas Tech University Press, 2002.

Clayton, Lawrence, and Wyman Meinzer, photographer. *Contemporary Ranches of Texas*. Austin: University of Texas Press, 2001.

Cochran, Mike, and John Lumpkin. *West Texas: A Portrait of Its People and Their Raw and Wondrous Land*. Lubbock: Texas Tech University Press, 1999.

Dewlen, Al. *The Bone Pickers*. Lubbock: Texas Tech University Press, 2002 (reprint).

Duke, Cordia Sloan, and Joe B. Frantz. *6000 Miles of Fence: Life on the XIT Ranch of Texas*. Austin: University of Texas Press, 1961.

Flynn, Robert. *North to Yesterday*. Fort Worth: Texas Christian University Press, 1985 (reprint).

Guy, Duane, ed. *The Story of Palo Duro Canyon*. Lubbock: Texas Tech University Press, 2001.

Haley, J. Evetts. *Charles Goodnight: Cowman and Plainsman*. Norman: University of Oklahoma Press, 1949.

Kelton, Elmer. *Hot Iron*. New York: Forge Press, 1998 (reprint).

McCathern, Gerald. *Quarantine*. Hereford, Tex.: Food for Thought Publishers, 2001.

McDonald, Walter. *All That Matters: The Texas Plains in Photographs and Poems*. Lubbock: Texas Tech University Press, 1993.

———. *The Digs in Escondido Canyon*. Lubbock: Texas Tech University Press, 1991.

Preston, Amarillo Slim, with Greg Dinkin. *Amarillo Slim in a World Full of Fat People: The Memoirs of the Greatest Gambler Who Ever Lived*. New York: HarperCollins, 2003.

Rathjen, Frederick W. *The Texas Panhandle Frontier*. Austin: University of Texas Press, 1985 (reprint edition).

Rose, Francis L., and Russell W. Strandtmann. *Wildflowers of the Llano Estacado*. Lubbock: Texas Tech University Press, 1990.

Steagall, Red, and Skeeter Hagler. *Born to This Land*. Lubbock: Texas Tech University Press, 2003.

Teichmann, Sandra Gail, ed. *Woman of the Plains: The Journals and Stories of Nellie M. Perry*. College Station: Texas A&M University Press, 2000.

Thomas, Jodi. *Beneath the Texas Sky*. New York: Zebra Books, 2001.

———. *To Wed in Texas*. New York: Berkley Publishing Group, 2000.

Thompson, Ronda. *Call of the Moon*. New York: Love Spell, 2002.

———. *Prickly Pear*. New York: Leisure Books, 2003.

Wauer, Roland H. *Butterflies of West Texas Parks and Preserves*. Lubbock: Texas Tech University Press, 2002.

Webb, Walter Prescott. *The Great Frontier*. Reno: University of Nevada Press, 2003 (reissue).

The Book Lover Tours the Southern Plains

Abilene, Archer City, Brownwood, Chillicothe, Cross Plains, Jacksboro, Quanah, San Angelo, Wichita Falls

If the Panhandle is about cowboys and cattle drives, the plains rolling south and east of Lubbock are about American Indians. Here is the place where the Comanches brought the white settlers' westward expansion to a halt and kept it at bay for forty years in some of the bloodiest fighting the frontier would see. The enforcers who would become the Texas Rangers first formed up here. The stories—of kidnap, rapine, torture and retribution—that would haunt generations after the fighting ceased were acted out here. The destruction of a proud warrior people defending their way of life was wrought among these gently rolling plains.

The Coming of the Horse

In 1598, Don Juan de Oñate brought into the country north of the Rio Grande an army of four hundred soldiers, 130 colonist families, uncounted numbers of priests, and seven thousand head of stock. The herds included three hundred mares and colts, prime samples of the tough mustang native to the arid areas of Spain. By 1700, every indigenous tribe in what would become Texas had horses of their own. A hundred years later, the Comanche people had bred vast herds of horses and had exploited them to become the leading military and economic force on the plains.

Free to follow the bison herds, able to provide fresh meat for every meal, empowered to overcome enemies less accomplished in waging war on horseback, the Comanches laid claim to the plains and held it. They put a swift end to the expansionist dreams of both the Spanish and the French and showed every inclination to do the same to the Americans moving in on them in the early part of the nineteenth century. The inevitable clash burst into all-out war in the 1830s as determined white settlers moved west, unprotected by fort or soldier, intent upon forging their way deep into Indian raiding and hunting grounds, pushing the frontier ever forward.

The Comanches saw these invading farmers and their families as easy game at first, as indeed they were to mounted warriors. Eventually, frontiersmen realized it was necessary to bring trained horsemen into the war to meet the Comanches on their own terms. Until then, they suffered, with hundreds killed, tortured, raped or captured.

But soon, settlers began to mount "ranging companies," bands of military irregulars to patrol the plains, track raiding Indians, and protect the homesteads. For forty years forts were built and armies mounted. The frontier advanced, receded, advanced again. In time, Texans adopted the Colt revolving pistol and learned to breed stronger horses. They also began systematically killing off the bison, which deprived the Indians of their economic and cultural backbone. The bloodiest fighting went on until 1875, when the war chief Quanah Parker finally gathered the remnants of his people and led them into surrender and life on the reservation.

The impact of those three hundred Spanish mares and colts still resonates today in the literature produced in this region of Texas. Comanches haunt our books, and part of their legacy is the cowboy himself, the farmer turned cowman who honed his riding skills to protect himself and his property from superior horsemen, as well as to herd his stock across the plains. Cowboy and Comanche alike inhabit our greatest stories and inspire our greatest writers.

The New "Western" Novel: Kelton, Flynn and McMurtry

To speak of the literature of the southern plains of Texas is to invoke the names of novelists Elmer Kelton, Larry McMurtry, Robert Flynn and the authors of a hundred years worth of a kind of popular novel called "the western." So many writers have set western stories on these far-reaching plains that it would take a chapter of this book to list them and their works. Among them, these West Texans created the twenty-first century's view of Texas and its past. The Indian wars, the trail drive, opening the west for settlement, and survival in a harsh land: these themes echo again and again, underscored always by the human element, the emotional price paid along the road toward modernization.

The frontier during the waning days and aftermath of the Civil War makes a dramatic setting for many of Elmer Kelton's works, the brutal clashes between Texans and Indian tribes a constant theme. One of his best novels, *The Wolf and the Buffalo,* follows two black slaves freed after the war as they join the army to fight the Comanches. Their unit is the Tenth U.S. Cavalry out of Fort Concho near San Angelo. The black men who make up that unit are called the Buffalo Soldiers by the Indians, who liken their hair to the mane of the buffalo. The stirring story is full of Indian medicine, racial conflicts, bloody fighting and the relentless threat of thirst on the dry plains.

Elmer Kelton

In a group of related novels, Kelton tells about the early Texas Rangers and their role in "resettling" Indians across the Red River onto reservations set up by the federal government. *The Buckskin Line, Badger Boy*, and *Way of the Coyote* recreate that era accurately.

Nor is Kelton reluctant to take on more modern themes. He explores the inevitable end of the open range and what it means to the cowboy way of life in *The Good Old Boys*; shows a rancher's struggle to maintain his independence while surviving the drought of the 1950s in *The Time It Never Rained*; and delves into a conflict between labor and management in *The Day the Cowboys Quit*.

Kelton's books carry his trademark historical reliability, as well as the kind of emotional impact that makes stories memorable.

Authenticity plays a role that may go unrecognized by engrossed readers with little interest in analyzing why a great read is a great read. But if Elmer Kelton says the trees growing near a certain creek were pecan trees, you can be sure that

ELMER KELTON: AMERICA'S FAVORITE WESTERN WRITER

Each year, the organization of authors called Western Writers of America bestows a Spur Award upon a novel that covers western themes and subjects. Elmer Kelton has won more of them than any other writer in history, so many, in fact, that this group of novelists, historians and other accomplished authors voted him "All-Time Best Western Author." The National Cowboy Hall of Fame has also honored him several times with its Heritage Award. He has honorary doctorates and lifetime achievement awards from prestigious universities. He also has the love and respect of the thousands of fans he's gratified in more than fifty years of writing novels about the West.

A World War II combat infantry veteran, Kelton began his writing career covering the farm and ranch news for the *San Angelo Standard-Times*, a job for which he was suited by both ranching experience and a journalism degree from the University of Texas at Austin. He plunged into the habit of winning Spur Awards in 1956, and hasn't given it up yet.

Elmer Kelton's Award-Winning Novels about Texas

1956 *Buffalo Wagons*, Spur Award for Best Western Novel of the Year, Western Writers of America

1971 *The Day the Cowboys Quit*, Spur Award for Best Western Novel of the Year, Western Writers of America

1973 *The Time It Never Rained*, Spur Award for Best Western Novel of the Year, Western Writers of America, and Western Heritage Award from National Cowboy Hall of Fame

1978 *The Good Old Boys*, Western Heritage Award from National Cowboy Hall of Fame

1980 *The Wolf and the Buffalo*, Texas Sesquicentennial Book, Texas Library Asociation

1981 *Eyes of the Hawk*, Spur Award for Best Western Novel of the Year, Western Writers of America

1987 *The Man Who Rode Midnight*, Western Heritage Award from National Cowboy Hall of Fame

1992 *Slaughter*, Spur Award for Best Western Novel of the Year, Western Writers of America

2002 *The Way of the Coyote*, Spur Award for Best Western Novel of the Year, Western Writers of America

pecan trees really grow beside that stream. He notices the details and relays them to us, the sounds of a prairie chicken, the way a horned toad moves, how you can tell whether a horse is corn-fed or grass-fed by its wind and its stamina.

His people are ordinary folks. Soldiers, cowmen, farm women, a young man heading west because his family's blackland farm will pass to his older brother and the place won't support both of them. His Indians are people, too, not movie extras, and their motives for bloodletting are always clear. That doesn't make them any less chilling when they set out to harry or attack the Texans we've been reading about. One Texan's scalp hanging from a warrior's belt, a Comanche will tell you, will do as well another.

Some of the same Comanches Kelton writes about show up as well in Larry McMurtry's *Lonesome Dove*, winner of the Pulitzer Prize for Fiction in 1986. The book begins its action so far south that raids across the border into Mexico are commonplace, but then cuts a swath across the lower plains and crosses the Canadian River heading for points north. Although McMurtry has said that this book was designed to debunk the Code of the West and demythologize the American cowboy, it has had the opposite effect. Readers are drawn to his tough, grizzled old ex-Rangers, Gus and Call, who kill bandits and Indians and keep pushing that herd, living the Code of the West and doing their part to open the frontier for the more civilized settlers who will follow. We are, in fact, willing to follow and watch them doing all those things for almost nine hundred pages.

In 1993, McMurtry returned to this set of characters (at least those who survived *Lonesome Dove*) in *Streets of Laredo*, a sequel. Then came the prequels, *Dead Man's Walk* and *Comanche Moon*, which spirited readers back to the time when Gus and Call were younger men, riding with the Texas Rangers.

Some of the books in this series have been more warmly received than others, but the cowpokes Gus and Call are as firmly ensconced in the pantheon of western characters as any ever created, and, taken together, the series forms a work of epic proportions rarely equaled in modern times.

Larry McMurtry was born in Wichita Falls and attended school in Archer City. Texan through and through, he followed the old dictum to write about what you know, and he captured the characters and conflicts of his native region with a realism that won him a large fan following throughout the nation. Wichita Falls, Archer City and other area towns figure prominently in his novels of more modern times, *Horseman, Pass By* and *The Last Picture Show* and its sequels, *Texasville* and *Duane's Depressed*.

Almost twenty years before *Lonesome Dove*, Robert Flynn wrote a trail-driving novel called *North to Yesterday*. It captured the human passion to be on the move, to seek out paths untaken. Funny and moving, with very untraditional "heroes," it won Flynn a Western Heritage Award from the National Cowboy Hall of Fame.

Flynn grew up in Chillicothe, a featureless, breeze-through hamlet on Highway 287 between Wichita Falls and Amarillo. The town is not much today except home to a few hundred folks and the ghosts of generations. And the setting, or at least its model, for Flynn's wonderful novel, *Wanderer Springs*.

At once one of the most complex and one of the most straightforward novels you will ever read, *Wanderer Springs* takes some getting used to. Flynn helps us out by providing a list of his 120 characters by way of a preface, identifying each by family descent or a salient feature of his or her life. With that many characters from three generations, and only three hundred and some pages in which to tell their stories, we know going in that those stories are going to be told fast. Flynn sets a brisk pace and never lets up. And he never wastes a word.

One character is described as "the sheriff who was given power because he looked like he had power," another as a woman "who lost the cows, her mind and her daughter," another as a man who "died in a fever epidemic and was plowed up every year," another—in what may be the best character description you're likely ever to read—as a man who was "one of the great howevers, who spent his life trying to become a human being."

And so on. Yes, it's funny. These enigmatic descriptions are borne out entirely by the stories told. But it's sad, too. There must be a literary term for the kind of writing that tells such sad things (and quite a few beautiful things) in such a funny way and makes it all sound like something you sat on your grandmother's porch and overheard, but a book like this comes from having lived among the people.

One more book about driving cattle deserves mention, this one a biography for nine- to twelve-year-old readers. *Trail Fever: The Life of a Texas Cowboy* by D. J. Lightfoot tells the true story of George Saunders who at the age of ten was riding out his first stampede and by seventeen was heading herds up and pointing them north for the long haul across the plains toward Kansas. Based on firsthand accounts first published eighty years ago, this book is fast-paced and entertaining, while maintaining a firm grip on the reality of the kind of life depicted.

Where the Indians Were

A little bit north and west of Robert Flynn country lies Copper Breaks State Park. On the Pease River near there, Cynthia Ann Parker, perhaps the most famed white captive in Texas history, was "liberated" from the Indian families with which she had lived since early childhood. She managed to take her daughter, Prairie Flower, into this new captivity with her, but she was forced to leave behind her husband, Peta Nocona, who she thought probably died in the battle, and her two sons. The oldest son was Quanah Parker.

Between them, Quanah Parker and his mother Cynthia Ann Parker have played starring roles in half a hundred books, fiction and nonfiction alike. In 1835, Cynthia Ann Parker at the age of nine was captured by Indians. She grew up with them, learned to love them, married one of them, and had his children. After twenty-five years among the people she considered her own, she was recaptured and returned to live with her blood relatives. The results were disastrous for her and the young daughter "rescued" with her. Her son, Quanah Parker, remained with the tribe and grew up to become the last great war chief of the Comanche people. He was also the leader who was able to negotiate with the white settlers when the time inevitably came that a means had to be found to move his people into the twentieth century.

Probably the most popular fictionalization of the story for the past twenty-some years has been *Ride the Wind* by Lucia St. Clair Robson. This is the kind of book that develops a fan following, with devotees who read it again every year or so. Yes, it's a romanticized version of the tale, but it's not a romance. In fact, the savagery of the attack by the Indians on Fort Parker in the first chapter may put off the reader seeking lighter entertainment. But this account is very close to that given by survivors and recorded by historians.

As Cynthia Ann's story advances, less is known about actual events and the author falls back on the devices of fiction, but fascinated readers will realize that her informed guesses about what transpired never fall very far from the truth. Her peers, Western Writers of America, were convinced enough of that to award the book their highest prize for fiction, the Spur Award, in 1983.

If an objective, painstakingly researched nonfiction account is more to your taste, you will find your needs well satisfied by Margaret Schmidt Hacker's *Cynthia Ann Parker: The Life and Legend.* Similarly, *The Last Comanche Chief: The Life and Times of Quanah Parker* by Bill Neeley will fill your need for historical detail about this last great leader, the way he and his people lived, and the adaptations they finally made to living among the white man. This is one history that moves as fast as a novel, with lots of verbatim witness accounts and colorful and lively detail. That Quanah Parker enjoyed having his photo taken is evidenced by the seventeen or so pictures of him that Neeley has rounded up for this book. Even more interesting is that many of them include the faces of some of Parker's multiple wives and children. The earliest was taken in 1880, the last in 1908.

Another well-respected biography is *Quanah Parker, Comanche Chief* by William T. Hagan, a retired history professor from the University of Oklahoma.

Lucia St. Clair Robson

Quanah Parker has cropped up in many novels, including Larry McMurtry's Pulitzer Prize–winning *Lonesome Dove*. An excellent fictional account for high school readers is *Quanah Parker: Comanche Chief* by Rosemary Kissinger.

The chronicle of the Comanche people as a whole is nowhere more completely recorded than in a fine history by T. R. Fehrenbach called *Comanches: The Destruction of a People*.

"The true human beings," Fehrenbach tells us they called themselves, even before they tamed the horse. Once astride that "engine of predatory conquest," they swept onto the Texas plains to stymie the plans for empire of Spanish and French alike and stand for most of a hundred years as a barrier against Anglo settlement in western Texas. To defeat them, the American government killed off the buffalo, turned the High Plains into a bison boneyard, and destroyed the economic underpinnings of their way of life.

From 1875, with the Indian threat diminished, the frontier advanced further in the next eight years than it had in the forty before.

The Kiowas fought as savagely and desperately as the Comanches. Led by their chief Santanta, they attacked a government wagon train near Fort Richardson in 1871. Author Cynthia Haseloff won a Spur Award for her historical novel based on these events, *The Kiowa Verdict*. Santanta was captured by troops commanded by General William Tecumseh Sherman, brought to trial in Jacksboro, and condemned to hang. After his sentence was commuted to life imprisonment and then reduced to parole, he continued to lead raids on white settlers from the reservation across the Red River. The prequel to *The Kiowa Verdict*, which Haseloff wrote the following year, is called *Santanta's Woman*. It tells the story of a white woman captured and inducted into the tribe by Kiowas; she learns to adapt well enough to live in peace with her captors.

Was the capture of women and children commonplace among the Plains Indians? According to Fehrenbach, it was an "ancient and universal" custom, a "survival measure" that helped them keep their population numbers stable. Without the extra hands brought into the tribe by the capture of young boys, the Comanches would not have been able to own and manage the enormous herds of horses that made up the wealth of the people. Torture, rape, enslavement, mutilation and murder of captives were commonplace. But so was adoption, marriage and genuine absorption into the tribe.

The families of captives were often left dead in the smoldering ruins of their frontier homesteads. There might be nothing for a captive to return to. Joining the tribe that provided food and shelter sometimes seemed the only option for captives.

When family members were left alive, as in Alan Le May's classic novel *The Searchers*, the effects were devastating. Tortured by uncertainty as to the fate of loved ones, relatives were helpless to follow across the trackless plains or, when they tried, unable to mount rescue against the numberless enemy. Le May's characters Amos Edwards and Martin Pauley refuse to give up despite the odds. After a brutal Comanche attack leaves most of their family dead and two young women taken, Amos and Marty embark on a quest that will consume years of their lives and make their names legendary among the tribes.

They quickly learn that one of the girls is dead; her long scalp is flaunted by a warrior dancing in triumph about a fire. Bent on saving the other or exacting retribution, the two men track the Indians relentlessly, carving for themselves in the process a permanent place in the lore of the West. One of Hollywood director

> ## WHAT EVER HAPPENED TO ZANE GREY?
>
> Zane Grey, the writer who first claimed the West as his own and devoted sixty-seven books to it, chose to set only a handful in Texas. Although Grey died in 1939, he still continues to be read, popular among both romance readers and fanciers of westerns. Most public libraries all over the state will boast several volumes. Among Grey's novels that take place all or in part within the Lone Star State are these:
>
> *The Trail Driver*, set partly along the Colorado River
>
> *The Lost Wagon Train*, with a dramatic crossing of the Pecos River at the legendary Horsehead Crossing
>
> *West of the Pecos*, with scenes in Langtry, Judge Roy Bean country
>
> *The Fugitive Trail*, set near the headwaters of the Brazos River
>
> *Stairs of Sand*, with scenes in Denton County
>
> *The Thundering Herd*, set unmistakably on the High Plains
>
> *The Lone Star Ranger*, restored and reissued as *Rangers of the Lone Star*, set in southwestern Texas
>
> For more on the geography of Grey's writings, well as essays about his life and work, see the fascinating web site of Zane Grey's West Society: www.zanegreysws.org.

John Ford's most absorbing films and certainly one of actor John Wayne's finest performances are embodied in the 1956 movie by the same name.

The history of the tribes that claimed the Red River Valley has been well documented, especially in two works by F. Todd Smith, *The Wichita Indians: Traders of Texas and the Southern Plains, 1540–1845* and *The Caddos, the Wichitas and the United States, 1846–1901*. Covering the time in the mid-sixteenth century when the Wichitas dominated the southern plains through the annexation of Texas to the United States, the subsequent moving of the tribes onto reservation lands, and the lives they were able to make there, these two books resound with both authority and detail.

Stories with a Lighter Touch

The whimsy of a waterfall built for tourists who come to what may be the least touristy town in Texas sets the tone for Paula Boyd's comic mystery novel, *Dead Man Falls*. She calls the city of her setting "Red River Falls," but don't let that fool you. It's Wichita Falls, not even thinly disguised. Jolene Jackson, Boyd's female sleuth, tells a fairly standard mystery tale, but with homespun humor, a keen eye for local customs, and a sharp ear for dialect. Jolene's comments on a rival's cranberry-colored workout suit gives us an example: "she looked like a mildewed bowl of art deco grapes."

An amusing and thoroughly engrossing women's novel (maybe you could call it a romance, though it offers more plot and deeper characterization than most such) is Jodi Thomas's *The Widows of Wichita County*. It's the story of five women whose husbands are all in some way involved in the oil business. When an oil rig explodes with all five of the men on it, four are killed, one survives so badly burned his identity is in dispute, and the women draw together to face the tragedies through strengthening friendships.

Romance plays a role, but it remains secondary to the character portraits of these five women. Teetering on the verge of stereotype, but never quite taking the plunge, Thomas reveals these women to us not only through their relationships to each other, but also through their relationships to clothes. One of them runs a fancy ladies' shop that doesn't deign to carry "women's sizes." Her sensibilities are offended by the thought of the beautiful lines of her expensive dresses being ruined by the lumpy figures of her two grown daughters. Another wears boxy sweaters decorated around the edges with letters of the alphabet or sweatshirts hand-decorated with Santa Claus figures. Another haunts bars and dresses like "a throwaway cowgirl." But just when you think you've pegged a character, Thomas veers away from stereotype, making for a stronger heading. I enjoyed getting to know these gals.

Thomas has been writing novels with Texas settings since 1988, most of them unabashed paperback romances and very popular with readers all over the country. Her Texas landscape is full of Wal-Marts and grain silos and oil-rig pumps "dancing to a tune they heard deep in the earth . . . dipping to the beat, trying to pull the melody to the surface, so that all could hear."

She has won awards from Romance Writers of America, has had books selected by Doubleday Book Club, and has seen her work on the Bestseller Lists of both *USA Today* and the *New York Times*. She is a Texas Tech Distinguished Alumni and writer-in-residence at West Texas A&M University. Visit her web site at www.jodithomas.com.

Cowboy poetry may sound like an oxymoron to the uninitiated, but the popularity of this form of literature makes it clear that plenty of folks appreciate it. For an introduction to the kind of quality work being done by today's poets, dip into an anthology edited by Robert McDowell, called *Cowboy Poetry Matters: From Abilene to the Mainstream: Contemporary Cowboy Writing*. McDowell is not afraid to engage the scholarly question of whether poetry can be relevant anymore. He shows just how relevant it is to the world these poets know, the world of work on the farm or ranch and fellowship among people and horses.

The collections of Texas poet Walter McDonald regularly garner literary awards. *All That Matters: The Texas Plains in Photographs and Poems* and *The Digs in Escondido Canyon* capture a clear-eyed view of this powerful land, untainted by sentimentality.

Perhaps you've never heard of Breckinridge Elkins, western hero. Or Bran Mak Morn, the Pict. What about Kull, the Atlantean? Or Conan the Cimmerian, who held the throne of Aquilonia in the Hyborian Age before the dawn of recorded history, and who has been brought to life on the screen by Arnold Schwarzenegger as Conan the Barbarian? All these vivid creations sprang from the brain of a strange young man who drew them and their fabulous settings from his imagination some seventy years ago and turned them into tales that still boast a huge fan following. From 1928 to 1936, Robert E. Howard poured out stories for the pulp magazines, especially *Weird Tales* and *Action Stories*. He lived with his mother in the tiny town of Cross Plains. When his mother became terminally ill, he killed himself. He was barely thirty years old.

Since then, Howard's works (none of which were published in book form during his life), and works by others based on them and on his characters, have enjoyed tremendous popularity. His own stories, collected, restored and edited by adoring fans, are widely available, as are derivatives and tributes by such well-known modern fantasists as L. Sprague De Camp and Harry Turtledove.

Howard's sonorous and word-rich style is mesmerizing, full of shadowy tombs and riders clad in silk and steel, of fantastic dark-haired women and "spider-haunted mystery." It is a style that looks easy to emulate, a miscalculation that has foundered many a would-be imitator.

If you want a taste of the real stuff, start with *Conan the Cimmerian*, written in 1932 and newly issued in 2003 by Del Ray Books.

For the tots, a charming children's tale by William Joyce is set in the city of Abilene. Readers from five to nine will enjoy *Santa Calls*, a tale of three Abilene kids who set off in a Yuletide Flyer for a great adventure in Santa's hometown, Toyland.

Robert E. Howard Home

Robert E. Howard Hero

Attractions in the Southern Plains

ABILENE AND THE FORTS TRAIL

If you're interested in the frontier forts so dramatically described in much of the literature about the Indian Wars, stop in Abilene at the combination visitor center and interactive historical experience they call **Frontier Texas!** (800-727-7704 or 915-676-2556). Located at North First and Cypress Streets, it features exhibits from the 1780 to 1880 frontier period and will introduce you to the **Texas Forts Trail** (or see www.texasfortstrail.com).

Between 1849 and 1881, the Texas and U.S. Armies fought more than two hundred battles against the native tribes of the plains. In support of that war effort, they built forts in the wilderness not only to house the soldiers but to protect settlers trying to carve homesteads out of ages-old Indian hunting grounds. These are the forts that sheltered and supplied the real-life counterparts of the soldiers written about by Kelton, McMurtry and their like.

Abilene sits pretty much in the middle of a trail of eight such frontier forts stretching from Jacksboro in the north to Eldorado on the southern end, and then east to Mason. You can join the trail anywhere along its length, but if you are in Abilene, you'll have to decide whether to head north or south to follow parts of the trail or to make the 650-mile loop that will take you to all eight sites.

Different degrees of restoration and preservation mark the different forts, ranging from the dramatic ruins at **Fort Phantom Hill** to the remarkable twenty-three preserved or restored buildings at **Fort Concho** (325-481-2646), which is a National Historic Landmark.

At **Fort Griffin State Park and Historic Site** (325-762-3592), you can see the official state herd of Texas longhorns. An outdoor spectacle enacted by the residents of the nearby town of Albany takes place during the last two weekends in June each year. **Fort Griffin Fandangle** (325-762-3838) features cowboys, Indians, round-ups, and parades. There will be fiddles and guitars, singers and dancers, poets and performers, as these descendants of pioneers re-enact their past, when Fort Griffin was part of the line of forts that helped tame the West for settlement by Texans.

One of the largest outposts of its kind when it was built in 1851, **Fort Belknap** preserves its past today in buildings maintained as a county park.

Fort Richardson State Park and Historic Site (940-567-3506) is the northernmost stop on the trail. Several restored buildings stand in an area so quiet even the mockingbirds seem to mute their songs. The town of Jacksboro lies just over the tree line, but this location feels so remote, you have only to squint your eyes to imagine the horsebackin' Comanches in the distance. A small but very professional interpretive center invites you to linger, and you can get a glass of iced tea or a hamburger later at the **Green Frog Café** (940-567-5711) in nearby Jacksboro.

If you're heading south from Abilene, stop off at **Buffalo Gap Historic Village** (915-572-3365), a collection of 20 history-laden structures, including a jail, store, bank, school and doctor's office, for a firsthand experience of life on the frontier. The village is 14 miles south of Abilene on State Park Highway 89. At **Abilene State Park** (325-572-3204), a few miles south of here, you can see more of the official Texas Longhorn Herd and some buffalo and stroll or picnic in the shade of some four thousand native pecan trees.

The next stop on the Forts Trail is the ruins of **Fort Chadbourne** (325-743-2555), with its historic cemetery. Then it's south to San Angelo and **Fort Concho**. **Fort McKavett** (325-396-2358) west of Menard and **Fort Mason** near the town of Mason complete the tour. If you wish to head north toward Brownwood from here, you can make your way to Fort Richardson at Jacksboro, then back south to Abilene.

In Abilene, World War II and more modern military history are also memorialized. The **12th Armored Division Memorial Museum** (325-677-6515) at 1289 North 2nd Street holds that historic unit's archives. The men of the Twelfth Armored Division are the soldiers who spearheaded the liberation of prisoners from eleven death camps in Nazi Germany and a Japanese concentration camp in Manila. While their exploits overseas are commemorated here, students from Abilene Christian College study the ruins of a nearby Army camp to learn more about the training and barracks life of soldiers readying for combat. They are in the process of preparing an extensive oral history based on interviews with veterans, which will be an invaluable addition to the historical materials. These men saw the horrors of the Holocaust up close.

The remains of **Camp Barkeley**, which housed more than sixty thousand men for training during World War II, are located on State Highway 277, between FM 1235 and FM 707. A historical marker stands at what was once the main entrance to the camp, about eleven miles south of Abilene. Once twice the size of the city nearby, Camp Barkeley was closed soon after the war's end.

At **Dyess Air Force Base**, a visitor center offers an overview of the history of the base, but visitors will especially enjoy the outdoor exhibits that line the main street into the base. **Linear Air Park** (915-793-2199) shows off about thirty airplanes flown in the wars of the twentieth century, from World War II to Operation Desert Storm. This is an absolutely irresistible display for aviation buffs and a surprisingly inspiring one even to those with only a general interest in military aircraft. An awesome part of our nation's commitment to freedom is on exhibit here.

You may enter any time during daylight hours. At certain times, an endless stream of military jets will be passing overhead, their pilots going about their daily training or duty, while you stroll among the planes: F-111, B-66, B-1B, C-130, KC-97L, and many more. Admission is free, but you will need to stop at the main gate for a temporary pass for your vehicle. And make sure your seatbelt is fastened. Air Police are persnickety about such details.

A very special art gallery sits on the corner of North First and Cedar Streets in Abilene. **The National Center for Children's Illustrated Literature** (325-673-4586) showcases artwork from children's literature and offers educational programs about the exhibited artwork to encourage creativity and its expressions among children. The nearby **Grace Cultural Center** (325-673-4587) at 102 Cypress Street offers history, art and a children's museum.

Brownwood

Two cemeteries in this area hold interest for book lovers. Greenleaf Cemetery is the final resting place of **Robert E. Howard** of "Conan the Barbarian" fame. Nearby Indian Creek Cemetery is the burial site of novelist and Pulitzer Prize–winning short story writer **Katherine Anne Porter**.

Brownwood is also home to the **Douglas MacArthur Academy of Freedom** (915-646-2502), which features papers from the World War II hero's estate and a series of exhibits focusing on the eternal human quest for freedom. The academy is a research and teaching facility affiliated with Howard Payne University, but it houses many treasures of historical interest. Guided tours are available, but hours may vary with the university's schedule, so call ahead. You'll find it on FM 2524 (Austin Avenue) at Coggin Street.

Cross Plains

In Cross Plains, the hometown of **Robert E. Howard**, a civic group has purchased the house that Howard lived and worked in from 1919 until his death in 1936. The house is open by appointment at 625 State Highway 36 West. Write to Project Pride, P.O. Box 534, Cross Plains, TX 76443.

The **Cross Plains Public Library** (254-725-7722) holds a treasure cache of Howard memorabilia, including first editions, original manuscripts and pulp magazines. Located at 149 N. Main Street, it is open 1–5 on weekdays.

Quanah

Just west of Chillicothe on Highway 287, you'll notice what look like four small volcanoes across the prairie to the south. They're about nine miles away. A more

THE BOOK LOVER
TOURS ARCHER CITY

During his early days as a student and aspiring writer, Larry McMurtry learned to deal in books to make a living, first the merely used, then the rare or antiquarian. By 1970, he was able to open his first bookstore in Washington, D.C. Today, he owns **Booked Up, Inc.** (940-574-2511) in Archer City, a store made up of four buildings that house several hundreds of thousands of "previously owned" books.

Real Book Lovers will make the trek to Archer City to browse in what is undoubtedly one of the largest bookstores in Texas. The journey is less than twenty-five miles from Wichita Falls, about 130 from Dallas, but don't expect to spend less than half a day sorting through the countless volumes. You may want to pack in your own supplies, a few cheese sandwiches and a bottle of water, perhaps. The town's population of less than two thousand seems to get along with not much more than a Dairy Queen and a Sonic Drive-in for dining out. The Dairy Queen, by the way, is the one mentioned in the title of McMurtry's memoir, *Walter Benjamin at the Dairy Queen*.

First editions, autographed copies, antiquarian volumes and plain old used books fill the store's neat shelves in a method that seems somewhat haphazard, but may hold a hidden pattern known only to the cognoscenti, or to those willing to hunt up somebody to ask. One thing you won't have to worry about here is being pestered by the help. There isn't any. Browse as long as you like through the sturdy white shelves in any of the buildings. When you've burdened your arms with all the tomes they can carry, lug them down the street to Building Number One. You can usually scare up someone there to take your money.

Many people who come here admit to being overwhelmed by the floor-to-ceiling rows upon rows of books. Others are amazed at how clean it all is. Most treasure troves of books, except in climate-controlled conditions, attract dust the way magnets collect nails. Many used book stores have customers sneezing within seconds of entering. Not this one. Some employee must live on one of those rolling library ladders, spending hours upon hours dusting books.

unlikely sight you will rarely see than these conical mounds rising from the flat earth. Only two to three hundred feet high, they seem to loom magically against a bright blue sky. To see them is to develop an instant longing to know what they are. The whole scene becomes even more intriguing when you learn that a community called **Medicine Mounds** once existed there.

That community is long gone now, but the name predated it and outlasted it. Comanche and Kiowa Indians thought these dolomite hills to be holy sites, imbued with healing properties.

According to Darwin Spearing, author of *Roadside Geology of Texas*, the mounds "are high-standing erosional remnants." In other words, they are all that's left to show us where the top of the soil once lay in this area. Everything else has eroded away. Today, gypsum is mined in this county by Georgia-Pacific and turned into wall board and other products.

If you want a closer look at the mounds, FM 91 from Chillicothe or FM 1167, which turns south about midway between Chillicothe and Quanah, will take you closer. The mounds are on private property, though, and are not open to the public.

In Quanah you will find an unprepossessing eatery billing itself as **Medicine Mounds Depot Restaurant** (940-663-5619) on the south side of Highway 287 near the east end of town. An old Santa Fe train station moved here from Medicine Mounds, still marked with bullet holes from holdups, it's a Texas Historic Landmark.

Enter this restaurant only if you are in search of authentic Texas cooking. You are unlikely to find spinach, raspberries or feta cheese on the menu in any form. What you will find is real chicken-fried steak swimming in real gravy, your choice of vegetables, including the green bean casserole your grandmother used to make with crunchy fried onions on the top, burgers made from either beef or buffalo, huge glasses of iced tea, and a waitress who worries that you didn't get enough to eat.

San Angelo

San Angelo's Visitor Information Center (800-375-1206 or 915-653-1206) at 500 Rio Concho Drive provides maps and brochures to guide you through the region.

Fort Concho National Historic Landmark (325-481-2646), with its beautifully-aged stone buildings, transports visitors right into the past. History thrives here, kept vital by a Living History program and supplemented by a schedule of re-enactments, tours, speakers, and concerts.

The first U.S. Army troops arrived at Fort Concho just before Christmas in 1867. A little over a year later, the first Buffalo Soldiers showed up. Until 1889, soldiers housed here ventured north into the staked plains and west into the Trans-Pecos, exploring, clashing with the resident Indians, escorting stagecoaches and wagon trains, ensuring delivery of the U.S. mail, and opening the way for farmers, ranchers, merchants and schoolteachers.

Today, volunteers portray the various units that once lived and worked at Fort Concho, including infantry, cavalry, artillery and Buffalo Soldiers, laundresses and officers' wives. They all sport authentic costumes, weapons, and equipment, and their displays are fun as well as educational. The landmark is in the six-hundred block of Oakes Street south of downtown.

The **West Texas Collection** at the **Porter Henderson Library** (325-942-2164) on the campus of Angelo State University houses many thousands of books, manuscripts, documents and photographs on the history of the Southwest, with emphasis on Texas and the San Angelo area. Genealogy, folklore and fiction round out the collection. Parking can be a problem on campus, so you will need to get a guest parking permit from the University Police Department (325-942-2071). They can direct you to the library parking lot. Hours vary with the university's schedule, so call for information.

WICHITA FALLS

The first question most visitors to this city ask is, "Where's the falls?" They'll tell you all about it at the **Wichita Falls Convention and Visitors Bureau** (800-799-MPEC or 940-716-5500) at 1000 Fifth Street. There may have been a falls here in the early days, but no one seems to know for sure exactly where. It could never have amounted to much. But in 1986, the city fathers finally woke up to the fact that if visitors wanted a falls, maybe they should give them one, so they built one—fifty-four feet of cascading water. It's easy to see if you're going south on I-44. If you want to get closer, you have to enter Lucy Park, which is accessible from U.S. Highway 277 West.

The city, the county, the falls, the river, the lake, even the Permian rock outcroppings in the landscape are all named for a tribe of Caddo Indians, the Wichitas, who lived in the Red River Valley before the white settlers claimed it for their own. Downtown, the **Wichita Theater and Opera House** (940-723-9037) brings in top-of-the-line musical entertainment, usually in the western vein. For a schedule of events, see www.wichitafallsdowntownproud.com.

A TREAT FOR THE BOOK LOVER: A FIRST-EDITION KING JAMES BIBLE

The Moffett Library
On the campus of Midwestern University.

Access to these special collections is controlled for their protection, but you can see them Monday–Friday 2–5, or by appointment (940-397-4757).

The library claims two unique collections, one covering the history of print and featuring such rarities as ancient maps and first editions of famous modern works. In the Nolan A. Moore III Heritage of Print Collection, you can glimpse a first illustrated edition of Milton's *Paradise Lost*, as well as a first edition of the *King James Bible* of 1611. The Criscoe/Lanasa Collection assembles research materials on award-winning children's literature.

A popular annual event here is the **Hotter'N Hell Hundred**, billed as "the largest sanctioned century bicycle ride in the country, possibly the world." If you fancy cycling one hundred miles in one-hundred-degree heat, this is the sport for you. The huge cycling-industry consumer and trade show will be of more interest to anyone for whom air conditioning is as important as oxygen. Thousands of participants, fans, and hangers-on crowd into the city for this event, so make your plans early.

The Reading Tour

Boyd, Paula. *Dead Man Falls*. Pine, Colo.: Diomo Books, 2000.

Fehrenbach, T. R. *Comanches: The Destruction of a People*. New York: DeCapo Press, 1994 (reprint).

Flynn, Robert. *North to Yesterday*. Fort Worth: Texas Christian University Press, 1985.

———. *Wanderer Springs*. Fort Worth: Texas Christian University Press, 1987.

Hacker, Margaret Schmidt. *Cynthia Ann Parker: The Life and Legend*. El Paso: Texas Western Press, 1998.

Hagan, William T. *Quanah Parker, Comanche Chief*. Norman: University of Oklahoma Press, 1993.

Haseloff, Cynthia. *Kiowa Verdict: A Western Story*. New York: Simon & Schuster, 1997.

———. *Santanta's Woman*. New York: Macmillan, 1999.

Howard, Robert E. *Conan the Cimmerian*. New York: Del Ray Books, 2003.

Joyce, William. *Santa Calls*. New York: HarperFestival, 1998.

Kelton, Elmer. *Badger Boy*. New York: Forge, 2001.

———. *The Buckskin Line*. New York: Forge, 2000.

———. *The Day the Cowboys Quit*. Fort Worth: Texas Christian University Press, 1994.

———. *The Good Old Boys*. Fort Worth: Texas Christian University Press, 1985 (reissue).

———. *The Time It Never Rained*. New York: Forge, 1999.

———. *The Way of the Coyote*. New York: Forge, 2001.

———. *The Wolf and the Buffalo*. Fort Worth: Texas Christian University Press, 1986 (reprint).

Kissinger, Rosemary. *Quanah Parker: Comanche Chief*. New York: Pelican Publishing, 1999.

Le May, Alan. *The Searchers*. New York: Buccaneer Books, 1999 (reprint).

Lightfoot, D. J., and John Bobbish, illustrator. *Trail Fever: The Life of a Texas Cowboy*. Houston: Hendrick-Long, 2003.

McDonald, Walter. *All That Matters: The Texas Plains in Photographs and Poems*. Lubbock: Texas Tech University Press, 1992.

———. *The Digs in Escondido Canyon*. Lubbock: Texas Tech University Press, 1991.

McDowell, Robert, ed. *Cowboy Poetry Matters: From Abilene to the Mainstream: Contemporary Cowboy Writing*. Ashland, Ore.: Story Line Press, 2000.

McMurtry, Larry. *Comanche Moon*. New York: Pocket Books, 1998.

———. *Duane's Depressed*. New York: Pocket Books, 1999.

———. *Horseman, Pass By*. New York: Simon & Schuster, 2002 (reissue).

———. *The Last Picture Show*. New York: Scribner Paperback Fiction, 1999 (reprint).

———. *Lonesome Dove*. New York: Pocket Books, 1991 (reissue).
———. *Streets of Laredo*. New York: Pocket Books, 1995.
———. *Walter Benjamin at the Dairy Queen*. New York: Touchstone Books, 2001.
Neeley, Bill. *The Last Comanche Chief: The Life and Times of Quanah Parker*. New York: John Wiley & Sons, 1995.
Robson, Lucia St. Clair. *Ride the Wind*. New York: Ballantine Books, 1992 (reprint).
Smith, F. Todd. *The Caddos, the Wichitas, and the United States, 1846–1901*. College Station: Texas A&M University Press, 1996.
———. *The Wichita Indians: Traders of Texas and the Southern Plains, 1540–1845*. College Station: Texas A&M University Press, 2000.
Spearing, Darwin. *Roadside Geology of Texas*. Mountain Press, 1991.
Thomas, Jodi. *The Widows of Wichita County*. New York: Mira, 2003.

✶3✶

The Book Lover Tours the Big Bend and Trans-Pecos

Alpine, Balmorhea, Big Bend National Park, Big Bend Ranch State Park, Del Rio, El Paso, Fort Davis, Guadalupe Mountains National Park, Lajitas, Langtry, Marfa, Midland-Odessa, Pecos

To get to El Paso by car, drive west until you lose all interest in living, and then it's just another 175 miles.

Highway miles from Dallas to El Paso total 609. Leaving from Lubbock, it's only 340, from Houston, 725. International airports in El Paso and Midland-Odessa tempt many visitors to fly into one of these cities and rent a car. There is much to see and experience in Big Bend Country, once you get used to the idea of how spread out it is.

Natural history holds the spotlight here. The beauties of the rough land are many, but they are subtle, except when they are banging you in the eye. There are mountains, the tallest in the state, and hummingbirds, more species than any other area can claim.

Seekers of the exotic can trudge through pale sand dunes at Monahans State Park, look for mysterious luminosities in the clear night air near Marfa, or swim near endangered fish at Balmorhea Springs. The McDonald Observatory in the Davis Mountains offers unrivaled views of earth's near neighbors, the planets, and "tours" of the night sky conducted by people who know the North Star from

Andromeda and can show you how to trace the outlines of the constellations. In Del Rio you can view pictographs four thousand years old.

And then there are the Chihuahuan Desert and the two Big Bend parks, one maintained by the state, the other a national treasure. If you came to Texas expecting cactus and have been disappointed till now, get ready for a treat. Not only does cactus grow here better than just about anywhere else, it is cherished here, studied here, and preserved, along with other sturdy native plants, in gardens, nature trails, parks and city landscapes. More than seventy species of cactus grow within the national park, the most of any park in the nation.

Plant and animal life, especially of the avian kind, live in abundance here, belying the reputation of the desert as a place without life. Bird-watchers will find hundreds of feathered species in habitats ranging from mountain to canyon. Javelinas and white-tail deer populations thrive on the succulents. Coyotes range widely, and mountain lion and black bear are not unknown.

The history of the area is entwined with Apaches, soldiers, outlaws, famed lawmen and brave folks delivering the mail. Towns were built around springs, natural wells, or other water sources, many of which were first claimed by Indians, then by Army garrisons. As the Indians were driven out, mining, especially of quicksilver, had a brief heyday, followed by farming along the northern bank of the Rio Grande, and then ranching, which proved terribly hard on the land, destroying much of the natural grassland. It was not until 1944 that the U.S. Government established Big Bend National Park along the river and began restoring the native flora.

Today, petroleum production, sheep and cattle herding, agribusiness, and tourism and recreation drive local economies. Midland-Odessa is the center of oil and gas production. El Paso is the state's fourth largest producer of dairy products and is a retail and distribution center for almost every product imaginable. Hunting and fishing opportunities abound throughout the area, and easy access to Mexico at several points attracts many tourists.

In almost every town, you will find some commercial enterprise set up and waiting to help you explore and enjoy the natural wonders of the area. Bird-watching tours, rafting adventures, equestrian rentals, chuck-wagon cookouts, jeep tours, fossil tours and even camel treks may be available, depending on where you are and when. Gliders, mountain bikes, kayaks and canoes may all be spotted at one time or another. No matter how unprepossessing a settlement might appear from behind your dusty windshield, take a moment to stop by the local chamber of commerce or visitor center and thumb through the local brochures. Adventures beyond your dreams may lie in almost any one of them.

And the writers who live in this challenging country? Well, they write mainly about the challenges of this country. Lyrically, graphically, sweepingly, they have captured the essence of what it means to live in Tom Lea's "Wonderful Country." Not surprisingly, they use more than words to do that. Books of photographs loom large on every bestseller list in the region.

Capturing the Beauty

The official State Photographer for Texas is Wyman Meinzer. His photographs have graced the covers of *National Geographic, Audubon, Texas Parks and Wildlife* and their like more than 250 times. Meinzer has documented the phenomenal beauty of his land, its life and its heritage, and the titles of his books speak their subjects: *Great Lonely Places of the Plains*; *Desert Sanctuaries: The Chinatis of the Big Bend*; *Texas Sky*.

Another Texas photographer who has paid tribute to this area is Laurence Parent, who, with writer Joe Nick Patoski, put together *Texas Mountains*, a chronicle of the ranges of far west Texas, including not only the Davis, Guadalupe and Chisos ranges but the less well-known ones, as well: the Beach, Chinati, Christmas, Eagle, Franklin, and Sierra Diablo. One hundred and twenty color photos make it hard to argue with this book's claim to document all the mountain ranges of Texas. *The Guadalupe Mountains of Texas*, with photographs by Michael Allender and text by Alan Tennant, offers a close-up view of some of the wildest scenery to be found anywhere, as well as an account of the area's prehistory, history and ecology.

A stark contrast to works in color, James Evans's black and white images in *Big Bend Pictures* have captured the fancy of many of the denizens of this area, the folks who call the Big Bend home. They perceive in it something of an antidote to the romanticism that color photography can't help lending its subjects. Evans sees not only the beauty in the land and people he photographs but their quirkiness, too, and he points his lens at humans as much as at cactus or mountain. *Big Bend Pictures* is a large-format book with 102 photographs and an appendix that reveals what drew the artist to each subject and what each means to him personally.

If photographs don't satisfy your thirst for natural beauty, there are books that will take you deeper into the geology, plant life, and animal populations of the Big Bend. If you just have to know what a quonker katydid is or how the Texas lyre snake catches a bat, or if you're one of those people who aren't comfortable if they don't know the names of the plants around them, supplemental reading is in order.

Reading about Nature

Highly recommended is *Naturalist's Big Bend: An Introduction to the Trees and Shrubs, Wildflowers, Cacti, Mammals, Birds, Reptiles and Amphibians, Fish, and Insects* by Roland H. Wauer and Carl M. Fleming. These two authors are heavy hitters in the natural resources specialty of the National Park Service, and it shows. If you want to find the habitat of the peregrine falcon, the canyon tree frog, or the giant dagger yucca, this region-by-region tour guide to the Big Bend will show you where to look. It will give you an overview of archaeology and history associated with each area, and the geology, too.

In spite of the wealth of information contained here, the authors are not indulging in false modesty to call their book "an introduction." The wealth of plant and animal life that inhabits this region could never be rounded up into a mere 208 pages and forty-three photographs. But these experts know exactly what to highlight for the visitor who wants to know more about the flora and fauna but doesn't want to pursue a degree in them.

If you are a truly committed "plant person," find a copy of the five-hundred-page *Trees and Shrubs of the Trans-Pecos and Adjacent Areas* by A. Michael Powell, a guide to more than four hundred species of native and naturalized woody plants. *Cactuses of Big Bend National Park* (not "cacti," you will note) by Douglas B. Evans describes most of the cactuses you can expect to see inside the park. Fifty-two color photographs add immeasurably to the book's usefulness.

Anyone similarly committed to bird-watching may find value in *Birds of the Trans-Pecos* by Jim Peterson and Barry R. Zimmer. This is not a field guide full of pretty color pictures to help beginners identify birds. It's basically a list of the species to be encountered here, all 482 of them, and a description of their preferred habitats and thus their distribution. Of little interest to the casual birder, it will prove an essential tool for the amateur naturalist or avid observer.

The beginning bird-watcher will be much more comfortable with *Stokes Field Guide to Birds: Western Region* by Donald and Lillian Stokes. Bird by bird, it provides a color photograph, a range map, a description, and notes about such behaviors as feeding and nesting. Quick indexes and color-coding become more helpful as you gain expertise in identifying bird families, and notes about where individual species rank in conservation remind bird stalkers how precious each really is.

The National Park Service maintains a very nice web site at www.nps.gov/bibe/birdpg.htm, where you can see a checklist and obtain an introduction to the birds of Big Bend National Park. It's always beautifully illustrated with current photos taken at the park.

One of the best kept secrets about this region of Texas is that up to nine species of hummingbird may be spotted here during fall migrations, more than in any other part of the state. Birders are becoming more aware of this phenomenon and more are pouring in every year to pursue sightings of species they've never seen before. If you plan to get in on the action, you may want to invest in the indispensable *Stokes Hummingbird Book: The Complete Guide to Attracting, Identifying, and Enjoying Hummingbirds* by Don and Lillian Stokes. Seventy color photos and eight range map drawings will help you sort out the tiny acrobats as they buzz by.

Butterflies of West Texas Parks and Preserves by Roland Wauer provides a fully-illustrated guide to the fifty butterflies most commonly found west of the Pecos, as well as to eleven "specialities" that live nowhere else but this region.

The crown jewel of the region's nature writing is a collection of some sixty literary essays called *God's Country or Devil's Playground*, edited by Barney Nelson. Writers who have known and loved, or sometimes known and feared, this rugged country present unique perspectives in such themed chapters as "Paradise Found and Lost," "Nature as Devil's Advocate," and "A Big Bend Sense of Place." Writers are on a par with contributors Walter Prescott Webb, Roy Bedichek and Ludwig Bemelmans.

Of Oil and Presidents

Human beings sometimes feel dwarfed by the immensity of this land and the apparent emptiness of much of it. But the folks who settled the Trans-Pecos, the ones who were tenacious enough to withstand the wind, the drought, and the isolation until the 1920s, often found themselves sitting upon riches almost beyond measure, a sea of oil. Since 1926, more than two billion barrels of the stuff have been pumped out of Ector County alone. Odessa, that county's seat, and its neighbor Midland now make up the working heart of West Texas Oil.

Oil booms attract people the way streetlights attract nighthawks, and among the families attracted to Midland-Odessa in the late 1940s was that of a new Yale graduate named George H. W. Bush, who was later elected forty-first president of the United States. His son, George W. Bush, who would become forty-third president, spent many of his formative years here and later returned as an adult, bringing his own bride, Laura, to start his family here. George W. Bush often cites the people and culture of Midland as significant in the forming of his values and beliefs.

As presidents, both George Bushes have been the subjects of many books, some objective, some laudatory, some vituperative. Since the elder Bushes now make their home in Houston, you will find books about them described in the section devoted to that area.

The younger Bush and Laura, his wife, have graced the covers of many a volume in the relatively short time they've held center stage in the nation's political life. For a taste of what fun it is to ridicule a Texan who aspires to the presidency, see the acerbic *Shrub: The Short but Happy Political Life of George W. Bush* by Molly Ivins and Lou Dubose. For a view from the other side, try *The Right Man: The Surprise Presidency of George W. Bush* by David Frum, the president's former speechwriter. Stephen Mansfield explores the role of Mr. Bush's religious faith in shaping his politics in *The Faith of George W. Bush*. For a look at the smart, charming and solid-as-a-rock woman behind the presidency, see *George and Laura: Portrait of an American Marriage* by Christopher Andersen. Even more insightful is *The Perfect Wife: The Life and Choices of Laura Bush* by Ann Gerhart.

Can a Western Novel Be "Literary"?

Until Larry McMurtry won a Pulitzer Prize with his trail-drive novel, *Lonesome Dove*, the idea of a "literary" western had the ring of oxymoron to a lot of people. But even before McMurtry made the West respectable, Tom Lea and Cormac McCarthy had captured the hearts of the literati of the Southwest with their landmark novels.

A pistolero on the Chihuahuan desert, war lords and war, murder and revenge, love and betrayal—all the elements are there for the potboiler western in Lea's *The Wonderful Country*, but it never happens. What we get instead is an artist's evocation of the beauties and mysteries of the borderlands and those who people them. In a voice so quiet it seems simple, Lea draws from both sides of the border to explore the nature of evil and to show the courage that the wild and wonderful land demanded of people whose values included compassion and tolerance. A painter, muralist and poet, as well as a nationally-recognized novelist, Lea captured the mountains, valleys, and rivers of the area around El Paso in a word portrait that remains as vivid today as in 1952, when the book was first published. It is still in print and readily available.

Not until Cormac McCarthy came along did another "western" novelist attract the attention of the literati. Set half a century later than *The Wonderful Country*, the three novels that make up McCarthy's *Border Trilogy* set off fireworks in the literary world, beginning with *All the Pretty Horses*. The *San Francisco Chronicle* called it "an American classic to stand with the finest literary achievements of the century." *The Crossing* and *Cities of the Plain* completed the work, a long and dramatic homage to the frontier life and an elegy for its end. But it took *Blood Meridian, Or, the Evening Redness in the West* for the critics to propel McCarthy into the ranks of America's acknowledged masters, like Melville and Faulkner.

Plot seems almost a marginal concern when you're immersed in McCarthy's pace and diction, but plot there is, with all the violence the movies have taught us to expect in stories set in such rugged lands. The other western conventions get turned on their heads. Here, Anglos are hunting Indians and collecting bounties on their scalps, and the language is so darkly compelling, the characters so abhorrent, the violence so undiluted that the effect for some readers will be horror. That is an emotional response that would have been acceptable to any of the Greek tragedians, but let the reader be warned.

Once Is Enough for Some Authors

More widely known outside of Texas and probably the most unlikely author ever to set a tale in these parts is Edna Ferber, born in Michigan and reared in Wisconsin. She was known as the greatest American woman novelist of her day, a day in which a "woman novelist" was carefully demarcated from the "real" kind. She managed, despite the handicap of her gender, to win a Pulitzer Prize for her novel set in Illinois, *So Big*.

Ferber's only connection to Texas is tenuous, yet one that many Texans treasure. She is the author of *Giant*, a novel about a ranching family that was set, and later filmed, in West Texas. The 1956 movie is better known today than the novel. Rock Hudson, Elizabeth Taylor, and James Dean, Hollywood superstars in their day, still hold the modern fan's attention, but so, perhaps surprisingly, does Ferber's prose. The language is dated but by no means antiquated, and her insights about race, class, and economic conflicts are still worth reading.

Like Ferber, modern mystery writer Nevada Barr has set only one novel in Texas, but it's a humdinger. *Track of the Cat* finds Barr's character, Park Ranger Anna Pigeon, assigned to Guadeloupe National Park and tracking down a killer who's trying to blame his depredations on the wild cougars that haunt these mountains and canyons. This is the first outing for Anna in an engaging series of mysteries set in National Parks around the country. Barr's works are usually several cuts above the expected in this genre. Once you've followed Anna into the desolate beauty of this Texas park, you'll want to know what she's doing in the parts of Carlsbad Caverns that aren't open to the public in *Blind Descent*, and how she got into Lake Superior's deep water in *A Superior Death*, and so on. Strong plots, strong characters and a gift for describing far-flung settings keep Barr at the top of her game.

Some Can't Get Enough

Even more colorful, and a lot more committed to a Texas setting, the mysteries by Marfa native Allana Martin deserve attention. Her character Texana Jones plays amateur sleuth on La Frontera, the borderlands of far southwest Texas. Western Writers of America honored her first novel, *Death of a Healing Woman*, and her skills at characterization and description have grown stronger with successive novels. Sixth in the series, and one of the most polished, is *Death of the River Master*, which finds Texana and her husband Clay fighting the justice system south of the border. The setting in Presidio and its across-the-river neighbor Ojinaga lets the author draw out the cultural and historical tensions that shape life in this region today.

Several collections of short stories by Texans with Hispanic roots illuminate life in the modern borderlands and their cities. Dagoberto Gilb has earned numerous literary awards for his *The Magic of Blood*, and *Woodcuts of Women* was similarly well-received in literary circles. *The Ghost of John Wayne and Other Stories* by Ray González resonates with a form of magical realism. He gives voice to history and myth, the land and the people, holy and sinful, blending the ancient past with the all-too-present now.

Sergio Troncoso's *The Last Tortilla and Other Stories*, firmly rooted in La Frontera where he grew up, reflects the concerns of modern Latinos, but Troncoso is not afraid to tackle the bigger issues—the existence of evil, for instance, and its relationship to what we commonly consider justice, truth and righteousness—as he does in his novel *The Nature of Truth*.

Another aspect of El Paso life is recorded in a book about the tradition of painting artworks on walls of public buildings. *Colors on Desert Walls: The Murals of El Paso*, with text by cultural arts historian Miguel Juárez and photographs by Cynthia Weber Farah, is a unique record of this art form.

Readers aged nine to twelve will be engrossed by the mystery, magic and suspense of *Treasure of Panther Peak* by Aileen Kilgore Henderson. They can revel in the wild adventures of Page, whose mother takes her to live in Big Bend National Park.

Texas Rangers, Bad Men, and Apaches

Novelist Zane Grey called the Texas Rangers the men "who made the great Lone Star State habitable," and certainly they have gone down in frontier lore as heroes without equal. But the casual investigator may be surprised at just how extensive that lore is, ranging from myth to scholarly dissertation. If you want something somewhere between, you'll find the works of Mike Cox solidly in the middle. Readable as only a veteran newshound can make them, historically reliable and well documented, Cox's accounts will hold your attention. They range from *The Texas Rangers: Men of Valor and Action* for young adults to *Texas Ranger Tales: Stories That Need Telling* and *Texas Ranger Tales II*, documenting the deeds of early Rangers both notorious and obscure.

If your interest is sufficiently piqued to send to you in search of more, look for the classic by Walter Prescott Webb, *The Texas Rangers: A Century of Frontier Defense* or *Lone Star Justice: The First Century of the Texas Rangers* by Robert M. Utley.

For an encyclopedic knowledge (literally) of the gunmen of the West, the outlaws and those who sought to bring them to justice, turn to the works of Leon C. Metz. His *Encyclopedia of Lawmen, Outlaws and Gunfighters* bears a hefty price tag and may thus best be perused in the reference room of a public library, but many of his less massive works are more accessible and every bit as winning.

One of the great things about Metz's books is the trustworthiness of his scholarship. Combine that with a flair for storytelling, and you get winners like *The Shooters*, with its portrayals of Billy the Kid, Butch Cassidy, the Earp brothers, Jesse and

Leon C. Metz

Frank James, the Dalton brothers, and others who had a way with a gun. Metz has also written extensively about the early days of El Paso, especially in *Dallas Stoudenmire: El Paso Marshall* and *Turning Points in El Paso, Texas*.

One lawman you will hear about as you travel in this area is "The Law West of the Pecos," Judge Roy Bean. From 1882 to 1903, Roy Bean served in the elected post of Justice of the Peace in the town of Langtry. He has a colorful reputation for being highhanded in keeping the peace on the frontier, but because the townspeople kept electing him, he must have been meting out the kind of justice they wanted. He held court in a saloon, which continued conducting its business even as he conducted his.

Jack Skiles, who grew up in the shadow of that saloon, began in the middle of the last century to collect oral history about the judge from anyone who might have known him or his contemporaries. The result is an authoritative and highly readable history called *Judge Roy Bean Country*.

Geronimo, Nana, and Mangas Coloradas. Cochise. Victorio. Those were names to strike a chill into the spines of Anglos vying with Chiricahua and Mescalero Apaches for control over this far corner of Texas and patches of its neighbors, Mexico and New Mexico. In 1880 Victorio, often called the best tactician of the lot, led a band of about three hundred warriors on raiding parties into Texas between El Paso and Fort Davis. Dispatched to deal with him were troops from the black Ninth and Tenth U.S. Cavalries, stationed at Fort Davis. These Buffalo Soldiers were already seasoned Indian fighters by the time they set out after Victorio and his band in 1880, fought them in a battle at Rattlesnake Springs, and chased them into Mexico.

Just about everyone who lived in the area was engaged at one time or another in fighting or tracking down Victorio, including civilians and Texas Rangers. It was Colonel Joaquin Terrazas of the Chihuahua state militia that finally cornered him at a place called Tres Castillas and put an end to his bloody career. Two excellent books that recount those events—one from the viewpoint of the Apache, the other from the Buffalo Soldiers'—are Eve Ball's *In the Days of Victorio: Recollections of a Warm Springs Apache* and *The Buffalo Soldiers: A Narrative of the Negro Cavalry in the West* by William H. Leckie. The first, a powerful and factual account for young readers grades six to nine, follows a fifteen-year-old Apache girl through the tragedy of the loss of her tribe and way of life. Another youth book on the subject, *Walks Alone* by Brian Burks, may be too strong for very emotional younger readers, but its lessons about fortitude and survival resonate for all. *Buffalo Soldiers* is a compelling account of the role played by African Americans in developing the frontier and making it safe from the depredations of Victorio and other warriors.

TREATS FOR BOOK LOVERS

University research facilities make their special collections available to the public.

Haley Memorial Library and History Center in Midland

1805 West Indiana Avenue
Midland 79701
432-682-5785

Range Life and a Master Historian

See an original bell from the Alamo Mission, cast in 1722. It's on display along with other historical artifacts, art, and photos.

Library Collections: A sanctuary for the works of some of the West's most accomplished and most honored historians and writers, the Library bears the name of historian and biographer J. Evetts Haley and houses twenty-five thousand volumes of printed and manuscript materials. Haley's collection alone holds manuscripts of seven hundred interviews he conducted over fifty years spent documenting life on the frontier.

Military history, early railroads, ranching, mining, social issues, politics and more are represented in the collections, which are open to serious researchers. The Erwin E. Smith Collection of over six hundred original negatives preserves a record of range and cowboy life second to none. The library also holds art shows and sometimes sells rare books.

C. L. Sonnichsen Special Collections Department

The Library at the University of Texas at El Paso
500 West University Avenue
El Paso 79968
915-747-6725

History, Fiction, and the Southwest

Book Collections: Holdings include collections based on the personal library of premier printer Carl Hertzog, military historian S. L. A. Marshall, Rabbi Vincent Ravel, C. L. Sonnichsen's western fiction library, a southwest and border studies collection, study of Chicano history and culture, the books and articles published by UTEP personnel, a rare books collection, and more.

Manuscript Holdings: 420 manuscript collections and fifty-two photograph collections detail local history. Material includes El Paso County records and documents from the Southern Pacific Railroad.

Border Heritage Center

El Paso Public Library, Main Library
501 N. Oregon St.
El Paso 79901
915-543-5401

Southwestern and Raza History

Holdings: The Southwest Collection began more than a hundred years ago as the library began to collect and preserve research and reference material,

(continued)

including manuscripts, clippings, architectural drawings, maps, and other material related to west Texas, New Mexico, Arizona and the Mexican states of Chihuahua and Sonora.

Raza: The Mexican American Collection brings together works of all types by and about Mexican Americans and is especially solid in fiction and poetry.

Genealogy: This collection reflects the ancestral heritage of families throughout the transborder area. It includes source material from not only West Texas, but from Mexico, Spain, Africa, and other nations, as well.

The Archives of the Big Bend
Bryan Wildenthal Memorial Library
Sul Ross State University
Alpine 79832
432-837-8123

Law and Photography

Archives: about five thousand books of Texas and regional interest. Manuscript collections include the papers of these personages: Texas Ranger Roy W. Aldritch; Texas lawmakers Benjamen F. Berkeley, E. E. Townsend, and Gene Hendryx; and historians Harry Warren and Jodie P. Harris.

Photography collections include the works of W. D. Smithers and Charles Hunter, Peter Koch, Mr. and Mrs. Carl Thain and Frank Duncan. Oral history collections are ongoing.

Attractions in the Big Bend and Trans-Pecos

ALPINE

The population of Brewster County is less than ten thousand, and well over half those folks live in Alpine. Just to emphasize how empty the spaces are out here—the state of Connecticut and the state of Rhode Island would fit within this county's boundaries. At the same time.

Downtown, pick up a walking (or driving) tour map from the Chamber of Commerce at 106 N. 3rd Street and enjoy learning about the history of the old buildings. Visit **Front Street Bookstore** on E. Holland Street. On the beautiful campus of Sul Ross State University, you'll discover an extensive collection of artifacts from all four of the different cultures that have claimed this land at one time or another in the **Museum of the Big Bend** (432-837-8143).

Drive 18 miles out of town, south on Texas Highway 118, and go agate hunting at the **Woodward Agate Ranch** (432-364-2271). Or head west on U.S. Highway 90 about three miles and take the kids to **Apache Trading Post** (432-837-5506). While they're checking out the souvenirs, you can investigate their fine selection of books, topographical maps and relief maps of the region.

A SPECIAL ATTRACTION FOR BOOK LOVERS

Welcome to Front Street Books in Alpine and Marathon

121 E. Holland Avenue in Alpine and next to the Gage Hotel in Marathon
Both stores are located on U.S. Highway 90
800-597-3360

www.fsbooks.com

Front Street Books serves an eclectic crowd, from Sul Ross University professors and students to first-time tourists looking for the best book to read about the Big Bend. "We tell them about *Adventures in the Big Bend* by Jim Glendinning," store owner Jean Hardy likes to say. "Not only is it the best, it's published by our very own Iron Mountain Press."

Deep inventories of new books, a stock of used and even antiquarian

Front Street Books Storefront

volumes, and the willingness to search out what the customer wants mark the attitude at this West Texas fixture. If they don't have the collectible or out-of-print edition you want, they'll help you ferret it out. Their web site offers the same range of services.

Something's always in the air here—book signings, authors reading from their books, creative writing workshops, open-mike nights. What more pleasant way to spend an evening than in the presence of fellow book lovers in Big Bend country? They never met a stranger here, so come on in.

Front Street Books Logo

Exploring Big Bend National Park

Hiking, exploring, mountain biking, river floating, bird-watching, stargazing, camping, nature watching, exclaiming at spectacular scenery and glorying in flamboyant displays of clouds and light—these are a few of the things to do here.

The key to enjoying this huge park is to remember that its 801,000 acres are not equally receptive to exploring by everyone. This is rough country. It gets very hot here in the summer. Fortunately, there are facilities for inexperienced hikers, as well as for the experts. Have fun, but know your abilities and keep track of your supplies, including gas and water.

In planning your trip, make use of the excellent web site offering live views and satellite images of the park at www.nps.gov/bibe/home.htm. You will find there not only local weather forecasts, temperatures and river levels but campground availability, as well. Maps, information about safety awareness, a birding checklist, a schedule of activities, rules about pets—it's all there. It even offers you a list of gas stations that serve the park area. The number to call for general information is 432-477-2251.

Another useful web site is maintained by Brewster County at www.visitbigbend.com.

Even if you've visited the web sites before arriving, a stop at one of the **Big Bend National Park Visitor Centers** before entering the park is a must. It's always a good idea to check road conditions and weather reports, and you will need permits for certain actions, such as river activities and camping at backcountry and primitive sites. The Park Headquarters is at Panther Junction. Other centers in Chisos Basin, Persimmon Gap and Rio Grande Village are open seasonally.

Big Bend National Park is truly one of the nation's greatest treasures. More than twelve hundred plant species live here, along with 450 species of birds, as well as all the animals you would expect in such an environment, from the western diamondback rattlesnake to the mountain lion. It holds the national park record for number of species of birds, bats and, yes, cacti (with sixty species) within its bounds.

As you might expect, birding is a flourishing activity around here. With habitats ranging from the river floodplain through the Chihuahuan Desert and into the Chisos Mountains, birds are adapted everywhere. Birders come here to add the scaled quail and the elf owl to their lists, as well as phainopepla, pyrrhuloxia and colima warbler. They track down Lucifer hummingbirds here, along with blue-throated hummingbirds and magnificent hummingbirds.

Terlingua Ranch is a commercial bird-watching tour company. They can customize a trip for you, load you up in a van and take you to the best sites. Or they will provide a knowledgeable guide to ride in your vehicle with you, steer you toward the "hot spots" and help you identify what you see. You can contact them at P.O. Box 507 Terlingua, Texas 79852, or call 888-531-2223. Be sure to ask about pricing options.

Go in April and May if you want to see the cactus bloom.

EL PASO

Three major museums tell the story of El Paso's rich culture and history. Missions, monuments, historic sites and smaller museums round out the picture.

University of Texas at El Paso hosts the **El Paso Centennial Museum** (915-747-5565), where the Chihuahuan Desert is the focus and plants are the star, at least in the display garden, which showcases more than four hundred species of native desert plants suitable for landscaping use in the arid Southwest. Two dozen planting beds around the rock buildings include a sensory garden, a contemplation garden, and beds that simply show off the beauty and utility of these unusual plants. Diversity, human and other, carries the show inside the museum, with exhibits about local birds and mammals, Native American cultures, and mineralogy.

See how entrepreneurial pioneers lived in a magnificent nineteen-room adobe house at **Magoffin Home State Historic Site** (915-533-5147), 1120 Magoffin Avenue. Joseph Magoffin brought the first street car company to El Paso, founded the first bank, spent decades in tireless public service and, beginning in the early 1870s, built this embodiment of Territorial Style architecture to house his family. Their original furnishings and decorations are still here, typifying the tastes of the Victorian era. When the last of the Magoffins died in 1986, the state acquired the property and continues to operate it as an educational facility for the public. Tours guided by knowledgeable docents are available, and the gift shop specializes in material about El Paso and the Southwest.

Holdings at the **El Paso Museum of Art** (915-532-1707) at 1 Arts Festival Plaza, a large and modern facility, include five thousand works of art. Highlights are European painting and sculpture from the thirteenth through the eighteenth centuries in the Kress collection, nineteenth- and twentieth-century American art, and both historical and contemporary art from Mexico and the American Southwest.

Perhaps of all El Paso's many historic exhibits and displays, the trail laid out for touring the city's **old missions** is the most alluring. It leads you through the lower valley to two missions built in the seventeenth century and one founded in the eighteenth, all restored and maintained and brimming with history. Nuestra

Senora del Carmen, established in 1681, is the oldest mission in the state. You can reach it from I-10 East by taking the Zaragosa exit. Nuestra Senora de la Conception del Socorro, founded a year later, lies on FM 258 South, as does the latecomer to this group, San Elizario Presidio Chapel from 1777.

If you time it right, a trolley tour will take you on the rounds of the mission trail and throw in stops at a history museum and an Indian cultural center, not to mention lunch. This "Trolley on a Mission" operates on Thursdays during the summer and on the fourth Saturday of each month from fall through early spring. For details, call 915-544-0062.

El Paso gives a nod to the Bard every September with the production of several of his plays. Since the event is staged outdoors, it's called **Shakespeare on the Rocks**. From June through August, the same organization presents **VIVA! El Paso**, the drama of the city's long and colorful history in music and spectacle. The McKelligon Canyon Amphitheater, home to both productions, lies in the shadow of the Franklin Mountains. Talk about a dramatic setting! For information about either presentation, call 800-915-VIVA or visit www.viva-ep.org.

Enjoying the Scenery in El Paso

The city of El Paso offers opportunities to enjoy spectacular views of dramatic scenery. The Wyler Aerial Tramway (915-566-6622) will take you to the top of Ranger Peak in the Franklin Mountains, affording you a view of seven thousand square miles of Texas, New Mexico and Mexico, not to mention the cities of El Paso and Juarez laid out below.

If you prefer to drive, don't miss the excitement of the eleven-mile long **Trans-Mountain Highway** (Texas Loop 375) that wends through the Franklin Mountains. From I-10 West, take Exit 6 and go into Franklin Mountain State Park. Head for Smuggler's Pass at 5250 feet. You'll find a place to park there, so you can get out and enjoy the view down the valley of the Rio Grande. There are trailheads nearby for hikers, but don't go out unprepared. This is true wilderness, and in the warmer months, temperatures are downright immodest and thirst is a hazard. In the winter you can get sleet out of a cloud that wasn't even there the last time you looked.

At 3401 Trans-Mountain Road, you will find **Wilderness Park Museum** (915-755-4332), devoted to depicting the lives of Native Americans, and a nature trail featuring native plants.

For a tamer adventure, explore the lower shoulder of Mount Franklin from **Richmond Street** or **Rim Road**. You'll get an eyeful of the cities below.

FORT DAVIS

With a population of 1,050 in a county whose population barely tops 2,000, this hamlet may be the ultimate place to get away from it all. However, because of scenery, history, hunting and bird-watching, tourism is a major industry, and folks around here know how to treat visitors. The Chamber of Commerce for Fort Davis (800-524-3015 or 432-426-3015), on the south side of the square, dispenses information about the area. At the wonderful old **Hotel Limpia** (915-426-3237 or 800-662-5517), they'll let you sit in rocking chairs on the wide veranda and listen to the hummingbirds buzzing the geraniums, wander around back and pet-talk with the fat yellow cat snoozing in the lavender bed, sample the wares in the quaint gift shops, even saunter across the street to the soda fountain for a burger.

Before you get too adjusted to this slower pace of life, drive over to the restored cavalry fort on the north edge of town, **Fort Davis National Historic Site** (432-426-3224), one of the best preserved of the Buffalo Soldier forts. On grounds covering more than four hundred acres, rock and adobe buildings that once held the troopers have been preserved or restored. It's a stirring monument to the cavalry and infantry companies who explored this region in the nineteenth century. After the Civil War, the Twenty-fourth and Twenty-fifth U.S. Infantry and the Ninth and Tenth U.S. Cavalry, all-black regiments, were posted here. They were charged with protecting travelers and mail and freight haulers on the trail between San Antonio and El Paso during the wars with the Comanches and the Mescalero Apaches.

MCDONALD OBSERVATORY

From Fort Davis, take Texas Highway 118 about sixteen miles north to the observatory's Visitors Information Center (432-426-3640 or 877-984-7827). It's difficult to explain the effect upon a traveler approaching McDonald Observatory of the glistening white domes rising from the desert and commanding the sky. You can see them from miles away through the clear, smogless air. That air, at an altitude of sixty-eight hundred feet above sea level, is one of the factors that attracted the stargazers here in the first place and still brings astronomers and research scientists here from around the world. This is one of the premier astronomical facilities in the world.

Fortunately, the observatory accommodates regular folks, too. They call it a public education outreach. All you need in order to enjoy a visit here is a sense of the drama of a star-swept night sky and curiosity about Earth's neighbors: the moon, the planets of the solar system, and the stars. If you can't bring those things with you, the staff here, who seem to love their jobs and the chance to tell others about the treasures of the sky, will instill them in you before you get away.

By all means, plan to join one of the "Star Parties" held Tuesday, Friday and Saturday nights to look through telescopes set up for the occasion. You'll get to examine whatever is most interesting that particular night through telescopes that range in size between eight and twenty-two inches. Then, someone who reads the skies as readily as you read a map of your hometown will take you out into the incredible darkness and show you how to trace out the outlines of constellations and identify stars by their relationships with them.

Take a sweater. It can get cool at night.

Plan to go back in the daytime, too, for a guided tour of the big research telescopes, maybe a peek at the surface of the sun, and to enjoy the exhibits, gift shop, and endless activities that are always underway. If you want to look through one of the really big telescopes, you'll have to get a reservation in early.

GUADALUPE MOUNTAINS NATIONAL PARK
HC 60 Box 400
Salt Flat, Texas 79847
915-828-3251 Headquarters Visitor Center
505-981-2418 Dog Canyon Ranger Station

For the most part, this is a hiking park. Vehicle access is limited. There's RV and tent camping here, but no lodging. Overnight stays require a permit and must be restricted to certain areas. You'll need one for backpacking and horseback riding, too. Check in at the Headquarters Visitor Center (915-828-3251) off U.S. Highway 62/180 near Pine Springs.

Besides being home to the highest mountain peaks in Texas, this wonderfully wild and rugged country holds gems of history, both human and natural, preserved in the unlikeliest of spots. Experienced hikers tromp the park's eighty miles of trail to see a vast diversity of plant life, remnants of a gigantic ancient fossil reef, forested canyons and more.

Six springs located within a three-mile radius made the spot where the **Frijole Ranch** was built irresistible to early settlers. Today, you can drive up to the house, now a museum that preserves pioneer life with perfect clarity not so much in the artifacts it houses as in its near-total isolation. About a mile east of the Headquarters Visitor Center on U.S. Highway 62/180, watch for the exit that directs you north to Frijole Ranch. You will drive through desert wildflowers, stirring up desert birds, toward a cool oasis of huge old trees and a collection of tiny buildings.

Get out of your car and look around and realize that at one time a sizeable family supported itself here as what we would call truck farmers. On fifteen acres near the house and the spring that fed their crops, they grew apples, peaches, apricots, plums, pears, figs, pecans, blackberries, strawberries, corn and other vegetables. When the time came to harvest crops, they piled them into a wagon, covered them with moistened strips of paper and linen, and hauled them for two days to Van Horn, sixty-five miles away. A visit here will give you a greater appreciation for your dinner salad tonight.

LAJITAS

The star attraction at Lajitas is **Warnock Environmental Education Center** (432-424-3327), on FM 170 east of town. The Center serves as a gateway to the Big Bend Ranch State Park, but you don't have to be headed into the park to enjoy this stop. This state park is wilder and less developed than the national park to the east, with no facilities except what you find at this center. Only experienced backpackers should venture into the park, and this is the place to get permits for different activities. Of course, anyone can appreciate the great selection of books and maps specific to the Big Bend offered by the gift store. And don't miss the 2-acre botanical garden set within the 99.9-acre site. You will see hedgehog, prickly pear and other cacti, and such wonders as Texas wolfberry, gumdrop tree and bird of paradise, all thriving in an area where the average rainfall is 8.9 inches a year.

LANGTRY-DEL RIO

Stop here to see where **Judge Roy Bean**, the famous "Law West of the Pecos" held court, saloon, opera house and all. Preserved and restored, these historic structures make for an entertaining stop. The visitor center (432-291-3340) features a noteworthy little botanical garden displaying desert plants, and the Texas Department of Transportation hands out tourist literature.

Whitehead Memorial Museum (830-774-7568) is an open-air museum at 1308 South Main Street. Made up of several beautifully-preserved buildings as a sort of "frontier village," this is the final resting place of Judge Roy Bean.

MARFA

Marfa is home to **El Paisano Hotel** (866-729-3669), headquarters for the Hollywood crew during its filming of Edna Ferber's novel *Giant* in 1955. A National Historic Landmark, it functions as guest lodging even today. You will find it at 207 North Highland.

Marfa also hosts one of the strangest attractions in the state, a viewing center that invites you to stare across the desert at night toward some treeless hills and try to distinguish the headlights of moving automobiles on the hillside road from what many people describe as "mysterious lights" that sometimes hover and dance in the same area. **Marfa Mystery Lights Viewing Center** is a raised deck that lets you investigate the phenomenon in comfort, but dress warmly; it can get chilly when the sun goes down. Don't forget to take your binoculars. You can reach the center by taking U.S. Highway 67/90 east for about eight miles.

MIDLAND-ODESSA

This metropolitan area maintains information centers at two locations, 109 N. Main (800-624-6435) in Midland and 700 North Grant in Odessa (800-780-4678).

The cities share a population of almost two hundred thousand. They lie in the heart of oil land. Several superb museums show just what that means, geologically, historically and culturally. But there's a lot more to these towns than oil. One boasts a replica of Shakespeare's Globe Theater and stages the Bard's plays every year. In the other, two future U.S. presidents lived at the same time. Today, a fine collection of vintage aircraft, many civic parks and swimming pools, and live musical and theatrical productions keep things hopping.

SHAKESPEARE ON THE PLAINS

Globe of the Great Southwest

On the Campus of Odessa College
2308 Shakespeare Road
432-332-1586 or
432-580-3177

You will be relieved to know that this recreation of Shakespeare's Globe Theater of London is not nearly as authentic as it first appears. It has air conditioning, for one thing, a fact that will appeal to you as a visitor to West Texas a great deal more than it would have to Will in his sixteenth-century location on the Thames. It has a roof, for another, which the original may not have needed, but this one does. Snug inside, productions can roll despite blue northers, dust storms, ice storms, or summer's quite unreasonable heat. Plumbing, carpeting and plush red seats set this theater apart, too, but patrons are so grateful to have such luxuries that they rarely come up as hurdles to real authenticity.

Here on the campus of Odessa College there stands an absolutely charming representation of the famous and ancient theater, one that keeps the stage hot for local fans and visitors alike. It fills its 410 seats not only for productions of the Bard's plays, but also for a full schedule of performances ranging from Broadway musicals to gospel singing. Its excellent acoustics (aided, one would think, by the roof) and professional management make it a delightful addition to the arts in Odessa.

Very close to the theater stands a recreation of the cottage owned by Shakespeare's wife, Anne Hathaway, in Stratford-upon-Avon. That's where you will find the **Shakespeare library** and archives. It's air conditioned, too.

Home to Two Presidents: George W. Bush Childhood Home and Presidential Museum

On the Campus University of Texas of the Permian Basin in Odessa

George H. W. and Barbara Bush lived in several different locations in both Midland and Odessa when they were a young and growing family just getting involved in the oil business in the 1950s and 1960s. Two houses that held both them and the son who would follow his father in the White House are still standing, as is a house that George W. and his wife Laura lived in as a young married couple. All these houses have now come under the supervision of the University of Texas of the Permian Basin.

The **Presidential Museum and Library** (432-363-7737) is housed at 4919 E. University in Odessa. The museum tells the story of the United States Presidency and the election process that creates and upholds it. An enormous collection of presidential campaign materials is organized according to eras, from the period of the Founding Fathers through expansion, wars and depression to the explosive growth of presidential powers after World War II and during the Cold War. It also shows how the presidency, diminished with the fall of Richard Nixon, was reclaimed and rebuilt by the presidents who followed.

The information gathered here ranges from the profoundest historical material to the silliest political cartoon. There is a collection of dolls to represent the dress and hair styles of all the First Ladies. And at the heart of it all stands **The Library of the Presidents**. The Library preserves more than forty-five hundred books and other documents regarding the presidency and offers them for in-house use to researchers.

Excellent historical, art and industry museums stand out in these two cities. **Ellen Noel Art Museum of the Permian Basin** (432-550-9696) features fine arts exhibits and a Sculpture and Sensory Garden at 4909 E. University Boulevard, on the campus of the University of Texas of the Permian Basin in Odessa. **Museum of the Southwest Complex** (432-683-2882) at 1705 W. Missouri in Midland claims not only art, including regional and native American pieces, but a children's museum and a planetarium, as well.

American Airpower Heritage Museum and Commemorative Air Force Headquarters (432-567-3009) at Midland International Airport is a must see for airplane buffs and World War II aficionados. Combat aircraft that is still perfectly flyable or has been restored to flying condition is shown in a changing exhibit that calls on a collection of more than 140 planes.

Permian Basin Petroleum Museum (915-683-4403) is located at 1500 I-20 West. With both indoor and outdoor exhibits of oil field equipment, it is the

TREATS FOR BOOK LOVERS

The Petroleum Museum Archives Center
1500 Interstate 20 West
Midland 79701
Take Exit 136 and stay on the north service road.
432-683-4509

Absolutely Everything about Oil

The petroleum industry (especially in the Permian Basin)—its history, growth, and economic and social impact—is preserved here in private papers, company records and other documents, sound recordings, film, photographs and maps.

Holdings include oil company and related association histories, newspapers from the early twentieth century, town and county histories, company and professional journals, and catalogs showing early tools and equipment, as well as graduate theses relating to petroleum, cattle, railroads and other local industry.

---

world's foremost museum dedicated to telling the story of petroleum production, covering both its technical and its social aspects, especially life in the early oil fields and boom towns. Its interactive exhibits explaining how oil is formed and how humans have been able to exploit it are simple enough for children to enjoy and fascinating to curious adults.

The Reading Tour

Andersen, Christopher. *George and Laura: Portrait of an American Marriage*. New York: William Morrow, 2002.

Ball, Eve. *In the Days of Victorio: Recollections of a Warm Springs Apache*. Tucson: University of Arizona Press, 1970.

Barr, Nevada. *Track of the Cat*. New York: Berkeley, 2003 (reissue).

Burks, Brian: *Walks Alone*. New York: Turtleback Books, 2000.

Cox, Mike. *Texas Rangers: Men of Valor and Action*. Austin: Eakin Publications, 1992.

———. *Texas Ranger Tales: Stories That Need Telling*. Plano: Republic of Texas Press, 1999.

———. *Texas Rangers Tales II*. Plano: Republic of Texas Press, 1999.

Evans, Douglas B. *Cactuses of Big Bend National Park*. Austin: University of Texas Press, 1998.

Evans, James. *Big Bend Pictures*. Austin: University of Texas Press, 2003.

Ferber, Edna. *Giant*. New York: Perennial, 2002 (reprint).

Frum, David. *The Right Man: The Surprise Presidency of George W. Bush*. New York: Random House, 2003.

Gerhart, Ann. *The Perfect Wife: The Life and Choices of Laura Bush*. New York: Simon and Schuster, 2004.

Gilb, Dagoberto. *The Magic of Blood*. Albuquerque: University of New Mexico Press, 1993.

———. *Woodcuts of Women*. New York: Grove Press, 2000.

González, Ray. *The Ghost of John Wayne and Other Stories*. Tucson: University of Arizona Press, 2001.

Henderson, Aileen Kilgore. *Treasure of Panther Peak*. New York: Turtleback Books, 1998.

Ivins, Molly, and Lou Dubose. *Shrub: The Short but Happy Political Life of George W. Bush*. New York: Vintage Books, 2000.

Juárez, Miguel, and Cynthia Weber Farah. *Colors on Desert Walls: The Murals of El Paso*. El Paso: Texas Western Press, 1998.

Lea, Tom. *The Wonderful Country*. Texas Tradition Series, no. 33. Fort Worth: Texas Christian University Press, 2002.

Leckie, William H. *The Buffalo Soldiers: A Narrative of the Negro Cavalry in the West*. Tucson: University of Arizona Press, 1999.

Mansfield, Stephen. *The Faith of George W. Bush*. New York: J. P. Tarcher, 2003.

Martin, Allana. *Death of a Healing Woman*. New York: St. Martin's, 1996.

———. *Death of the River Master: A Texana Jones Mystery*. New York: Thomas Dunne Books, 2003.

McCarthy, Cormac. *All the Pretty Horses*. New York: Vintage, 1993 (reprint edition).

———. *Blood Meridian; or, The Evening Redness in the West*. New York: Vintage, 1992 (reissue edition).

———. *Cities of the Plain*. New York: Alfred A. Knopf, 1998 (reprint edition).

———. *The Crossing*. New York: Alfred A. Knopf, 1994 (reprint edition).

Meinzer, Wyman. *Desert Sanctuaries: The Chinatis of the Big Bend*. Lubbock: Texas Tech University Press, 2003.

———. *Great Lonely Places of the Plains*. Lubbock: Texas Tech University Press, 2003.

———. *Texas Sky*. Austin: University of Texas Press, 1998.

Metz, Leon. *Dallas Stoudenmire: El Paso Marshall*. Norman: University of Oklahoma Press, 1993 (trade edition).

———. *Encyclopedia of Lawmen, Outlaws and Gunfighters*. New York: Facts on File, 2002.

———. *Turning Points in El Paso, Texas*. El Paso: Mangan Books, 1985.

Nelson, Barney, ed. *God's Country or Devil's Playground*. Austin: University of Texas Press, 2002.

Patoski, Joe Nick, and Laurence Parent. *Texas Mountains*. Austin: University of Texas Press, 2001.

Peterson, Jim, and Barry Zimmer. *Birds of the Trans-Pecos*. Corrie Herring Hooks Series, no. 37. Austin: University of Texas Press, 1998.

Powell, A. Michael. *Trees and Shrubs of the Trans-Pecos and Adjacent Areas*. 2nd ed. Austin: University of Texas Press, 1998.

Skiles, Jack. *Judge Roy Bean Country*. Lubbock: Texas Tech University Press, 1997.

Stokes, Donald, and Lillian Stokes. *Stokes Hummingbird Book: The Complete Guide to Attracting, Identifying, and Enjoying Hummingbirds*. New York: Little Brown & Company, 1989.

———. *Stokes Field Guide to Birds: Western Region*. New York: Little, Brown & Company, 1994.

Tennant, Allen, and Michael Allender. *The Guadalupe Mountains of Texas*. 2nd ed. Austin: University of Texas Press, 1997.

Troncoso, Sergio. *The Last Tortilla and Other Stories*. Tucson: University of Arizona Press, 2000.

———. *The Nature of Truth*. Evanston, Ill.: Northwestern University Press, 2003.

Utley, Robert M. *Lone Star Justice: The First Century of the Texas Rangers*. New York: Oxford Press, 2002.

Wauer, Roland. *Butterflies of West Texas Parks and Preserves*. Lubbock: Texas Tech University Press, 2002.

Wauer, Roland H., and Carl M. Fleming. *Naturalist's Big Bend: An Introduction to the Trees and Shrubs, Wildflowers, Cacti, Birds, Reptiles and Amphibians, Fish and Insects*. Rev. ed. College Station: Texas A&M University Press, 2002.

Webb, Walter Prescott. *The Texas Rangers: A Century of Frontier Defense*. 2nd ed. Austin: University of Texas Press, 1965.

✶4✶

The Book Lover Tours North Central Texas and the Metroplex

Arlington, Dallas-Fort Worth, Denton, Gainesville, Irving, McKinney, Mesquite, Sherman-Denison, Tioga, Waco, Weatherford

The area we call North Central Texas is defined by the Red River on the North and the Brazos where it runs through Waco to the south. Dallas forms its eastern border, Weatherford its western. Not large in size by Texas standards, the area holds large cities Dallas and Fort Worth and suburbs that stretch the population into the millions.

Quarter horse ranches line rural stretches of many highways outside the cities, and wheat vies with sorghum for room in the fertile fields. Beef cattle have replaced the buffalo that once darkened these prairies. Recreation, especially water-related, and spectator sports are major industries in an area where early farmers fought native tribesmen for access to water and the deep, black-clay soil that was proving so uncommonly rich for production of cotton, vegetables, grains and stock feed. In the end, the farmers won, and major transportation routes sprang up to handle the commerce in farm and ranch products. In the 1850s cross-country trails for gold seekers passed through here leading the way to California. The Butterfield Overland Mail stagecoach trail crossed the Red River near Sherman, and later, both Sherman and Denison became transportation nexuses. And two cities grew along the banks of the Trinity River that would between them come to define Texas in the minds of many: Dallas, home to a world-popular television show by that name, and Fort Worth, known everywhere as "Cowtown."

Dallas-Fort Worth Metroplex

Today, it's hard to drive or fly into the Dallas-Fort Worth Metroplex, with its five million people spread over a couple of thousand square miles, and believe the area ever had much identity beyond this great urban expanse. In truth, Dallas was a commercial center almost from its inception. John Neely Bryan built the first cabin on the Trinity in 1841. By 1849, there was a newspaper serving a population of almost a thousand, and several stores, schools and churches had sprung up to support them. You might say that Dallas had been a town just waiting to happen. It was a natural stopover for cattle drives, a place to stock up on supplies, as well as a destination for immigrants from Europe.

During the Civil War, the city served as an administrative center and then became a transportation hub with the arrival of railroads. The establishment of a Federal Reserve Bank fed growth in the banking industry. In the twentieth century, insurance, fashion, telecommunications, construction, real estate, an international airport, and professional sports drove the economy. Dallas entered the twenty-first century as a leading tourist destination and national convention center.

The violence that marked so many frontier towns always seemed less prevalent here, and something happened in 1856 that was to shape the future of this city in ways that no frontiersman could have predicted. A group of European intellectuals, enamored of socialist ideas, tried to create a utopian society in the area. They called it La Reunion. When it failed, a few hundred survivors moved into Dallas, bringing with them not only their idealism but their educations in science and the arts. Soon, other cultivated Europeans joined them. Their contribution to the culture then emerging in the young city is still felt today with the mature city's commitment to the arts, as well as in the educational systems it supports.

Fort Worth, in contrast, was the wild, wild west from the beginning. Established as a military camp in 1849, it was abandoned by the Army in 1853, and the fort's deserted buildings sheltered settlers, giving them a frontier foothold and a chance to turn their attention to serving the new cattle-drive business, which burgeoned, especially after the Civil War. Cowboys, buffalo hunters, gamblers and gunmen: Fort Worth saw them all. The coming of the railroads and the end of the trail-driving era turned the town into a meatpacking center and a distribution point for beef. Stockyards, auction and exchange grounds, and rodeos bolstered the Fort Worth identity, one it still bears proudly today. It is and always has been "Cowtown."

Butch Cassidy and the Sundance Kid put in an appearance here, as did Comanche Chief Quanah Parker, gambler and gunman Luke Short, gangsters Bonnie and Clyde, and such civilizers as newspaper publisher Amon G. Carter. In the end, Fort Worth, like Dallas, evolved into something no frontiersman could have predicted—a center for the arts and education.

In the twenty-first century, the DFW Metroplex is no longer just two cities or even just two counties. Every county that shares a border with Dallas or Tarrant County has become part of the complex, and every town within a hundred miles of its outposts falls under its sway. Commuters from as far away as Bonham, Greenville, Mineral Wells and Corsicana drive into the metropolis to work, shop and play.

The complex of cities we call the Metroplex forms a vast stronghold for higher education, both public and private. Members of the education community range from the University of North Texas and Texas Woman's University in Denton to Baylor University in Waco, from Texas Christian University in Fort Worth to the University of Texas at Dallas, Southern Methodist University, Texas Southwestern Medical Center, and others to two-year college systems with multiple campuses in several counties.

Along with its commitment to education, the Metroplex nourishes writers and other artists. For Book Lovers reading their way through Texas, this area offers special riches in cultural and historical collections at universities and museums. Perhaps less expected is the army of popular novelists that call the Metroplex home. Sandra Brown leads the pack.

Love and Death in the Metroplex

Romance and romantic-suspense novelist Sandra Brown has earned so many slots on the New York Times Bestseller List that there's no point in trying to pin down how many. By the time you read this, the number will have grown from the current fifty-something. Furthermore, not only do her novels make the list, they debut on the list, often joining one or two of their sisters already perched there. That's how sure her fans are that each new title will be as satisfactory as the last.

Having made such a virtue of predictability, Brown finds herself the butt of some critical disdain. Even in the world of popular literature, critics often slight her or ignore her. Booksellers, however, love her. As of this writing, she has more than sixty titles in print in more than thirty languages. Worldwide, her books have sold seventy million copies. Do you think she cares what the critics think?

The settings for Brown's novels are Texas, New York, the world. Sometimes even Fort Worth or Dallas. Her characters are often Texan, even if they find themselves in exotic locations, like South Carolina or New Mexico. Sex—or, as it's usually called in this genre, romance—of the steamy kind always plays large in these tales. Among Brown's many novels with a strong Texas connection are *Standoff*, full of characters from the Metroplex who find themselves in hot water in rural New Mexico; *The Crush*, about a Fort Worth surgeon pursued by two men, a cop and a psychopath; and *Hello, Darkness*, set in an Austin that's home to ex–porn queens, teenage sex clubbers, a sex-addicted dentist, and one or two really sordid characters.

Romance is not the only genre flourishing in the Metroplex. Mystery and suspense novels are numerous. These are often actually set in Dallas or Fort Worth, and most seem to share a sardonic sense of humor. Here are a few examples.

A. W. Gray's *Bino's Blues* stars his series character Bino, a six-and-a-half-footer with a tough manner and a heart of gold who stirs up the murky waters of law and politics in Fort Worth. Gray has a gift for minor characters and a sneaky way with humor that may have you laughing out loud in the library reading room. His mysteries featuring a female attorney in Dallas appear under the pseudonym Sarah Gregory. They include *Capitol Scandal* and *The Best Defense*.

Fashionista and college professor Chloe Green serves up a look at the seamy side of the fashion world in *Going Out in Style*, a murder mystery that includes beauty advice. And Laurie Moore, educated to teach school but having spent a couple of decades in law enforcement, makes us laugh with *The Lady Godiva Murder* and *Constable's Run*. Howard Swindle hits a more sardonic note with

---

A TREAT FOR THE BOOK LOVER: SANDRA BROWN FOCUSES ON TEXAS

Some of romantic-suspense novelist Sandra Brown's most exciting novels take place in Texas, where she was born and reared. From Waco to Austin and from prairie to vale, she knows the land and the people and portrays them as only a native could. Look into some of these novels set in the Lone Star State. A printable list of all Brown's books is available at her web site, www.sandrabrown.net.

Another Dawn
The Crush
Hello, Darkness
Mirror Image
Relentless Desire
Standoff
Sunset Embrace
Texas Chase
Texas Lucky
Texas Sage

Jitter Joint, about a cop in rehab for a drinking problem. He runs into a killer who's cheerfully tagging each of his victims with one of the Twelve Steps made famous by Alcoholics Anonymous.

But if you want really gruesome laughs, turn to Doug Swanson, whose private investigator Jack Flippo hangs with some of the trashiest women and dumbest thugs ever to bounce around the Dallas underworld. Try *96 Tears* or, if you can stand a comic take on the idiocy that seems to have enveloped Dallas in the aftermath of the Kennedy assassination, read *Umbrella Man*.

DALLAS: HISTORY OF A CITY

The history of the DFW area has been documented in several books, including *Dallas Then and Now* by Ken Fitzgerald, a pictorial history of the changes the city has undergone. But one of the most compelling accounts is found in *The Lives and Times of Black Dallas Women* by Marc Sanders and Ruthe Winegarten. It's the 160-year history of the "guts, gumption and go-ahead" that fueled the rise of black women from slavery to leadership in the modern community.

Early on, black women identified education as the pathway to equality, and they pursued it for themselves and their children with a single-mindedness that took them from one-room segregated schools into the largest universities in the state, not just as students but as teachers, and finally administrators, as well. No more inspiring stories have ever been told than those of the nameless women who worked as laundresses, domestic servants and schoolteachers so their granddaughters could work on school boards and city councils and the state legislature.

Dallas was home to the first black female dentist in the South, but during the nineteenth century, women of any race found most professions closed to them. Teaching, nursing and social work opened up little by little, but most black women who rose out of domestic service or manual labor did it through entrepreneurship. They founded businesses, they bought real estate, and they brought African-American art and performance to Dallas. They opened boarding houses and took in sewing. They developed cosmetology products. They opened funeral homes. By the middle of the twentieth century, they were making their mark in law, medicine, government and business.

This book starts off with a horror story about a young slave woman who in 1853 killed a white man who had probably sexually assaulted her. She was sentenced and hanged as a murderess. The authors tell that story not to exploit the bitterness it raises but to elevate their narrative to the story of women who survived despite outrage and deprivation. The backdrop goes from Emancipation

THE HISTORY MERCHANT

2723 Routh Street
Dallas 75201
214-979-0810

www.historymerchant.com

"Tired of fast-food bookstores? Try browsing and reading in the quiet and unhurried ambiance of an eighteenth-century London bookshop." That's the invitation proprietor Richard Hazlett issues to the serious bibliophile looking for the most elegant bookshop in town. If you've been seeking a fine leather-bound edition by a seventeenth-century author, a signed first edition by Sir Arthur Conan Doyle, or all twenty-three first-edition volumes of the longest biography ever written in the English language, you just might find it here in this wonderful store that specializes in the rare and the antiquarian. If things like archival paper, vellum binding, and twenty-four-carat gold trim make you happy, you're in the right place. History, biography and classic literature are the stock in trade here, and Mr. Hazlett is just the expert to have at your side while you shop.

The History Merchant

through the Civil Rights Era and ends on a note of pride and dignity, with a focus on the contributions black women will make in the future of Dallas.

Also of interest is Rose G. Biderman's *They Came to Stay: The Story of the Jews of Dallas, 1870–1997*. Archivist, curator and historian, Biderman illustrates the Jewish influence on the religious, social and business development of Dallas.

The role that Dallas, especially the neighborhood known as Deep Ellum, played in the development of vernacular music in this country is not generally well known. In fact, just like Beale Street in Memphis and Bourbon Street in New Orleans, Elm Street in east Dallas was a center for the development of uniquely American music, including blues, jazz, gospel and country, during the 1920s and 1930s. An amazing book documents that amazing era: *Deep Ellum and Central Track: Where the Black and White Worlds of Dallas Converged* by Alan B. Govenar and Jay F. Brakefield. Discographies, photographs, and a bibliography round out the text.

Assassination

The most famous event in the history of Dallas took place on November 22, 1963. Any serious inquiry into the events of that day must begin with the report issued by the President's Commission charged with its investigation, the *Warren Report*. The official U.S. Government conclusion was that Lee Harvey Oswald took a rifle to the sixth floor of the School Book Depository in Dallas and fired it three times, killing President John F. Kennedy and seriously wounding Texas Governor John Connally. Controversy still rages over that conclusion and perhaps always will.

Countless books have chronicled the events of that day, including one written by four young broadcast journalists who worked in Dallas media, witnessed the assassination and its aftermath, and reported it to the world. *When the News Went Live: Dallas 1963* by Bob Huffaker, Bill Mercer, George Phenix and Wes Wise shows the reporters seizing the opportunity to make broadcast history, immersing themselves in developing events, even while grieving with the rest of the shocked nation. This book recreates the "all the air suddenly sucked out of the room" sensations that struck most Americans when they fully realized what was happening down there in Dallas.

Nellie Connally, who was riding in the limousine with her husband John and the Kennedys, offers a unique perspective in her book *From Love Field: Our Final Hours with John F. Kennedy*. Other worthy accounts of the assassination and its aftermath include *The Day Kennedy Was Shot* by Jim Bishop and *The Trial of Jack Ruby* by John Kaplan and Jon R. Waltz. Most historians agree that the account of events given by sensationalist movies like *JFK* and *Ruby* is not grounded in evidence.

FORT WORTH IN HISTORY

An account of *How Fort Worth Became the Texasmost City* is novelist Leonard Sanders's compilation of historic documents and photographs delineating the city's heritage, including the seamy side that all cities have. The writing is vivid, coherent and dramatic, supplemented by photos of meat carcasses hanging in a 1912 meat market; of ladies in hats, gloves, and long skirts at tea; of the first fire station, the first mercantile company, the finest soda fountain in town, and many other gems, all marking the development of the town Sanders calls "Texasmost."

Judy Alter and Jim Lee, both writers themselves, have sketched a portrait of what they call "*the* typical Texas city" in the words of others. A compendium of poetry, stories, essays and novel excerpts, *Literary Fort Worth* introduces us to the voices of many Fort Worth writers.

DENISON, HOME TO A U.S. PRESIDENT

The history of Denison is the history of travel in the Red River Valley. That heritage is laid out in Sherrie S. McLeRoy's *Black Land, Red River: A Pictorial History of Grayson County, Texas*, a complete photographic and narrative overview of the history of Grayson County from the first Native American tribes to the last decade of the twentieth century.

According to McLeRoy, the earliest settlements in Grayson County sprang up as fording places across the quicksand-dangerous river. Indian tribes fiercely defended the rich land against the encroachments of farmers and other settlers. By the early 1840s, their determined resistance had almost succeeded in driving back the invaders, but by 1845, the government had built military forts in a line from Austin to the Red River, as well as a road to supply them. That road came to be called Preston Road for its terminus at the trading post village called Preston, and it brought the army with it. By the end of the decade, major east-west roads had been pushed through, routing folks toward gold-crazy California. Indians tried to hold out, but treaties and reservations were their future.

Within a hundred years, the Army Corps of Engineers decided to tame the Red River. They ended up with the largest rolled earthfill dam in the country. Today, Denison Dam impounds Lake Texoma, an enormous recreational paradise that attracts millions of visitors and millions of dollars every year.

Dwight David Eisenhower

Dwight David Eisenhower, World War II hero and the nation's thirty-fourth president, was born in this railroad town in 1890. The small family home is now a museum amidst a state historical park. Eisenhower served as Supreme

Commander of the Allied invasion of Europe, as president of Columbia University after the war, and as Supreme Commander of NATO forces in 1951. As President of the United States, he began school desegregation in America, sending federal troops into Arkansas to enforce the Court's orders. "There must be no second class citizens in this country," he declared.

Books about Eisenhower, in war and in peace, number in the hundreds. You can find biographies, political histories, military accounts, and personal memoirs about the man on the shelves of every library in the State of Texas. A popular favorite is *General Ike: A Personal Reminiscence*, written by the general's son, historian John S. D. Eisenhower.

Don't look for too much objectivity in this book. Even professional historians view their subjects through lenses colored by personal perceptions. John adored his father and has given us, in effect, a testament to a great man. Somehow, that seems alright; the general was adored by a lot of Americans, and many who went into the forests of the Ardennes with him shared the view of the man depicted here.

General Ike covers the war years. For a more comprehensive biography, see Stephen E. Ambrose's *Eisenhower*, a 640-page condensation of an earlier two-volume work. It's highly readable, thorough, and not quite as adoring as John Eisenhower's book.

Gainesville

The big game hunter Frank "Bring 'Em Back Alive" Buck was born in Gainesville in 1884. His family soon moved to Dallas, but it is in Gainesville that his legacy is preserved in a zoo that bears his name.

Frank Buck traveled around the world to trap, bring back to America and sell exotic animals at a time before politics had attached itself to such enterprises. A real entrepreneur, he leveraged his exotic animal business into entertainment production, with books, films, comics, radio shows and circus performances based on his exploits.

He wrote seven books, including *Bring 'Em Back Alive,* during the thirties, and an autobiography, *All in a Lifetime,* in 1941. Surprisingly enough, these books are still quite readable. Exotic locales, wild animals hunted and in captivity, python attacks: they roll out one escapade after another for the armchair adventurer. A bestseller in 1930, *Bring 'Em Back Alive* made Buck into a movie star, too, a hero as glamorous as Babe Ruth.

The modern reader who wants to sample the best Buck stories will dip into the work of Steven Lehrer, who has collected and edited nineteen selections into a single volume, *Bring 'Em Back Alive: The Best of Frank Buck*. With a knowledgeable and sensitive introduction, Lehrer helps us see the famous hunter in the context of his own times.

SHERMAN
Sherman became a major transportation crossroads in 1849 when the "California Trail" forged by the gold-seeking Forty-niners made its way through here, as did the Butterfield Overland Coach. The Butterfield carried mail and passengers six days from St. Louis to Sherman, another six to El Paso and then eleven more across the great American wilderness to San Francisco. The entire journey cost $200 and covered 2,757 miles. In 1848, the local cattle industry was born with the import of two Durham cows and a bull, bought from Queen Victoria's herd in England, shipped to New Orleans, and then freighted by wagon to Sherman.

Quantrill and the James Brothers
On August 21, 1863, William Clarke Quantrill led 400 Confederate guerillas in a raid on the Union-supporting town of Lawrence, Kansas. They robbed and burned the town and left more than 150 civilians slaughtered. A couple of months later, he brought his men to Sherman for a bit of rest and recreation. There, they promptly began robbing, killing, and otherwise terrorizing the local residents. Complaints to the Army headquarters in Bonham brought orders for Quantrill's arrest, but he slipped across the Red River and continued his depredations

---

A TREAT FOR THE BOOK LOVER: "THE BOOK OF KELLS" REPLICA

Rare Books Collection, George T. and Gladys H. Abell Library Center

Austin College
900 N. Grand
Sherman 75090-4440
903-813-2490

The Julio Berunza Collection on Alexander the Great holds about nine hundred books, maps and other documents, both ancient and modern.

Collections of nineteenth-century periodicals, modern European history, literature and culture, modern religion and theology, and Texas and the Southwest studies are of interest primarily to researchers in these fields.

Of more general interest is a fine-art facsimile of *The Book of Kells*, a ninth-century illuminated manuscript, issued in a limited edition in 1986. The manuscript is universally considered one of the finest surviving specimens of the illuminator's art. You can see this replica in the window of the Heard Rare Books Room in the library.

throughout Kansas and Missouri. The Yankees got him before too much longer, and he died in a Union prison the same year the war ended.

Frank and Jesse James, Cole Younger and "Bloody" Bill Anderson rode with Quantrill and have ties with Sherman, as does lady outlaw Belle Starr. Jesse and Frank's sister lived and taught school here after the Civil War. They are said to have visited her more than once.

Well over a dozen books have chronicled the escapades of guerilla leader William Quantrill, some fiction and some claiming not to be. *Quantrill of Missouri: The Making of a Guerilla Warrior* by Paul R. Petersen argues that the man was a military leader, respected by his followers, misjudged by history. He was a brilliant soldier engaged, with the likes of the James Gang, in what these days would be called terrorism, taking the war home to the folks supposed to be safe behind enemy lines. The standard biography, still well regarded by scholars, is *William Clarke Quantrill: His Life and Times* by Albert E. Castel. The University of Oklahoma has recently reissued this classic.

Various other well-chronicled ruffians hung out around Sherman from time to time. One of the less celebrated local gunmen of the period was John Selman, who killed notorious gunslinger John Wesley Hardin, a native of Bonham, who had by then accounted for the deaths of over thirty people.

Violence and disorder on the frontier were not limited to men or even to grownups. Few more harrowing tales have ever been told than that of Olive Oatman. At the age of thirteen, she watched horrified as Indians clubbed to death her father, her pregnant mother, her three sisters and one brother. Another brother, left for dead, survived his head injuries and later made his way back to civilization. But Olive and her seven-year-old sister were taken captive by the rampaging Apaches. Her story of captivity, slavery, starvation, and ultimate survival is only one of the inspiring true stories in Sherrie S. McLeRoy's *Red River Women*.

Another blood-chilling version of the captivity of Olive and her sister Mary Ann Oatman is found in a

Sherrie McLeRoy

young adult book called *The Ordeal of Olive Oatman: A True Story of the American West* by Margaret Rau. It doesn't sugarcoat the treatment of the two girls, but it does indicate some of the motivations behind the Indians' behavior.

Tioga

On a lighter note, take this quiz.

What Texan born in Tioga . . .

- . . . has five stars in Hollywood's Walk of Fame, one each for radio, recording, movies, television and live performances?
- . . . recorded the very first certified gold record, followed by a dozen more?
- . . . recorded the first song to "go platinum"?
- . . . recorded the original versions of "Rudolph the Red-Nosed Reindeer," "Here Comes Santa Claus," and "Back in the Saddle Again"?
- . . . gave Roy Rogers his first break in films?
- . . . made 635 recordings and appeared in ninety-three feature films?
- . . . owned the California Angels baseball team before they became the Anaheim Angels?
- . . . and has his birthday celebrated in Tioga with a lively festival every September?

Answer: The actor, singer, producer, songwriter, baseball manager, tireless performer, World War II Army Air Corps pilot, entrepreneur and multimillionaire, the singing cowboy Gene Autry.

Autrey's autobiography, *Back in the Saddle Again*, chronicles his rise from farm boy to Hollywood legend and has provided inspiration to many a fellow aspirant to fame and riches. It's highly readable, even today, especially for one who lived through any of the times he writes about.

The Gene Autry Songbook, edited by Alex Gordon, includes words and music to the songs that had your grandparents humming: "Don't Fence Me In," "Have I Told You Lately that I Love You?," "Tumbling Tumbleweeds," "You Are My Sunshine," and more. A delightful children's book based on one of Autry's most popular works, *Here Comes Santa Claus*, has been illustrated by the gifted Bruce Whatley. This song was honored as one of the top holiday songs of the century in 1998 by the American Society of Composers, Authors and Publishers (ASCAP). If you're musical, you'll be glad to see the lyrics, piano music and guitar chords included. The book is suitable for ages three and up.

Waco

A pleasant, mid-sized city on the Brazos River with a history rich in Tonkawa, Wichita and Waco Indian lore; several small but proud museums, a zoo, symphony, and theater; and home of the much-respected Baylor University, the name Waco is known around the world as a synonym for almost unthinkable horror.

In 1993, religious leader David Koresh and seventy-three of his Branch Davidian followers died in a conflagration set off while their compound near the city was under attack by U.S. Government forces. After a fifty-one-day siege by the United States Bureau of Alcohol, Tobacco and Firearms, the U.S. Justice Department approved a plan to use a gas against the compound which they later admitted could have been incendiary and thus a major cause of the holocaust that followed its use.

David Koresh began having regular conversations with God at the age of twelve. Two-sided conversations. In an interview published by Dick J. Reavis in his riveting *The Ashes of Waco: An Investigation*, Koresh's mother can't say why he dropped out of school in the eleventh grade. "My own life was in so much turmoil at the time," she remembers, "that maybe I didn't notice."

Held back in early grades by a learning disability, Koresh managed to maintain average grades in high school, pulling down good ones in deportment. He was never arrested, never disturbed the peace. He was fond of music, guns and the Bible.

But the U.S. Government said he had begun stockpiling weapons in the compound where he lived as a young adult with his followers and that he intended to use them in an attack on the government. There were stories of drugs and orgies. It turned out, according to several accounts, that the worst things of which he was actually guilty before the fighting broke out may have been sexual, and his followers let him get away with them. He took a twelve-year-old girl as a wife; he declared many women his concubines and made them off-limits to the other men.

The tale is told by a surviving Davidian, David Thibodeau, in *A Place Called Waco: A Survivor's Story*, raising issues of religious tolerance and the roles played by the media. Stuart A. Wright's compendium of essays by social scientists, religious historians and others suggests that federal force was excessive and unjustified in *Armageddon in Waco: Critical Perspectives on the Branch Davidian Conflict*.

There's More to Waco

Fortunately, Waco is as full of beauty as any city in Texas, which helps offset the aura of strangeness that seems to cling stubbornly to its name. In old homes and gardens, it has no rival in its size; the Brazos River meanders past miles of lovely municipal parkland. A major university campus lends dignity with its traditional red brick buildings and white columns. And what must surely be one of the loveliest libraries in the nation is found here—the **Armstrong Browning Library**, housing the memorabilia of two poets who were lovers and then man and wife, Robert Browning and Elizabeth Barrett Browning.

TREATS FOR BOOK LOVERS IN NORTH CENTRAL TEXAS AND THE METROPLEX

Armstrong Browning Library

Baylor University
Corner of Speight Avenue and 8th Street
P.O. Box 97152
Waco 76798-7152
254-710-3566

www.browninglibrary.org

Poets and Lovers

This library is the world's largest and most complete collection of works by and about the Victorian poets Robert Browning and Elizabeth Barrett Browning, as well as memorabilia and personal possessions of the couple.

Armstrong Browning Library in Waco

The library serves as a research facility devoted to the works of the Brownings and their contemporaries, especially Matthew Arnold, Alfred Lord Tennyson, Charles Dickens, and John Ruskin, housing the largest collection of such material in the world. The ambition of its caretakers is no less than to include a copy of every book and article ever published on the Brownings and their work. Paintings, sculptures, showcases, Victorian furniture and the scholarly silence that fills the rooms make the place seem as much museum as library. And it boasts what may be the largest collection of stained glass windows found outside a church in the world, fifty-six gorgeous windows, to be exact, all brilliant illustrations of themes from the Brownings's poetry.

The love story of these two gifted poets, Robert Browning and Elizabeth Barrett, has been told many times. One account that uses the lovers' own words to tell their story is edited by Peter Washington. *Robert and Elizabeth Barrett Browning: Poems and Letters* draws together selections from their poems, as well as from letters they wrote to each other. Editions and collections of their works can be found in every library in America.

University Libraries Special Collections

Willis Library, University of North Texas
P.O. Box 305190
Denton 76203-5190
940-565-2769

www.library.unt.edu/rarebooks/collections

Most materials cataloged online at http://iii.library.unt.edu.

From McMurtry to Music

Many marvelous volumes, archives and manuscripts are to be found in this library of enormous resources.

Collections include rare books and Texana, with literature, history of printing, travel, miniature and small books, such as Bibles, almanacs and chapbooks; maps from 1597 to 1900; history, both local and state, with much material from the private library of Anson Jones and his family; manuscript collections of writers, including Larry McMurtry and Warren Norwood; first editions by Larry McMurtry and Katherine Anne Porter, and much more.

Weaver Collection includes children's literature, early textbooks, folk and fairy tales, works of major authors and illustrators, books about dolls and games, and books in special formats, such as miniatures and pop-ups.

The university also has libraries devoted to music (www.library.unt.edu/music), one of the largest at any university in the country, and oral history (www.library.unt.edu/ohp), as well as government documents and the papers of several prominent people.

The Woman's Collection

Blagg-Huey Library
Texas Woman's University
Main campus off Bell Avenue
Denton 76204
940-898-3751

www.twu.edu/library/collections.htm

Use of rare books and collections should be arranged in advance.

All about Women

Holdings: A major research collection on the history of American women, centered on many thousands of books, including women's biographies, manuscripts and other documents, and photographs. Contains the University Archives, with research material on the history of women's education, and an international collection of cookbooks, a chronicle of culinary and cultural history.

Some of the material, including the cookbooks, is available from the open stacks; some is accessed through the university's online catalog.

Eugene McDermott Library

University of Texas at Dallas
P.O. Box 830643
Richardson 75083-0643
972-883-2570

www.utdallas.edu

Collections: Airplanes, Stamps and Botany

History of Aviation: Two and a half million—that's about how many pieces this shrine to aviation history preserves in its archives and library.

The Wineburgh Philatelic Research Library documents philatelic and

(continued)

postal history. Holdings include philately of the British Commonwealth, Mexico, Western Europe, and South America, as well as the Confederacy and the United States.

The Louise B. Belsterling Library spotlights works about botany, including a 1499 volume called *Herbarium Latinum*. It's open for research only, and you will need a special appointment to see the books in this collection.

William A. Blakley Library

University of Dallas
1845 East Northgate Drive
Irving 75062
972-721-5328

www.udallas.edu/Library

Rare and Irish—Texan, Too
Rare book collections include Texana and Irish interests.

Mary Couts Burnett Library

Texas Christian University
TCU Box 298400
Fort Worth 76129
817-257-7117

http://libnt2.lib.tcu.edu/SpColl/Index.htm

Special Collections: A Wide, Wide Range
Speaker Jim Wright Collection; archive of the Van Cliburn International Piano Competition; William Luther Lewis Collection (literature, including nine hundred first editions); TCU Archives and Historical Collection; Newcomer-Pate Luxembourg Collection; Mayfield Collection (on western outlaws and gunmen); George T. Abell Collection (antique maps); works of Anthony Trollope; books on Abraham Lincoln, the American presidency, vice presidency, and first ladies.

DeGolyer Library

Southern Methodist University
6404 Hilltop Lane
Dallas 75205
214-768-2012

www.smu.edu/cul/degolyer

World Class in Every Way
SMU's immense library system includes world-class libraries in law, the arts and humanities, business, science and engineering, history, theology and other wide-ranging interests. The special collections are housed in the DeGolyer Library.

Holdings include rare books, manuscripts, archives, pamphlets, maps and other documents. Subjects range from women of the Southwest, to an oral history of the performing arts, to historical railroad records and photographs, and other material relating to business, transportation, science and literature. Writers whose papers are collected include Horton Foote, Paul Horgan, Stanley Marcus, and Lao She.

Historic newspapers, as well as the personal and business papers of the DeGolyer family and of former U.S. Congressman Earle Campbell are found here. The Doris and Lawrence H. Budner Theodore Roosevelt Collection contains thousands of items relating to the life and times of Theodore Roosevelt. The library is also strong in the history of European discovery and exploration of the New World, Spanish colonialism, and the American continent west of the Mississippi.

> **Special Collections**
> Central Library, 6th Floor
> University of Texas at Arlington
> 702 College Street
> Arlington 76019
> 817-272-3393
>
> http://libraries.uta.edu/
> SpecColl/index.html
>
> The university strongly encourages researchers to call before visiting any of the collections.
>
> **Too Much to Name**
> Many of the materials in the collections are listed and described in a handbook that is available online or at the reference desk in the Special Collections Library. Called *A Guide to Archives and Manuscripts in the Special Collections Division at The University of Texas at Arlington Libraries*, it can be accessed from the web site listed above.
>
> There are thirty thousand volumes, thousands of linear feet of manuscripts, 3.6 million photographs and negatives, and countless materials in other formats in this collection focused on Texas, the history of Mexico between 1810 and 1920, the Mexican American War of 1846–1848, and cartographic history, especially of the American Southwest and the Gulf area of Texas.
>
> Manuscripts include a group in Spanish, dating from the sixteenth century, letters and documents of early Texans, and the papers of selected modern authors, businessmen and other Texas leaders. Collections of newspapers, commercial photographs, graphics, maps and other materials are also available.

Attractions in North Central Texas and the Metroplex

DENISON

Denison has two dozen art galleries maintained by local artists, many of them quite gifted, a winery tasting room, well-stocked antique shops and, just a block or two north of Main, some of the best barbecue in North Texas. It all gets a special boost every spring in an **Arts and Wine Renaissance Festival** that features tastings from a range of Texas wineries, street entertainment and lots of good food. In April, the **Lakefest Regatta**, the third largest charity regatta in the country, takes place on nearby Lake Texoma.

Parades, street festivals, shows and fairs mean something fun going on most of the time. But even without the thrill of special events, Denison offers the visitor much over which to pause. Contact the Chamber of Commerce (903-465-1551) for details at 313 W. Woodard Street.

Dwight David Eisenhower was born in a house sitting amid a tangle of tracks from three different lines. The family soon moved on, but the house in which the future president was born was preserved. Restored now to its 1890 appearance, it forms the heart of **Eisenhower Birthplace State Historic Site**. Located at 208 East Day Street, it's operated by Texas Parks and Wildlife.

Another namesake of the former president is **Eisenhower State Park** (903-465-1956), a popular spot on Lake Texoma for water sports and camping. American bald eagles often fish below the dam here in winter, launching from the tall trees on the north side of the river and dropping like feathered anvils into the waters to snatch up prey. The white giants floating on the waves and ducking occasionally for fish are pelicans.

More prime birding awaits you on the eleven thousand acres of water, shoreline, creeks, woods and prairie that make up **Hagerman National Wildlife Refuge** (903-786-2826). More than 300 species of birds have been identified here since the refuge was established in 1946. You can find an online checklist by going to www.usgs.gov and then typing "Hagerman" into the Search box.

You'll find birds on this refuge any time of the day, any day of the year, but if you want spectacular sightings, don't miss the migrating geese and other waterfowl that winter here by the thousands.

Other Denison sites of interest include the **Red River Railroad Museum** maintained by the Katy Railroad Historical Society at 104 E. Main Street. Besides historical documents and artifacts from the early days of railroading, you'll get to see a diesel engine, caboose, tank cars and gondola up close. For hours, call 903-463-6238.

History is well served also at **Grayson County Frontier Village** (903-465-2487) located west of Exit 67 from Highway 75, a collection of nineteen early homes, stores and a school. Excellent restoration and maintenance make this a museum worth visiting.

Oh, and about that barbecue. The Doyle family has been turning out brisket, ribs, hotlinks and all the right vegetables for decades at **The Hickory House**, 630 W. Woodard St., just two blocks north of Main Street. Plain, simple, and always delicious, their barbecue holds its own with that of the more famous houses.

SHERMAN

Sherman's Convention and Visitors Council (903-893-1184 or 1-888-893-1188) can be found at 307 W. Washington Street. The city's festivals include the **Arts Festival** in September, which attracts vendors of all sorts of handmade crafts to display their wares under the autumn sun and brings in visitors looking for not only crafts but art as well. A juried show highlights festivities. Musical entertainment is first class, and parades, a 5K walk, a bike rally, and innumerable activities keep the show rolling. Only a few blocks away, an annual **Hispanic Celebration** takes place at the same time, attracting music and spicy food lovers from miles away. Also in September, a **National Aerobatic Competition** at Grayson County Airport allows more than fifty aerobatic pilots to compete in spectacular flying events.

GAINESVILLE

A comfortable fifty years old, the **Frank Buck Zoo** (888-585-4468 or 940-665-2831) fills a park cooled by tall trees with a collection of birds and animals that is worth stopping for if you have zoo enthusiasts in the car. It won't exhaust either your feet or your patience, and over one hundred thousand people a year think it's entertaining or educational enough for a stop. Other Gainesville attractions include the **Santa Fe Depot Museum**, which takes advantage of a newly-restored 1902 depot to show off three main displays: the role of transportation in the area's development, Gainesville's Coca-Cola industry and the Community Circus that called Gainesville home for more than three decades. A fascinating footnote to history is found in the display of artifacts associated with the Harvey House restaurant chain and the women who worked there. Another recent renovation has converted the old city hall building into the **Morton Museum of Cooke County** (940-668-8900), where area history is covered in changing exhibits. The building sports a Texas Historical Marker and a stunning stained glass skylight that will make your whole day look better.

TIOGA

This is more village than town, but the whole shebang turns out to pay tribute to Gene Autry, their favorite native son, every year. They hold a public festival featuring one live band after another, dancing, cowboy storytelling and recitation, vintage movies, pony rides for the kids, Indian dancers and old-timey fiddlers, plus food and western arts and crafts. For specific dates, call 866-408-4642 or visit www.geneautryfestival.com.

Dallas-Fort Worth Metroplex

If you plan more than a pass-through visit to this area, do yourself a favor and acquire a copy of a guidebook by Robert Rafferty and Loys Reynolds called *The Dallas-Fort Worth Metroplex* from Lone Star Guides. It covers thirteen of the cities that make up the Metroplex area, giving for each a brief history, contact information for local visitor and information centers, a listing of prominent museums, interesting historic places, and parks, gardens, and nature centers. It also includes information about local colleges and universities, music and theater venues, and attractions designed especially for kids.

This is the reference that tells you about the Chisholm Trail Roundup and Chief Quanah Parker Comanche Pow Wow in Fort Worth, the Sammons Center for the Arts, a jazz venue in Dallas, the hot-air ballooning activities in Plano, the Children's Learning Center in Arlington, the Owens Spring Creek Farm in Richardson, and hundreds of other places to see and things to do.

Arlington

Arlington's Convention and Visitor Center (817-265-7721) is at 1905 E. Randol Mill Road. The web site is www.arlington.org.

Six Flags over Texas (817-640-8900), the two-hundred-acre amusement park, is situated in the city of Arlington, between Fort Worth and Dallas. **The Ballpark at Arlington**, home of the American League's Texas Rangers baseball team, is there, too. At the ballpark, **Legends of the Game Baseball Museum and Learning Center** at 1000 Ballpark Way (817-273-5600) offers a deep look into the history of America's favorite sport. Of particular interest are exhibits from the Negro League and more than 140 items from the Baseball Hall of Fame. Interactive exhibits and programs especially for youth use the sport to teach lessons about math, science and history.

Dallas

The **Dallas Visitor and Convention Bureau** will send you a complete kit of information about what to do and see in Dallas. You can order it online at www.visit dallas.com/visitors/. You can also print maps of area transportation routes and DFW and Love Field Airport layouts from this site. Or you can go by the **Visitor Center at the Old Red Courthouse** (214-571-1301) at 100 Houston Street to pick up maps and brochures. You can check your email here, too, and use the Internet.

With seven thousand restaurants, Dallas has more eateries per capita than New York City. And with just as great a variety. If you're a stranger to these parts, you may think there's a preponderance of Tex-Mex cafes and steakhouses, but truth to tell, you can find almost anything you want to eat in this city, and often at very reasonable prices. Well, prices range from the super-luxurious **Mansion on Turtle Creek**'s (214-559-2100) four-course tasting menu, which nudges $100, to the local El Chico's less-than-ten-dollar fajitas. Whether you long for Thai, Indian, Italian, Japanese, Ethiopian, Middle Eastern or Southwestern fare, you will find it in Dallas or one of its close-in suburbs. Check up on what's cooking at www.guidelive.com/section/restaurants/.

Fair Park

Dallas attractions are scattered far and wide, but many of them cluster inside the huge state fair grounds called **Fair Park** (214-670-8400). The **Cotton Bowl** stadium is there, home of the annual New Year's Cotton Bowl. **The Age of Steam Railroad Museum** (214-428-0101), with the world's largest steam engine as its prize exhibit, is at 1105 Washington Street. **The Museum of Natural History** (214-421-3466) depicts the lives of indigenous American animals in attractive natural settings. An IMAX theater anchors the **Science Place** (214-428-5555) with its fascinating illustrations of science at work. Use the Grand Avenue entrance to the park.

Texas Discovery Gardens (www.texasdiscoverygardens.com), one of the true undiscovered treasures of the state, lies behind the 1936 Horticulture Building at 3601 Martin Luther King Boulevard, just inside the park. On a sunny summer day there, an alert visitor can count twenty to thirty different species of butterflies feeding on the flowers and herbs planted especially to attract them.

Women's Museum: An Institute for the Future (214-915-0860) at 3800 Parry Avenue seeks to memorialize the contributions of women to America, using interactive and electronic media, as well as more traditional exhibits.

African-American Museum (214-565-9026) at 3536 Grand Avenue near the entrance to Fair Park showcases fine African-American art and delineates the roles of African-Americans in the history of the country.

Fair Park is also home to the **State Fair of Texas** each fall, as well as numerous other annual shows, trade fairs, ethnic celebration and circuses.

Downtown Dallas

Among many fine collections, spanning the world and time from ancient Mesopotamia to modern decorative arts, the North American collection is the heart of the **Dallas Museum of Art** (214-922-1200, 1717 N. Harwood at Ross). Its store of regional Texas art from the twentieth century is unrivaled. Its European collection is especially strong in works from the eighteenth, nineteenth, and twentieth centuries, featuring the work of Monet, Pissarro, Rodin, Degas, Gauguin and others.

Everything about the modern facility at **Dallas World Aquarium and Zoological Garden** (214-720-2224, 1801 N. Griffin Street) is designed to bring nature close to humans, while protecting the two of them from each other. You can walk below a see-through bridge of water teeming with bright tropical fish, watch otters dive in a pond of their own, and look down on a crocodile so close it almost seems you can count its teeth. A rainforest with cascading waterfalls shows off birds, monkeys and other creatures.

Fresh fruit and vegetables, flowers, potted herbs, arts and crafts all star in the **Dallas Farmer's Market** (214-939-2808), which is open 7–6 every day at 1010 S. Pearl Street downtown. This is one of the largest outdoor markets left in the country. In season, you will find peaches from Weatherford, cantaloupes from Pecos, tomatoes from Canton, and throughout the winter, truckloads of vegetables from the Rio Grande Valley. Pick up bedding plants in the spring and summer, pumpkins for autumn decorations, even trees and shrubs for winter planting.

You'll also find a dazzling array of garden ornaments, specialty food products, and jewelry, pottery, and assorted gift items from Mexico. The American Institute of Wine and Food often sponsors **cooking demonstrations and classes** taught by local chefs. Call 214-653-8088 for information.

The great performance halls of New York and London have won much-deserved reputations for beauty and excellence in acoustics and service to their audiences. The **Morton H. Meyerson Symphony Center** (214-670-3600) at 2301 Flora Street is in that same heady class. The top-ten-rated Dallas Symphony Orchestra calls it home. Designed by architect I. M. Pei, with acoustics designed by Russell Johnson, it offers a musical experience matched only by the finest. Call for a schedule of performances or visit the web site, www.dallassymphony.com/.

Old City Park (214-421-5141), a village at 1717 Gano Street, depicts Texas life between 1840 and 1910, with a bank, offices, a blacksmith's shop, a church, and dozens of other buildings.

Also downtown is **Pioneer Plaza**, a tableau in bronze that will whisk you right out of the twenty-first century back into the days of the cattle drovers. Want to know what it would have looked like? Cowboys herding longhorns through rough country, across a stream, down a hill, through native grasses and wildflowers—this is what it would have looked like at the height of the cowboy days, only with everything at 140 percent of real-life size.

Picture that and you've got the feel of Pioneer Plaza, a four-acre representation of an early cattle trail, with three bronze cowboys on bronze horses, herding forty bronze longhorns along a very natural-looking trail and across a stream. This is the kind of exhibit you just can't keep your hands off of, full of powerful details and historical significance and just plain fascinating to get up close to. This tableau is the second-most-visited site downtown.

The Sixth Floor Museum at Dealey Plaza (214-747-6660, 411 Elm Street) draws more visitors than any other site in Dallas. A historical sign marks the spot where the motorcade was passing when the shots were fired that assassinated President John F. Kennedy. Dealey Plaza spells out the other details of that terrible day and its aftermath. You can take an elevator to the sixth floor of the Texas Book Depository, where Oswald knelt to fire the shots. After you've explored the museum, you may want to add your thoughts to the archives being collected from the public by writing in one of the "Memory Books" offered for your input.

Around Dallas
When you just have to get away from concrete, brick, asphalt and steel for a while, discover a treasure buried deep in the heart of the city. **Dallas Arboretum and Botanical Garden** (214-515-6500) is sixty-six acres of huge trees, green lawns, colorful flower beds, and waterfront, one of the best nature stores anywhere, and a full schedule of nature-related activities for both children and grownups. Lots of fun sculptures, many representing native animals, hide among the plantings or decorate the water features. A spring spectacular of azaleas, a summer full of colorful annuals and native perennials, and holiday decorations in the fall and winter mean something to see here any time of the year. You will find this first-class public garden at 8625 Garland Road.

The **Dallas Zoo** (214-670-5656) boasts everything you would expect in a large modern zoo, but its major strength lies in its twenty-five-acre "Wilds of Africa," which creates six major habitats and fills them with the appropriate animal and bird inhabitants. A monorail ride will take you through, past the Chimpanzee Forest, the Gorilla Conservation Research Center, the wattled cranes, meerkats, okapi and various other creatures of Africa. There's also a two-acre zoo just for children, an Endangered Tiger Habitat, and more. Special events for the family, such as presentations by zookeepers featuring different animals, go on throughout the year. You'll find the zoo at 650 South R. L. Thornton (I-35 East).

Denton
Two major state universities ensure sports, arts, music, and theater, most of the year, as well as galleries and museums. Texas Woman's University offers, among other exhibits on the campus, **Gowns of the First Ladies of Texas** (940-898-2000), showcasing inauguration gowns and other dresses of various governors' and presidents' wives. A charming chapel built in 1939, **Little Chapel-in-the-Woods**

(940-898-3644), contains ten lovely stained glass windows illustrating women serving the needs of fellow humans.

On the University of North Texas campus, the **Murchison Performing Arts Center** (940-565-4647) and the high-domed **Sky Theater** (940-565-3599) will broaden anyone's experience, with unmatched acoustics in the one and a high-tech planetarium in the other.

Fort Worth

Fort Worth absolutely bustles with places to go and things to do, eating Mexican food, barbecue, and chicken-fried steaks perhaps chief among them. Every city has its legendary restaurants and cafés. Some of Fort Worth's seem to be located in out-of-the-way industrial areas or tucked into unprepossessing neighborhood locations. If you're interested in the authentic way of food in this part of Texas, take the time to seek out one or two of them.

Joe T. Garcia's (817-626-4356), which started out sixty years ago in a private home, with customers helping themselves to beer from the family fridge, is now a large, friendly establishment still serving Tex-Mex beans, enchiladas and tacos family style at 2201 N. Commerce Street near the Stockyards. They're open every day, but at the busiest times these days you may need reservations. And they don't take credit cards.

For barbecue, check out **Angelo's** at 2533 White Settlement Road (817-332-0357). They don't take credit cards either, but they serve beer in quintessentially frosted mugs and slap onions and dill pickles on the sliced brisket sandwiches unless you appeal to them not to.

And no visit to Texas would be complete without a steak from **Cattleman's** at 2458 North Main Street. A Stockyards fixture since 1947, this hearty restaurant will be glad to run your plastic. Take a peek at their extensive menu at www.cattlemenssteakhouse.com/. If you run out of ideas for places to eat, look at www.guidelive.com/section/restaurants/.

It's easy to divide Fort Worth into neighborhoods, since attractions seem to clump together, somehow. We can talk about the Stockyard District, the Cultural District and Downtown as distinctive areas. Be sure to stop by any of the several Visitor Centers around the city to pick up brochures about other attractions and find out the latest on the rodeos, exhibits, arts performances, and other events that keep Fort Worth lively.

Fort Worth Cultural District Visitor Center lies in the heart of the Cultural District. From here, you will take in some of the best collections of art in the country on the one hand and first-class botanic gardens and zoo on the other.

The **Amon Carter Museum** (817-738-1933) at 3501 Camp Bowie Boulevard is about American art, with a very sophisticated collection that includes masterpieces by such artists as Alexander Calder, Thomas Cole, Stuart Davis, Thomas Eakins, Winslow Homer, Georgia O'Keeffe, John Singer Sargent, and Alfred Stieglitz. But the heart of the museum, the work that brings natives and visitors alike back time after time, is the paintings and sculptures of two geniuses that shaped and honed our modern perceptions of the cowboy and Indian as surely as did the words of Zane Grey or Larry McMurtry.

Frederic Remington and Charles M. Russell captured the cattle stampede, the Indian chase, the cavalry sergeant, the bucking bronco and the longhorn cow in oils and bronze, about four hundred examples of which form the base for this collection of American art. Other holdings include the works of several key American photographers—Eliot Porter, Laura Gilpin, and others—and scenes of the West painted by early explorers, and more.

Like much else about Fort Worth, this beautiful museum maintains an air of pleasant accommodation for visitors, with the politest security guards imaginable. That lack of pretension, backed by a solid offering of culture, carries over to the **Kimbell Art Museum** (817-332-8451) just down the slope from the Carter at 3333 Camp Bowie. A collection that includes the likes of El Greco, Rembrandt and Picasso and facilities that have hosted exhibits from the most important museums in the world sit quietly among the big shade trees and invite visitors to wander about, exploring the galleries at their leisure.

Unlike the Amon Carter, with its emphasis on the American, this museum was designed from the beginning to house art from all cultures and periods in all media. Quality was to guide selection. That philosophy has led to the acquisition of important European works and exquisite collections of Pre-Columbian and African art, as well as Classical, Egyptian, and Near Eastern antiquities.

One of the best-kept secrets here, by the way, is the buffet restaurant which serves elegant and delicious soups, salads, sandwiches and desserts at embarrassingly reasonable prices at lunch and stages a light dinner buffet with a wine selection on Friday evenings. For details or reservations, call **The Buffet Restaurant** at 817-332-8451, ext. 277.

Glance across the street from the Kimbell's east entrance, and you will see the latest addition to the city's arts scene, the **Modern Art Museum of Fort Worth** (817-738-9215 or 866-824-5566) at 3200 Darnell Street.

Dedicated to preserving and displaying art developed after World War II, this concrete, steel, and glass structure showcases works in a wide range of styles and media. Forty-foot tall transparent walls, massive concrete columns, an acre and a half reflecting pond, and an outdoor sculpture garden add up to a venue unmatched for viewing the latest in artistic output.

Back up Lancaster Street from the Modern Art Museum and across from the Amon Carter Museum sits the **Fort Worth Museum of Science and History** (817-255-9300), with its IMAX theater, planetarium and hands-on fun activities for kids.

South of the Science and History Museum lie the **Will Rogers Memorial Complex** (817-871-8150), where the stock shows are held, and the **National Cowgirl Museum and Hall of Fame** (817-336-4475), the world's only museum devoted to celebrating the women of the West, from bronc busters to artists. The geodesic-domed **Casa Mañana Playhouse** (817-332-2272) at 3101 Lancaster is a theater-in-the-round noted for musical and dramatic performances.

From the cultural district, University Drive leads south toward the parks, gardens and zoo. This area doesn't have its own visitor center, but its attractions are easy to find. First, on your right as you travel south on University, you will see the entrance to **Fort Worth Botanical Garden** (817-871-7686), the oldest such public planting in the state. It includes a ten thousand-square-foot conservatory with tropical plants and birds, a Rose Garden and a first-class Japanese Garden.

An excellent restaurant is hidden amid the foliage on Rock Springs Road, which runs between the Visitor Center and the Japanese Garden. Catch lunch or Sunday brunch at **The Gardens Restaurant** (817-731-2547) for a gourmet treat at very reasonable prices.

About a mile south of I-30, you will find the home of one of the largest collections of animals in the Western Hemisphere at the **Fort Worth Zoo** (817-759-7555). Animals from Africa, Australia, and around the world live in relative comfort and safety here. A tropical rain forest for chimpanzees, gorillas, and other primates; a koala exhibit; a naturalistic aviary for large birds of prey; a herpetarium for close-up views of many different kinds of snakes; habitats for tigers, bears, elephants and rhinos; a place to view newborn animals—there is enough to see here to occupy most of a day.

Heading north toward the legendary Fort Worth Stockyards, many visitors make their first stop inside the Stockyard grounds at **The Fort Worth Stockyard National Historic District Visitor Center**, 130 E. Exchange Avenue. Folks come to this Historic District today to eat and shop, visit museums, catch a rodeo or Wild West show, ride a horse over a portion of the Chisholm Trail, take a historical walking tour, or board a restored vintage steam train for an excursion. Or maybe to bend an elbow and watch the bull riding inside the world's largest honky-tonk.

Oh, and catch a concert by a big-name country music star, of course. Cattle drives, hay rides, petting zoos, parades and countless other activities invite you to experience a taste of the old West. Top it all off with a meal at **The Lonesome Dove Western Bistro**, where you can enjoy an appetizer like braised wild boar ribs with Lonesome Dove BBQ Sauce and housemade pickles or maybe a dinner of hand-cut buffalo rib eye with serrano–lime compound butter. Prices are about what you'd expect from a top-notch restaurant, and this is one.

Look for these exciting sites to visit within the District:

Stockyards Station. Shopping and restaurants. Board the Tarantula Steam Excursion train here for a round trip to the suburb of Grapevine. 140 E. Exchange Avenue, 817-625-RAIL.

White Elephant Saloon. Live music every night. 106 E. Exchange Avenue, 817-624-1887.

The Lonesome Dove Western Bistro. 2406 N. Main Street at Exchange, 817-740-8810.

Billy Bob's Texas. World's biggest honky-tonk. www.billybobstexas.com. 817-624-7117.

Stockyards Championship Rodeo. Hosts competitions frequently throughout the year. 123 E. Exchange, 817-625-1025.

Stockyard Collections and Museum. Livestock Exchange Building, 131 E. Exchange, 817-625-5087.

Texas Cowboy Hall of Fame. Museum inside horse barns on E. Exchange Avenue, 817-626-7131.

Fort Worth is not one of those cities that roll up the sidewalks and send everyone out to the suburbs when the sun goes down. Nightlife keeps the **Downtown Entertainment District**, called **Sundance Square**, vibrant through the evening hours. You'll find a schedule of current events at the Visitor Center in the Sanger Building, 415 Throckmorton. Downtown, you can shop for cowboy duds, eat in classy restaurants, visit museums and galleries, and enjoy musical performances in one of the world's top venues for classical performances.

Cattle Raisers Museum (817-332-7064) at 1301 W. 7th Street depicts the history of ranching and wrangling from the beginning into the present day.

At 309 Main Street, **Sid Richardson Collection and Museum** (817-332-6554) displays works by famed western artists Frederic Remington and Charles M. Russell. **Bass Performance Hall** (817-212-4280) at 555 Commerce hosts performances by the famous and gifted, from classical guitarists to stand-up comics, year-round. It's built of white Texas limestone, with a couple of Texas-sized (forty-eight-foot) angels sculpted into the façade. Inside, sweeping staircases and faultless acoustics help make this one of the leading opera halls in the world. See the web site (www.basshall.com) or call for an update on current offerings.

Outside of the downtown area, Fort Worth offers a **Nature Center and Refuge** (817-237-1111) for bird watching and the country's second-largest sports facility at **Texas Motor Speedway** (817-215-8500 or www.texasmotorspeedway.com). There's room here for more than 150,000 race fans at one time, and they fill the place up several times a year, with both Indy-style and NASCAR races.

Hillsboro

Hill College Harold B. Simpson History Center (254-582-2555) maintains both a museum and a library at 112 Lamar Drive. Both will delight history buffs with an interest in the role Texans have played in the nation's wars.

The **Texas Heritage Museum** at Hill College tells the story of Texans in combat, especially in the Civil War and World War II, with galleries devoted to "the Blue and the Gray" and Audie Murphy, the most decorated soldier of World War II.

Besides the museum, the **Confederate Research Center** holds more than five thousand books, as well as manuscripts, maps and photographs relating to the Civil War. Microfilm of the service records of Confederate soldiers from Texas, newspapers published during the war, and other historical documents make it an outstanding research center on this subject. World Wars I and II are the subjects of another three thousand volumes. Researchers may use this library, but only by appointment (254-582-2555 ext. 242).

Irving

Home to **Texas Stadium and the Dallas Cowboys**, Irving offers sights ranging from a tour of the stadium (972-554-1804) to a tour of a major movie studio. **Las Colinas Movie Studios** (972-869-FILM) at 6301 N. O'Connor Road is, at one hundred thousand square feet, the largest sound stage complex between the coasts. Movie, commercial, and television productions are staged here, with complete facilities for music, film, video and multimedia. On the tour behind the scenes, you'll learn how movies create illusions through special effects, makeup and costume, and the manipulation of sound and light. Actors of the stature of Meryl Streep and Kevin Costner have worked here on such movies as *Silkwood* and *JFK*. David Bowie, Garth Brooks, and Eric Clapton have rehearsed or recorded here. Call for tour times or see www.studiosatlascolinas.com.

McKinney

They might as well have called this place "Texas in the raw," because **Heard Natural Science Museum and Wildlife Sanctuary** (972-562-5566) is all about Texas—its plants, animals and minerals—as nature intended it to be. There are three areas to explore. Inside, the museum focuses on the natural history of Texas, displaying native flora and fauna, fossils, and minerals. Outside, a garden shows off native trees, shrubs, grasses, and flowers, more than two hundred species of them.

Then, the wildlife sanctuary's four miles of nature trails lead you to explore almost three hundred acres of prairie, bottomland and limestone escarpment, all with their full complement of birds, insects, and other critters. Hiking trails range from an easy path paved for strollers and wheelchairs to a more challenging mile-and-a-half through some serious woods. Most trails will showcase wildflowers, especially in the spring. Night hikes are a special treat, but they are always guided and require reservations.

An excellent nature-centered gift store adds much to your experience here, with everything from serious books on astronomy and geology to stuffed caterpillars for the tots.

The Heard is located on FM 1378; take Highway 5 south from McKinney and watch for the turnoff to the east. A map is available from the web site: www.heardmuseum.org.

Mesquite

Country music, chuck wagon barbecue and the explosive action you find only when professional rodeo cowboys mount up—that's what comes with the **Mesquite Championship Rodeo** at 1818 Rodeo Drive, and what more could you ask? How about souvenir shops, pony rides for the kids, calf scrambles, cowboy poker and more, all in air conditioned comfort? You can even rent a luxury suite and find out what it means to really indulge yourself. It all goes on every Friday and Saturday night from April through September. You can buy tickets online (www.mesquiterodeo.com), or call 972-222-BULL(2855) or 972-285-8777.

Waco

Look for **Waco Convention and Visitors Bureau** (800-922-6386 or 254-750-8696) at Exit 335B from I-35.

A town of just over one hundred thousand, Waco has made itself into an educational, cultural, historical and recreational center. It has historic homes worth touring, including a plantation house built before the Civil War that anchors a modern botanical garden; the unique Armstrong Browning Library, which is the largest and most comprehensive collection of Browningiana in the world; museums of local history and a zoo.

The shade of trees huge and ancient awaits you at **Earle-Harrison House and Gardens on Fifth Street** (254-753-2032, 1901 N. Fifth Street), an 1858 mansion with sweeping verandas and a rose arbor seventy-five feet long, draped with antique roses that bloom and bloom and bloom. Can you imagine a better place for a picnic on a warm spring afternoon? Roses, garden ornaments, an herb bed, a pond garden, and blooming flowers cover five acres. You can enjoy the garden alone or tour the house, too.

If you still don't have enough of the Old South, investigate the **historic homes of Waco** that are open on weekends and some holidays. Call 254-753-5166 for a schedule.

Homestead Heritage (254-829-0417) in Elm Mott just north of Waco is the place to go if you want your kids to get a really clear picture of what life was like before cell phones and fast-food restaurants. Bring them to this historic village to see a blacksmith forging wrought iron, a potter throwing a pot on a wheel, and a carpenter shaping a plank with a hand plane. This is a working farm built and maintained by a faith-based group intent upon preserving traditional skills and passing them on through the generations. The fruits of the daily labor help sustain the operation with gifts, beeswax candles, handmade furniture, canned goods and many other unique treasures for sale from a two-hundred-year-old restored barn.

You are free to walk around the village, so wander past the blacksmith shop to find the herb garden if you like to see basil and rosemary, parsley and thyme. The fragrant harvest from this working plot goes straight into products for sale to the public.

Once a year, during Thanksgiving weekend, the village invites everyone to a free **Craft and Children's Fair** where even more homesteading skills are demonstrated, like weaving, quilting, and leatherwork, and soap, candle and cheese making.

From I-35, take Exit 343 and turn west on FM 308, then, after about three miles, turn right (north) on FM 933. Look for a sign and turn left (west) onto Halbert Lane. No pets are allowed.

Texas Ranger Hall of Fame and Museum at Fort Fisher (254-750-8631, at 100 Texas Ranger Trail in Waco) preserves the essence of the law enforcement organization known as the Texas Rangers. From their inception in the 1820s into the modern day, Rangers have played a special role in the shaping of Texas. Besides exhibits from famous cases, such as the shotgun found in the car in which Bonnie and Clyde met their deaths, there is a **Research Center** that houses a collection of Ranger-related memorabilia and archives case studies, documents and photographs. Genealogy material and oral history accounts round out the collection. Take Exit 335B, I-35 at University Parks Drive.

Draw a tall glass of sweet, dark liquid, dunk a ball of pure white vanilla ice cream in it, smother the top with whipped cream and top it off with a cherry. You're in the soda fountain where not only the Dr. Pepper Float but Dr. Pepper itself were invented, now the **Dr. Pepper Museum and Free Enterprise Institute** (254-757-1024, on South 5th Street). But there is more here than nostalgia and a great soda treat. The Free Enterprise Institute is designed to teach young people about how advertising and marketing work and the role they play in the relationship between producer and consumer. It also shows them how a soft drink invented in a Texas drug store can become the basis of a multinational corporation.

Strecker Museum in the Sid Richardson Building on the Baylor University campus (254-710-1110) on S. 4th Street is where museums started in Texas, or at least those that stayed in operation. In 1856, the first mineral specimens, shells and fossils were gathered and classified. Today, the Strecker sits on the campus of Baylor University, its collection augmented by plant and animal studies, traces of the area's earliest human inhabitants, and a huge trove of mammoth bones discovered near area rivers in 1978.

Martin Museum of Art (254-710-1867) on the Baylor campus and **Art Center Waco** (254-752-4371) at 1300 College Drive bring painting, sculpture and other arts to the city's mix. The **Texas Sports Hall of Fame** (254-756-1633) at 1108 S. University Parks Drive celebrates famous Texas athletes, like Byron Nelson, George Foreman, and Nolan Ryan.

Waco Suspension Bridge and River Walk has a history. In 1866, if you lived on one bank of the Brazos River, it wasn't easy to visit the other. So Wacoans brought in the bridge-design firm that would later design New York's Brooklyn Bridge, and they started sinking piers into the sandy riverbed in 1869. One year later, the bridge opened, the first single-span suspension bridge ever built west of the Mississippi. It was 475 feet long. For the next few years, more cattle than people crossed it, as it became part of the Chisholm Trail, bringing much prosperity to Waco. The only traffic allowed on the bridge these days is foot traffic.

The best views of the bridge, which is located between Franklin Avenue and Washington Avenue, are from the River Walk, a paved strolling area that runs along the south bank of the river for about a mile and a half. You can enter it from University Parks Drive or Martin Luther King Drive.

WEATHERFORD

Douglas G. Chandor was a portrait artist. Winston Churchill sat for him, as did Franklin Roosevelt. Some of his work is still displayed at the National Gallery in Washington D.C. But it was his skill at garden design that led him to create the garden that bears his name, **Chandor Gardens** (817-613-1700, 711 W. Lee Street). He combined ancient Chinese elements with such formal English features as a bowling green, built a waterfall and other water features in this prairie setting, and left a legacy of unmatched charm.

The Reading Tour

Alter, Judy, and Jim Lee. *Literary Fort Worth*. Fort Worth: Texas Christian University Press, 2002.
Ambrose, Stephen E. *Eisenhower*. New York: Simon & Schuster, 1983.
Autry, Gene. *Back in the Saddle Again*. New York: Doubleday, 1978.
Autry, Gene, and Oakley Haldeman. *Here Comes Santa Claus*. Illustrated by Bruce Whatley. New York: HarperCollins, 2002.
Bacon, D. C., and D. B. Hardeman. *Rayburn: A Biography*. Lanham, Md.: Madison Books, 1989 (reprint).
Biderman, Rose G. *They Came to Stay: The Story of the Jews of Dallas, 1870–1997*. Austin: Eakin Publications, 2001.
Bishop, Jim. *The Day Kennedy Was Shot*. New York: Gramercy Press, 1984 (reprint).
Brant, Marley. *Jesse James: The Man and the Myth*. New York: Berkley Publishing Group, 1998.
———. *The Outlaw Youngers: A Confederate Brotherhood*. Lanham, Md.: Madison Books, 1995.
Brown, Sandra. *The Crush*. New York. Warner Books, 2002
———. *Hello Darkness*. New York: Simon & Schuster, 2003.
———. *Standoff*. New York: Warner Books, 2000.
Buck, Frank. *Bring 'Em Back Alive: The Best of Frank Buck*. Edited by Stephen Lehrer. Lubbock: Texas Tech University Press, 2000.
Castel, Albert E. *William Clarke Quantrill: His Life and Times*. Norman: University of Oklahoma Press, 1999 (reprint).
Connally, Nellie. *From Love Field: Our Final Hours with John F. Kennedy*. New York: Rugged Land, 2003.
Eisenhower, John S. D. *General Ike: A Personal Reminiscence*. New York: Free Press, 2003.
Fitzgerald, Ken. *Dallas Then and Now*. San Diego, Calif.: Thunder Bay Press, 2001.
Gordon, Alex. *The Gene Autry Songbook*. Miami: Warner Brothers Publications, 1997.
Govenar, Alan B., and Jay F. Brakefield. *Deep Ellum and Central Track: Where the Black and White Worlds of Dallas Converged*. Denton: University of North Texas Press, 1998.
Gray, A. W. *Bino's Blues*. New York: Simon & Schuster, 1995.
Green, Chloe. *Fashion Victim*. New York: Kensington Mass Market, 2003.
———. *Going Out in Style*. New York: Kensington Mass Market, 2001.

Huffaker, Robert, et al. *When the News Went Live: Dallas 1963*. Dallas: Taylor Trade Publishing, 2004.
Kaplan, John, and Jon R. Waltz. *The Trial of Jack Ruby*. New York: Macmillan, 1965.
McLeRoy, Sherrie S. *Black Land, Red River: A Pictorial History of Grayson County*. Virginia Beach, Va.: The Donning Company, 1993.
———. *Red River Women*. Plano: Republic of Texas Press, 1996.
Moore, Laurie. *The Lady Godiva Murder*. New York: Five Star Books, 2002.
Petersen, Paul R. *Quantrill of Missouri: The Making of a Guerilla Warrior*. Nashville, Tenn.: Cumberland House Press, 2003.
Rafferty, Robert R., and Loys Reynolds. *Lone Star Guide to the Dallas-Fort Worth Metroplex*. Dallas: Taylor Trade, 2003.
Rau, Margaret. *The Ordeal of Olive Oatman: A True Story of the American West*. 2nd ed. Greensboro, N.C.: Morgan Reynolds, 2003.
Reavis, Dick J. *The Ashes of Waco: An Investigation*. 2nd ed. Syracuse, N.Y.: Syracuse University Press, 1998 (reprint).
Sanders, Leonard. *How Fort Worth Became the Texasmost City*. Fort Worth: Texas Christian University Press, 1986.
Sanders, Marc, and Ruthe Winegarten. *The Lives and Times of Black Dallas Women*. Edited by Harry Robinson Jr. Austin: Eakin Publications, 2003.
Shirley, Glenn. *Belle Starr and Her Times*. Norman: University of Oklahoma Press, 1995.
Stiles, T. J. *Jesse James: Last Rebel of the Civil War*. New York: Knopf, 2002.
Swanson, Doug. *96 Tears*. New York: HarperCollins, 1999.
———. *Umbrella Man*. New York: Putnam, 1999.
Swindle, Howard. *Jitter Joint*. New York: St. Martin's Press, 2000.
Thibodeau, David. *A Place Called Waco: A Survivor's Story*. New York: PublicAffairs, 1999.
Wright, Stuart A., ed. *Armageddon in Waco: Critical Perspectives on the Branch Davidian Conflict*. Chicago: University of Chicago Press, 1996.

✳5✳

The Book Lover Tours Central Texas and the Hill Country

The Hill Country, the Perfect Water Trail, Bats and Caves, Austin, Burnet, Fredericksburg, Ingram, Kerrville, Mason, San Marcos, Stonewall, Vanderpool

The Hill Country, an area of rugged limestone hills rolling west of Interstate 35 between Georgetown and San Antonio, is famous for its waters, though few of its crystal streams would be called "rivers" anywhere else. It's the wildflower capital of the state, but the ground is so hard, dry and alkaline that little else will grow there. As for its "hills," well, not even the famous Texan propensity for claiming largeness could elevate their name.

The Comanches who held such fierce dominion over most of Texas before Anglos arrived never made much of a connection with the Hill Country, except to harry settlers they saw as encroachers, but misleading reports about the region's potential as farmland brought thousands of Germans across the seas to settle here and leave their mark on the region. You will see the fences and houses they built out of stone because that was the only building material at hand. Towns and villages sport names like New Braunfels, Boerne, Gruene, and Fredericksburg.

In spite of such contradictions, many people consider the Hill Country one of the most beautiful parts of Texas and certainly one of the most desirable to visit. It's a land of cool springs and limpid pools, of clouds of bats at dawn and twilight, of caves unmatched for beauty and adventure. In spring, when fields and roadside ditches full of bluebonnets echo the deep hue of the sky, **wildflower hotlines** become available, so you can check every day for the best places to view the flowers. (One is 800-452-9292.) In the fall, maple trees where no maple trees ought to be create a legendary spectacle of foliage in Lost Maples State Natural Area, and birds so rare as to be considered trophy sightings frequent that same park.

The rocky rangeland provides enough browse in some areas for cattle, in others for sheep and goats. The dark green trees that dot the hills are juniper, usually called cedar by the locals, plus live oak or shinnery oak. The lighter, filmy-looking foliage is mesquite. The cactus is generally prickly pear (nopal). Alongside streams, cypress grows.

The whole area is riddled with caves large and small, many of them open for your inspection and some with a history of use by ancient peoples or eighteenth-century outlaws. Spring-fed streams send millions of gallons of cold water up to the surface to tumble down hillsides or dig out canyons. Floating down such streams in an inner tube is a sublime experience on a hot day, and opportunities to throw your tube in the water abound. If you don't have a tube, don't worry. Someone will be glad to rent you one.

Hunting is another popular attraction here, with seasons for deer, turkey, quail and dove. Roads are narrow and colorful towns often little more than hamlets. Summers are hot and dry, winters cool and dry. McCulloch County, the geographical center of the state of Texas, sees about twenty-six inches of rainfall a year. Most towns boast a museum, a swimming site, an annual festival, or all three.

The Hill Country attracts artists and artisans as does no other part of the state. Hundreds of painters, sculptors, potters and woodworkers, artists and crafters show and sell their unique wares, and one-of-a-kind art galleries spring up in the most unlikely places. The village of Wimberley alone hosts half a dozen galleries.

Such music legends as Willy Nelson, Stevie Ray Vaughan, Janis Joplin, George Strait, and Robert Earl Keen have deep connections to Austin. Thousands of people gather in Kerrville in the spring to immerse themselves in nonstop music, and Gruene is home to the oldest dancehall in Texas, whose rafters ring endlessly from the exertions of both emerging and well-known musical artists. Wherever you go in this area, music and other live entertainments await.

Writers Like the Hill Country, Too

More novels have been set in Austin than in any other Texas city except Houston. The writer that some credit as the best ever from Texas, Katherine Anne Porter, was born in Indian Creek and spent her childhood in the Hill Country. James Michener chose to live his last days here. William Sydney Porter, who gained fame under the pen name O. Henry, lived in Austin for a while, married a local girl, and began his writing career. You may remember him for his Christmas story, "The Gift of the Magi."

Although Katherine Anne Porter left Texas as a young adult to live in Europe, New York, and other such far-removed locales, her best novels and short stories reflect her Texas roots. When she died, she was buried in an old Texas cemetery beside her mother, just as she had instructed.

Porter's most honored book was 1965's *Collected Stories*. It garnered both a Pulitzer Prize and a National Book Award. She has also been widely read for such masterpieces as *Pale Horse, Pale Rider, Ship of Fools*, and *The Leaning Tower*. Porter's writing style gives the impression of simplicity, but it catches the cadence of country talk and the subtlety of human relationships in a way that sneaks up on unwary readers. It can yank them out of their lives and into the mind of an eighty-year-old woman who lies dying at the turn of the last century surrounded by her family, or of a farm wife rearing a mentally handicapped son, or of a young girl first understanding something of the facts of life as she watches her hunter brother find unborn babies in a rabbit he is disemboweling.

Some of Porter's stories, set in the aftermath of the Civil War, examine the relationships between former slaves and the families they had served. One memorable character is Nannie from "The Old Order": "Nannie, born in slavery, was pleased to think she would not die in it. She was wounded not so much by her state of being as by the word describing it. . . . Still, Emancipation had seemed to set right a wrong that stuck in her heart like a thorn."

Porter may be the most prestigious writer to come out of the Hill Country villages, but she may not be the most famous one. The work of Fred Gipson, born in Mason, was probably more widely read during the 1950s and 1960s when he was producing New York Times Bestsellers like *Hound-Dog Man* and *The Home Place*. And at least two of his novels—*Old Yeller* and its sequel, *Savage Sam*—have been favorites of young people for decades, but their realism in portraying life on the frontier makes them highly readable for any age. Brave dogs, willing to fight and die to protect their masters; smart dogs, able to contribute to a family's ability to endure hardship: these are staples that continue to resonate with readers after almost half a century.

And James Michener, of course, was a voice heard 'round the world. "Obsessively detailed" is how one of his admirers described his storytelling style. Often starting with an idea so large it had to be expressed in only one or two words, like *Texas, Legacy*, or *The Source*, Michener's grand sagas reflect the author's own adventurous nature and insatiable curiosity about man in his infinite variety. His first published work, *Tales of the South Pacific*, may be his most widely recognized, for it won a Pulitzer Prize for its depiction of life in the Pacific Islands during World War II and was adapted by Rodgers and Hammerstein as the perennially popular musical *South Pacific*.

Michener learned to love Austin while he lived there during his research for the mammoth historical novel he called simply *Texas*. He made his home there from 1985 until he died at the age of ninety in 1997, the author of thousands upon thousands of published pages.

The Hill Country is home to many prolific writers, but few produce as much work as the modern writing duo Susan and Bill Albert. They have coauthored almost one hundred books, including about sixty young-adult novels. Writing as Robin Paige, they create mysteries set in the British Isles during Victorian times, utilizing famous settings, as in *Death at Glamis Castle*, and introducing famous people, such as Arthur Conan Doyle in *Death at Dartmoor*.

Susan Wittig Albert also sets mystery novels in a town between Austin and San Antonio, where her protagonist, China Bayles, sells herbs and runs a tea room called Thyme for Tea, in between uncovering unsavory secrets in the small community and solving murders. Each of these novels revolves around a different herb, and they are full of herbalist lore, even recipes, and puns are the order of the day. *Indigo Dying* is about both using the indigo plant to produce dye and the heroine's effort to keep a village from dying. *A Dilly of a Death* features Phoebe the Pickle Queen, and so forth.

Among mysteries set in Austin, two that recreate the city's earliest days compel special interest. In Edwin Shrake's *The Borderland*, Republic of Texas President Lamar has just set about "creating Austin in the heart of a river valley favored by savages," and he and others are investing in "commercial lots along the spring-fed creek that was being renamed Congress Avenue and would run from the river to the square reserved for the new capitol building."

Historical figures from Sam Houston to Bigfoot Wallace appear in *The Borderland*, and much of its action, including battles with Comanches, is based on true events, but, with its swift pace, over-the-top characters and hint of magical realism, you will be reading superb historical fiction without thinking of it as a historical novel.

Drawing on historical events and characters, Steven Saylor recreates the Austin of the 1880s with the sure touch of a historian and invites William Sydney Porter (O. Henry) into it with a novelist's flair. In *A Twist at the End,* Porter returns to Texas from his Manhattan home to become involved in solving a serial murder.

Another serial killer appears in Mary Willis Walker's Edgar Award–winning *The Red Scream*, in which Austin journalist Molly Cates discovers that the state is about to execute the wrong man. Much scarier is *Under the Beetle's Cellar*, in which author Walker shamelessly endangers a busload of children and keeps her readers glued to the pages like the master of suspense she is. *All the Dead Lie Down* takes us to downtown Austin, where a plot is in place to blow up the state legislature.

Bill Crider pursues violence in the same venue with *The Texas Capitol Murders*. Rick Riordan's *The Devil Went Down to Austin* brings high tech onto the scene, as does Steven Saylor's *Have You Seen Dawn?* For a touch of humor with your mystery, turn to Ruby the Rabbi's wife in *Never Nosh a Matzo Ball* by Sharon Kahn. Or forget the mystery and go straight for the funny bone. Get acquainted with Kinky Friedman.

Be warned. Not everyone enjoys the kind of wide-open, often scatological, always irreverent humor personified in such Friedman titles as *Meanwhile Back at the Ranch, The Love Song of J. Edgar Hoover, God Bless John Wayne*, and *Elvis, Jesus and Coca Cola*. Others find it irresistible. His books sometimes come across as a series of one liners, sort of what Larry, Moe and Curly might have produced had they been as smart as the Marx Brothers and grown up in Texas. But many readers find a lot of zany charm in the purportedly autobiographical tales of a former country-western singer turned Manhattan private eye, and Friedman's genuine love for animals endears him to anyone who shares it. The animals in his stories don't actually speak, but Friedman treats them as if they were human, often producing some of his best lines, as in this brief observation from *Meanwhile Back at the Ranch*:

> "It's almost good to be alive," I said, paraphrasing my father.
> The cat did not respond. She did not believe in paraphrasing anybody. If a cat can't quote things precisely, the cat nearly always prefers to remain silent. If people pursued this same feline wisdom, there'd be a lot fewer misunderstandings, a lot fewer wars, and a lot fewer people ripping off Oscar Wilde at cocktail parties.

The real-life Kinky, just like the fictional one, maintains a large-scale animal rescue foundation in the Texas Hill Country. **Utopia Rescue Ranch** (830-589-7544) near Medina will be glad to help you adopt a dog or accept your donation toward neutering a cat. You can see photos of pooches and other assorted homeless ones at www.utopiarescue.com.

A quite remarkable population of writers of speculative fiction also finds refuge in the Hill Country. Michael Moorcock, born British but Texan by choice, leads the pack. For a taste of his powers, dip into *Blood: A Southern Fantasy*, where an alternate world faces annihilation as a tear in the fabric of reality leads to chaos, where Bourbon Street and the Rue Dauphine exist in a South that is not the South you know.

Bruce Sterling joins Moorcock at the forefront of modern fantasists. His futurist visions were seminal to the cyberpunk movement. His latest efforts have been more directed toward environmental issues, as in *Heavy Weather*, about the effect of global warming, or by speculations about biotechnology, in *Holy Fire* and *Distraction*.

Neal Barrett, Jr., has produced a string of novels in more than one genre. *Dead Dog Blues* starts with the murder of a Black Lab, and that's only the first of the bizarre events that keep the story rolling. Dark humor, colorful characters, smart and sassy women and a small-town Texas setting make this mystery a winner. But it is the science fiction he's been writing since the 1960s that has earned Barrett the most fame. He novelized the movie *Judge Dredd*; penned *Batman*, *Spider-Man* and *Babylon 5* novels; and wrote *The Treachery of Kings*, in which animals take human shape. Then he wrote *Interstate Dreams*, which is not quite fantasy, not quite reality, and, full of quirky characters and recognizable Texas settings, is being hailed as a significant work. It draws deeply on Barrett's seemingly inexhaustible fund of very dark humor.

That same propensity for finding humor in the darkest alleyways of human existence fuels the best work of Austinite William Browning Spencer, whose *Irrational Fears* and *Zod Wallop* find human redemption among lunacy and addiction. The latter novel, especially, is like a strange, modern fairy tale, in which the characters, and then the readers, find the line between real and imaginary a messy blur.

Fantasy of another kind sparks the category romances of Annette Broadrick, more than fifty of them, in fact. She often sets them in the Hill Country and peoples them with Texans. Broadrick is almost as prolific is Peggy Moreland, who calls the heroes of her Silhouette Romances "contemporary cowboys." They must show courage, honesty, willingness to protect the weak, and most of all, a tender heart.

Biography and Other Facts

When it comes to nonfiction, the life of one man dominates the field: the thirty-sixth president of the United States, Lyndon Baines Johnson. He was such a towering figure, not only in his native Texas but in the nation and the world, that his biography by Robert A. Caro will cover almost four thousand pages when the fourth volume is completed.

Caro takes us from the Hill Country of Johnson's birth into World War II in *The Path to Power* and to his election to the U.S. Senate in 1948 in *Means of Ascent*, showing how he built a power base from which he was able to extend his reach to shape history. Both volumes won the National Book Critics Circle Award for biography. *Master of the Senate* covers the 1950s, when Johnson was pushing civil rights legislation through the Senate, until he accepted the nomination as John F. Kennedy's running mate in 1960. When completed, the fourth volume will recount Johnson's accession to the presidency upon the assassination of John F. Kennedy, his Great Society and War on Poverty, and his role in the war in Viet Nam.

Master of the Senate won both a Pulitzer Prize for biography and a National Book Award for nonfiction. Caro begins it with a quote from Woodrow Wilson: "When you come into the presence of a leader of men, you know you have come into the presence of fire; that it is best not incautiously to touch that man; that there is something that makes it dangerous to cross him."

Caro knows his immense subject intimately and understands storytelling. You won't read any of these volumes in one day, but their contents will be with you forever.

If you just can't get enough of Austin, or think you might want to spend a week or longer, equip yourself with the most complete and up-to-date guidebook you can find. *Insider's Guide to Austin* by Hilary Hylton and Cam Rossie is a good one. Whether you're looking for an African-American bookstore, tickets to a UT Longhorns football game, the newest shopping mall, an authentic barbecue joint, or the skivvy on local events from gardening to nightclubbing, this is your resource. Another great guide for anyone planning to venture into the countryside any time between March and November is Chandra Beal's *Splash across Texas! The Definitive Guide to Swimming in Central Texas,* four hundred good-humored pages about where to go to cool off.

Austin for Book Lovers

Austin today is a Book Lover's paradise, not least because it's home to the largest university in the state, a fact that certainly adds to the impression that everyone here is a bibliophile. Students lug books around, just as they do on any campus, and it's not uncommon to spot a gangly teenager striding down the sidewalk, backpack flopping from a shoulder, nose wedged firmly in a book. Huge old oak trees invite people to sit in the shade and lose themselves in reading, and there are something like sixteen libraries located on site.

Among the university's contributions to the writing arts is a graduate program offering a Master of Fine Arts degree through the James Michener Center for Writers, one of the many endowments the Pulitzer Prize–winning writer bestowed on the university after he moved to Austin in the 1980s. The program is key to bringing renowned and influential novelists, playwrights and filmmakers to town to talk about their work.

And the university produces writers, of course, among the best in the state. Folklorist J. Frank Dobie, naturalist Roy Bedichek and historian Walter Prescott Webb first lit the torch of literary fervor on the campus, starting with the 1928 publication of Dobie's *Tales of Old-Time Texas*. Today, the torch is carried by such talents as poet Betsy Berry, short story writer Rafael Castillo, essayist and biographer Don Graham, and others.

Beyond the campus, Austin proves its commitment to books and writing with innumerable book stores, both general and specialized, many of which regularly host readings, author appearances and book signings, and even how-to-write workshops. Hundreds of writers and would-be writers live in the area. Romance writers, mystery writers, and children's writers all sponsor active chapters of their national organizations here. But two things mark Austin above all others as the literary mecca of not just Texas but the Southwest. One is the Texas Book Festival and the other is the League of Texas Writers. They both invite the public to join them in the celebration of reading and writing.

Texans Celebrate Reading and Writing

The **Texas Book Festival** (512-477-4055), held annually in late fall on the grounds of the capitol, is quite simply one of the premier literary events in the country. Writers famous and aspiring, local and international publishers, booksellers large and small, and readers of every ilk gather to celebrate the best in Texas literature. Galas, award ceremonies, a book fair, author readings, panels and workshops, parties and children's entertainment turn the State Capitol Complex into a fairground for Book Lovers.

A poetry slam may be going down at a local coffee house, free for the price of a latte, while the likes of Sandra Brown or Elmer Kelton gather at a black-tie affair at the Marriott. Children's authors visit schools to read their works, and over the entire weekend, published authors host workshops and panels or talk about their work with the reading public.

Best of all when you attend this festival, you don't have to feel guilty for indulging yourself in a weekend of pleasures. The whole event is a fundraiser to benefit the public libraries of Texas, with former Texas First Lady Laura Bush serving as honorary chair. Get all the details at www.texasbookfestival.org.

The second literary phenomenon that sets Austin apart is the twelve-hundred-strong organization of writers called the **League of Texas Writers** (512-499-8914).

What started two decades back as the Austin Writers' League is now one of the country's largest regional organizations representing writers.

The League sponsors workshops, classes, and retreats with famous writers, as well as contests, awards and grants. Mentoring and networking play important roles, as do critique groups and special interest groups. And each July, this organization makes possible the fulfillment of every aspiring writer's dream—the opportunity to meet one-on-one with a literary agent and talk about their work, with their Agents, Agents, Agents Conference.

Most of the League's activities are open to nonmembers (though at a slightly increased cost). You can find information about both membership and the latest classes and outings by dropping by the office at 1501 W. Fifth Street, Suite E-2, 12–6 Tuesday through Friday. Or find everything you need to know at www.writersleague.org.

TREATS FOR BOOK LOVERS: ANNUAL LITERARY CELEBRATIONS IN AUSTIN

Texans love books so much they declare the entire month of May **Texas Writers Month** every year and in Austin the whole town goes to the books. Authors sign books in stores all over the city. Poets read poetry aloud, mystery writers hold panel discussions for the public, and children's authors hold storytelling sessions with schoolagers.

The **O. Henry World Championship Pun-Off** is a pun-writing contest that's open to everyone. It's been held in Austin for more than a quarter of a century on the first Sunday in May. The **O. Henry Museum** (512-397-1465) will be able to tell you the details of this year's event, as will almost any local bookstore.

Other events to watch for are the spring **book sale** held by the **University of Texas Press** (512-471-7233) and the **Jewish Book Fair** (512-331-1144) sponsored by the Jewish Community Association of Austin, which brings in the likes of Nobel Prize winner Elie Wiesel each year in November to kick off a two-week celebration of Jewish Book Month.

In April, poets congregate in Austin from around the world to read their poetry to anyone who will listen. The **Austin International Poetry Festival** (512-349-9883) gives audience to all who fancy themselves gifted in the poetic arts. It's a wide-open, non-juried festival with room for all: slam poets, performance poets, literary poets and Poets Laureate. If you want to participate by reading your work aloud, you can find more information at www.aipf.org. Or you can just attend and immerse yourself in today's happening poetry.

TREATS FOR THE BOOK LOVER: HILL COUNTRY LIBRARIES

The University of Texas Specialty Libraries

Besides its general libraries that serve faculty and staff, the University of Texas at Austin operates three specialty libraries whose quality and subject matter attract readers and researchers from around the world.

The Center for American History
512-495-4515

www.cah.utexas.edu

The history of the United States forms the focus of this enormous collection of print, sound, and photographic resources. Special collections include Texas History, History of the South, UT Archives, Congressional History, Western Americana, Special Historical Collections, Archives of American Mathematics, Histories of Media and Touring Entertainment and much more.

Lyndon Baines Johnson Library and Museum

2313 Red River Street
512-916-5137
www.lbjlib.utexas.edu

Holdings include documents donated or collected from the period covering the 40-year public career of the thirty-sixth president of the United States. Huge photographic, oral, and audio-visual collections supplement the more than forty-five million paper records. A manuscript research room is available. Museum exhibits include selections from fifty thousand items of historical note and a replica of the Oval Office (built nearly to size) as it appeared during the Johnson presidency.

The Harry Ransom Humanities Research Center

Located on UT Campus in Austin at the northeast corner of 21st and Guadalupe Streets.
512-471-8944

www.hrc.utexas.edu

A world-class archive of fine art and literature, the center holds five million photographs and a collection of one hundred thousand works of art in addition to the thirty million manuscripts and one million rare books at the heart of its collections. A 1455 Gutenberg Bible and paintings by Frida Kahlo and Diego Rivera join manuscript collections of such major authors as T. S. Eliot, Ernest Hemingway, James Joyce, D. H. Lawrence, Isaac Bashevis Singer, and Tennessee Williams.

Beyond the University of Texas: Other Libraries in Austin

Other specialty libraries in Central Texas offer specialized reading and research opportunities.

Lorenzo De Zavala State Archives and Library

Texas State Library
1201 Brazos Street
512-463-5480

This is the official repository for the records of the government of Texas from the eighteenth century forward. All three branches of government make their documents available to the public through this resource. It also serves as a federal depository library, receiving and holding all documents and publications distributed by the Depository Library Program of the U.S. Government Printing Office, more than 1.5 million items at this time.

A genealogy collection provides access to indexes of Texas records of vital statistics, to service and pension records, including some from the Confederacy, to tax rolls and other county records, to selected city directories and other resources.

A vigorous **Talking Book Program** (800-252-9605) is part of this library system. It lends books and other printed material, through the mail, to folks who can't deal with regular print for one reason or another. More than eighty thousand titles are offered in recorded form, as well as large print and braille.

Austin History Center
9th and Guadalupe Streets
512-974-7480

The Austin History Center is a division of the Austin Public Library. Here are found the documents and photographs that record the history and affairs of Austin from 1839 to the present. A wonderful old building holds an excellent collection of books, maps and photographs, as well as thirty-five thousand architectural drawings and thousands of linear feet of primary research material—unpublished letters, records, and personal papers, pertaining both to private individuals and to businesses and civic organizations.

Invaluable research guides helping users find their way among the voluminous material include "African American Sources," "Census Information," and a collection of materials on Charles Whitman, the infamous "Tower Sniper."

Special Libraries Outside of Austin

Universities in Central Texas cities besides Austin are home to valuable collections.

Southwestern Writers Collection
Albert B. Alkek Library
Texas State University
San Marcos 78666
512-245-2313

Some of the most respected writers in the literary history of Texas are represented here, starting with Álvar Núñez Cabeza de Vaca, whose *La relación y comentarios* was the very first book written about Texas and the Southwest. But filmmakers and musicians who have contributed to the state's culture are honored here as well. Holdings include manuscripts, personal papers, documents, photos and artifacts relating to the lives and work of writers whose ranks include the likes of J. Frank Dobie, John Graves, A. C. Greene, Elithe Hamilton Kirkland, Dagoberto Gilb, Cormac McCarthy, Larry McMurtry, Sarah Bird, Katherine Anne Porter, and others.

The Cabeza de Vaca book, in a 1555 edition, forms the centerpiece of a special Hispanic Writers Collection, which features such material as twelve thousand songs recorded by Mexican Americans from the 1920s to the 1980s, as well as primary source material about Tejano music and musicians, including sources for Joe Nick Patoski's biography of

(*continued*)

Selena. Tomás Rivera and Tino Villanueva are among the writers represented.

The *Texas Monthly* Archives, recording the first twenty-five years of that magazine's existence, are also housed here, along with those of *Hispanic*.

The Film Archives have six hundred film and television screenplays and the papers of playwrights, directors and actors, such as Sam Shepard, William Broyles, Jr., and Tommy Lee Jones. But the star of the collection is the Lonesome Dove Archive, which holds material, scripts, memos, sketches, photos, and so forth, detailing every aspect of the film's production, from planning to shooting to distribution.

Many kinds of music are represented in the Texas Music Collection, bringing material to light on the careers of Willy Nelson, Stevie Ray Vaughan, and Selena, and reminding us why Bob Wills was called the King of Swing. Joe Nick Patoski, a long-time *Texas Monthly* editor and observer of the Texas music scene, collected decades worth of material that now supports this unique collection.

Superb specimens of Southwestern and Mexican photography are preserved and exhibited in the Wittliff Gallery, ranging from vintage to modern, from historical in value to artistic.

Old Yeller Exhibit

Mason County M. Beven Eckert
Memorial Library
410 Post Hill
Mason
325-347-5446

Historical and genealogical archives pertinent to Mason County are available here, but a wonderful attraction is the exhibit area dedicated to Mason resident Fred Gipson of *Old Yeller* fame. Books, photos and memorabilia are highlighted by a delightful life-size bronze monument called "A Boy and His Dog," by Texas artist Garland Weeks.

Cushing Library and Archives

Texas A&M University Libraries
Campus of Texas A&M
Bryan/College Station
979-845-1951

This bastion of science and engineering is a fitting repository for both the University's Archives of Science and Technology and an outstanding Science Fiction Research Collection. A Literature Collection also holds significant sets of the works of American and British authors of the nineteenth and twentieth centuries, ranging from Rudyard Kipling to William Faulkner. The huge library comprises some 173,000 printed volumes and a quarter million or so photographs, as well as original artworks in many media. Collection subjects run from ancient history to the history of Texas A&M, with strengths in many subject areas, including Texana and Americana, natural history, nautical archaeology, and more.

The George Bush Presidential Library and Museum

1000 George Bush Drive West
College Station 77845
979-691-4000

bushlibrary.tamu.edu

Thirty-eight million pages are needed to document the history of George Bush's presidency, his vice presidency that preceded it, Dan Quayle's vice presidency, and Mr. Bush's extensive career; and they are all preserved here in a state-of-the-art research facility and museum. A million photographs and thousands of videotapes ensure a complete record of the life and service of the forty-first president of the United States.

Books & Java in the Heart of the Hill Country

1642 FM 2673
Canyon Lake 78133
830-964-6060

www.booksandjava.com

Michael and Sherry Doyle invite you to join them in two of their favorite pursuits: reading a great book about the Hill Country and drinking a steaming cup of coffee at the same time. This unique book store serves up both attractions to all comers, including the fishers, boaters, water-skiers, tubers, rafters and nature lovers that visit this community. Introducing folks to local writing talent is their special pleasure. When asked to name their favorite books by Hill Country authors, here's the list they offered:

Walking the Choctaw Road by Lake Canyon's own Tim Tingle

History of Sattler and Mountain Valley School in Comal County, Texas 1846–1964 by Alton J. Rahe, another local writer

The *Dear Lizzie* series of books published by yet another, William H. Jacobs

Bone Dry by Ben Rehder, set in the Hill Country

Growing Up Simple in Texas by award-winner George Arnold of Fredericksburg

The Doyles will special order books and do book searches for you while you enjoy your latte. Retired teacher Sherry makes sure a classy selection of books for children is always on hand.

Books & Java Bookstore in Lake Canyon

Attractions

AUSTIN AND THE HILL COUNTRY

In 1839, three and a half years after the fall of the Alamo, the government of the Republic of Texas cast an acquisitive eye on a spot in the Colorado River Valley. The natural springs there, the trees and hills and limestone cliffs must have looked pretty impressive compared with the coastal plains around Houston, where state government was then seated. So they set about moving the capitol to Austin. It was a pretty spot then, and today, well over half a million in population growth later, it's a pretty spot still. Adding to the natural beauty of the setting are numerous city parks, a state park, a nature preserve, a botanical garden, and an internationally celebrated wildflower center.

A good place to begin a tour of Austin is with the **Capitol Visitors Center in the State Capitol Complex**. Built of native granite, topped by a statue of the Goddess of Liberty, whose head rises more than three hundred feet into the air, and packed full of history, the Capitol makes an impressive show looming over the city. A guide will take you on a tour of the most important buildings, if you like, or you can enjoy the grass and trees that make the complex an oasis of greenery, while you thumb through the leaflets and maps from the Visitor Center.

If art is on your agenda, you'll find this a gratifying city. **Austin Museum of Art** has two locations, one near the State Capitol at 823 Congress Avenue and the other at 3809 W. 35th Street. Their focus is modern art. To see what's going on in Mexican and Latino culture, tour the vivid **Mexic-Arte Museum** (512-480-9373) at 419 Congress Avenue.

Elisabet Ney Museum (512-458-2255) at 304 East 44th Street showcases a large collection of the famous sculptor's output. Ney came to Texas from Germany in 1870, built herself a beautiful little neoclassical studio in the woods

A TREAT FOR THE BOOK LOVER: ALL ABOUT WILLIAM SYDNEY PORTER, AKA O. HENRY

True Book Lovers will be enamored of the cottage where William Sydney Porter lived out some of his thirteen years in Austin. It's now a museum under the auspices of the city's Parks and Recreation Department and has been named the state's first National Literary Landmark. The **O. Henry Museum** (512-472-1903) at 409 E. Fifth Street exhibits artifacts and memorabilia related to Porter's time in Austin.

O. Henry fans will find riches, too, in the O. Henry Room of the **Austin History Center** (512-974-7480) at 810 Guadalupe Street, where letters, poems and manuscripts in the author's hand may be seen, along with the magazines that featured and illustrated his stories and several hundred books, some of them rare or first editions. Clippings, photographs and bibliographies round out this fine collection.

of Hyde Park, and became the most influential figure of her time on the development of the arts in Austin and Texas. Stephen F. Austin and Sam Houston posed for her life-sized figures, as did some of the most celebrated of Europeans, including the storyteller Jacob Grimm.

History, in the form of the "Story of Texas," finds its fullest expression in the **Bob Bullock State History Museum** (512-936-8746) at the corner of Congress Avenue and Martin Luther King Boulevard. Theater seats that shake when an oil gusher comes in on screen—they're in the multisensory Texas Spirit Theater, part of a full-floor exhibit on how Texans create and seize opportunities for growth, both creative and economic. Artifacts of Texas history from before the first European explorers to the 1900s take up another floor, showing the theme of how Texans have lived on the land. The tale of how the Lone Star State won its independence and handled the next hundred years after that requires yet another.

Many of the exhibits and attractions here are Texas-sized, including a sixty-foot video wall showing the time line of the state's history. Interactive stations along the way allow you to pause and soak up as much detail as you like. A four-hundred-seat **IMAX** theater can show both 2-D and 3-D films and keeps them rolling, with subjects that can range from dinosaurs to NASCAR.

Besides history and art, much of Austin's charm lies in its dedication to preserving natural history. Nothing personifies that ideal better than the **Lady Bird Johnson Wildflower Center** (512-292-4200) at 4801 La Crosse Avenue, where nature trails, wildflower meadows, butterfly plantings and many small cultivated beds educate the public in the use of native plants in the landscape. Wildflowers put on their biggest shows in the spring. Native plant and seed sales are held in both spring and fall. The gift shop here is second to none, with its wildflower theme, and you will find an excellent selection of gardening books.

For a more traditional look at gardening, don't miss **Zilker Park Botanical Garden** (512-477-8672). Plantings light up the park from the azaleas of early spring to the old roses that rebloom in fall, but two of the most interesting features are the Japanese Garden, which shows just how oriental a Texas garden can be made to look using native or adapted plants, and the Hartmann Prehistoric Garden, built around fossils and dinosaur tracks discovered on the grounds.

Austin Nature and Science Center (512-327-8181) at 301 Nature Center Drive leads hikers and strollers through nature trails in what is essentially downtown Austin. Call for directions. For more hiking through undisturbed natural habitat and the chance to spot some rare bird species, head for **Wild Basin Preserve** (512-327-7622). Watch for endangered species golden-cheeked warbler and black-capped vireo. **McKinney Falls State Park** (512-243-1643) offers hiking trails, campsites, and playgrounds. You can bird-watch, hike, swim, canoe and explore some 740 acres.

There is one more bit of natural lore that any visitor to Austin needs to know about, and that is the city's reputation as home to the nation's largest **urban bat colony**. About eight months out of the year, a million and a half bats sleep every day, all day, clinging to the crevices on the underside of the **Congress Avenue Bridge** over Town Lake. No one notices them while they sleep, but when they wake up at dusk and take off to begin a night of foraging for mosquitoes and other insects, they form a living tapestry across the evening sky that no one can ignore. From spring to fall, but especially in August, people gather near the bridge to watch the spectacle.

Texas Hill Country Wine Trail, an association of about sixteen wineries scattered throughout the region, works together to make sure something exciting is going on at some winery in the area just about all the time: wine tastings, vineyard tours, book signings, bottle signings, live music, gourmet dinners, and even fine art shows and sales. To see what's coming up, visit either www.texaswinetrail.com or www.texasfineartandwine.org.

On the Trail of the Perfect Water Experience

Water, and the lack or scarcity thereof, defines much of the Hill Country. Without the rivers that rise here and the streams that feed them, this land would seem as inhospitable as much of the far western part of the state. But the waters are here, springing forth in mighty gouts from places in the earth the Native Americans considered holy, or splashing in gurgles and murmurs from crevices and banks, or rolling in from the northwest through rugged canyons to join up with local streams.

Here are found both the longest and the shortest rivers flowing wholly within the state. The Comal rises from springs inside New Braunfels and trundles off for two and a half miles to join forces with the Guadalupe. The Colorado flows through about six hundred miles of Texas, stocking a series of reservoirs along the way, lakes so beautiful that it's easy to forget their utility as water and power providers for growing cities and see them only as pleasure providers.

Fishing, boating, swimming, and other water sports keep the surface waters of all these lakes busy. Parks and publicly maintained areas make access easy to most. If you want a bass as big as you can haul into the boat, **Lake Buchanan** is for you. If pretty scenery is just as important, head for **Lake LBJ** or **Inks Lake**. **Lake Marble Falls** appeals to water-skiers and hosts a cigarette boat race each year. Boating is also popular on the lakes in the city of Austin, **Lakes Travis** and

Austin and Town Lake. Other lakes include **Canyon Lake**, about twenty miles north of New Braunfels, offering a wide range of water sports. Find out what's going on at all these waterways any time of the year at www.highlandlakes.net.

Away from the big lakes, along innumerable spring-fed streams, gentler water sports are practiced. In San Marcos, you can float over the head waters of the San Marcos River and peer through your boat's glass bottom at springs giving up 150 million gallons of pure artesian water every day. A bit further down the river, you can wade or swim in those waters, or rent an inner tube and float gently down the stream. In fact, wading, swimming, sitting under miniature water "falls," tubing and just generally splashing about in clear, cold waters are the activities you will remember best from a trip into the Hill Country.

Memorable for its facilities and ease of access to water activities is **Blanco State Park** (830-833-4333) on U.S. Highway 281 in the city of Blanco. There are camping facilities from rough to comfy and places to fish for perch, catfish and bass, as well as room for the kids to play. In Boerne, you'll find the more rugged **Guadalupe River State Park** (830-438-2656). Both day-use and camping sites are available, with good access to the river. If things quiet down after all the canoeing, mountain biking and splashing about, you might spot the rare golden-cheeked warbler in the woods here.

Garner State Park (830-232-6132) lies near Concan on the Frio River. Facilities range from campsites with nothing but water available to comfy cabins with kitchens. Study rock formations in the deep canyons, do a little from-the-car birding while you explore miles of country road, or hop right in the water. This park offers lots to interest children, like miniature golf, and several miles of paved hiking trails. Make your reservations early if you plan to be here overnight. It's a very popular spot.

Outside Johnson City, **Pedernales Falls State Park** (830-868-7304) offers some spectacular scenery, as well as exciting opportunities to play in the water, watch birds and other wildlife, ride horses (bring your own), picnic, fish or bike. Similar attractions are available at **South Llano River State Park** (325-446-3994) near Junction.

At New Braunfels, you can select the kind of water recreation you want. How does a dip in a spring-fed pool under ancient oak trees sound? **Landa Park** on the Comal River is what you're looking for. It also has plenty of traditional attractions for kids, like swings and a miniature train. Or you can choose the sixty-five acres of high-tech water rides, slides, waves and coasters at **Schlitterbahn** (830-625-2351), or an adventurous raft, canoe or camping trip along the **Guadalupe River**.

For information, contact the New Braunfels Visitor Center (800-572-2626). No one in New Braunfels gets away dry.

In **San Marcos**, stroll along the walkway beside the river of the same name and explore five different city parks. The water here has just come out of the enormous springs at its headwaters and is still as clear as water gets, with its temperature a constant seventy-two degrees all year. Bring your snorkeling mask if you want to explore underwater, or plan to rent an inner tube and float around all afternoon. You can get a tube, plus a ride back to where you entered the river, from **Lion's Club Tube Rental and River Taxi** (512-396-5466.) To get a look at the springs themselves, take a glass-bottomed boat tour at **Aquarena Center** (512-245-7570) in San Marcos. A 5,400-gallon aquarium holds special interest as the home for four federally protected fish, the San Marcos Salamander, the Fountain Darter, the Texas Blind Salamander, and the San Marcos Gambusia.

In San Saba, both **Mill Pond Park** and **Reisen Park** provide sanctuaries, complete with swimming facilities. Playground equipment and big old oak and pecan trees invite families to linger here. Wimberley is home to the evocatively named **Blue Hole** (512-847-9127), a spot on Cypress Creek, where you can swing out over the water on a rope strung from a huge cypress tree to plunge into the water. Privately owned, this park offers some camping sites, as well as day use. No glass or pets in the park, please.

Many of the streams and rivers in the Hill Country, including dry beds, are susceptible to dangerous flash flooding. Pay attention to any signs that alert you to heed sirens or other warnings, and take them seriously.

BATTIER AND BATTIER

Austin may be home to the largest urban bat colony in the nation. But what about the bats who prefer the country life to life under a noisy city bridge? In the Hill Country, the flying mammals have lots of choices for home sites. If you long to see millions upon millions of them darkening the sky as evening falls, plan a trip outside the capitol city, perhaps to **Devil's Sinkhole State Natural Area** (830-683-2287) near Camp Wood. You will need to make a reservation for a guided tour to see the one million Mexican free-tailed bats there.

Much more accessible viewing can be found at **Old Tunnel Wildlife Management Area** (830-238-4487) near Fredericksburg, where about two million Mexican free-tailed bats swarm into the air every night from June through October. There are observation decks and, on Thursday and Saturday only, batwatching tours conducted by Texas Parks and Wildlife personnel. A bat-watching deck is open daily and is free, but you will need to make a reservation and pay a fee for the tour.

Reservations are required, too, for a tour of Stuart Bat Cave in **Kickapoo Cavern State Park** (830-563-2342), north of Brackettville. In a very undeveloped area, this 1068-foot-long cave may challenge your outdoor skills. The trip is strenuous enough to require a liability release, and you will need to bring your own source of light and other gear, as well as your own drinking water. Access to the park is restricted, so you must call for reservations.

But why not make it easy on yourself? The very best viewing of vast hordes of bats in Texas is available free, if you can find the spot, at **Eckert James River Bat Cave Preserve** (325-347-5970). It's less than twenty miles southwest of Mason, but you will need to call for directions. The Nature Conservancy of Texas and Bat Conservation International own and manage the property which houses some four million bats. It opens for the public 6–9 in the evening Thursday through Sunday, from the middle of May until early October, with a Preserve Steward on hand to explain what you're seeing. Donations are accepted on site.

CAVES YES, BATS NO

Not every cave in Texas is occupied by hordes of bats, much to the relief of many. Some folks are less than fond of bats, it seems. That doesn't mean they have to pass up some of the most remarkable scenery in Texas—that which lies underground in spectacular caves. If you want to explore a cave, get out your sturdy, low-heeled shoes, and pick up a light sweater. Paths are usually paved, but some may be bare rock, and temperatures deep in the earth may feel chilly, especially if you come in on a hot summer afternoon.

Inner Space Cavern (512-931-CAVE) lies a mile south of Georgetown on I-35. It's easy to get to and offers great rewards for a bit of physical effort. If you've never explored a cave before, this is a good one to start with. The otherworldly sights are beguiling, the three-quarter-mile trail is paved, and there's always a tour guide nearby. Be sure to ask the one leading your group to alert you when you are walking directly beneath the Interstate Highway. You'll never know, otherwise.

Similar beauties await you in pretty **Cave without a Name**, outside Boerne (830-537-4212). **Longhorn Cavern State Park** (830-598-CAVE) near Burnet offers tours of about one and a quarter miles and a constant temperature of sixty-four degrees.

A Quick Tour of the Hill Country

BURNET

If you want to spend some time among jackrabbits and eagles, maybe take a seventy-foot cruise boat across a lake and up a river, watch for wildflowers or bald eagles, and spend your evenings peering through a telescope at an endless sky brimful of stars and planets, **Canyon of the Eagles** may be for you (512-756-8787). It's a 940-acre resort on Lake Buchanan, with a modern lodge plus campsites, twelve miles of hiking trails, five miles of beach, and the chance to glimpse rare or endangered bird species, all set among the modest hills and scrubby woods around Lake Buchanan. **Vanishing Texas Cruise** (512-756-6986) docks its all-weather cruise vessel here and takes visitors out to explore the wilderness without having to stir from their comfortable seats. In the winter, bald eagles are a special lure, but the boat ride is fun any time. **Eagle Eye Observatory** houses a sixteen-inch Ealing Cassegrain telescope for your stargazing, or you can bring your own optics. Star parties are scheduled year-round. Musical entertainments and storytelling sessions are frequent at the lodge.

FREDERICKSBURG

For a town of fewer than ten thousand, Fredericksburg has made quite a name for itself. "The new Aspen," "the bed and breakfast capital of Texas," "the toast of Central Texas," and certainly, "historic," "friendly," and "full of great places to eat" are a few of the sobriquets you'll hear heaped on this picturesque city, settled in 1846 by Germans direct from the Old Country. More than three hundred bed and breakfast and guest house accommodations surely put Fredericksburg in competition with the best B&B areas of the state.

Camping and RV sites are available, too, as well as guest ranches. You'll want to stop by the **Visitor Information Center** (830-997-6523 or 888-997-3600) at 302 East Austin, because when you're not eating, sleeping, or visiting with the friendly locals, you will find a feast of attractions here.

The Admiral Nimitz State Historic Site and National Museum of the Pacific War (830-997-4379) is right downtown at 340 E. Main Street. Inside, explore the rich history of Fredericksburg and learn about one of its most famous native sons, Admiral Chester Nimitz. Exhibits detail the Pacific Theater of World War II both during and after the campaign. A small but fine Japanese garden is full of symbolism. A Memorial Wall for the fallen and a plaza recognizing the ten U.S. presidents who saw military duty during World War II round out the display.

Ever see a butterfly wrangler? Don't miss your chance at **Fredericksburg Butterfly Ranch** (830-990-0735) at 508 W. Main. They don't actually brand the native butterfly species who live here, but they do arrange it so you can observe them in all their life stages, from cocoon to magnificent winged beauty. The gift shop holds everything butterfly-related you could ever dream up, from feeders to stuffed toys, and the 1846 house is worth seeing for itself. Stop by here and enjoy the butterflies and the gardens planted for them.

On Milam Street, discover the organic herb garden at **Fredericksburg Herb Farm** (800-259-4372), with its day spa, restaurant, and even bed and breakfast facilities. The garden is lovely, and the gift shop features absolutely everything herby, including gourmet foods like lavender champagne vinegar and personal care products like mint and eucalyptus body soak, all made with the herbs that are grown right here.

Of equal interest is a farm east of town on U.S. Highway 290 that's dedicated to growing wildflowers for their seeds. At **Wildseed Farms** (830-990-1393), bluebonnets, coreopsis, phlox and other native flowers bloom as row crops in expansive fields visible from the road. The most spectacular shows appear when the fields are in bloom in the spring, but there's always a reason to stop here in any season. Besides bluebonnets, the Market Center Store stocks the seeds for poppies, larkspur, cosmos and other showy annuals, along with all the wildflowers that make good landscape plants. You can find a Texas-themed t-shirt, jewelry or specialty foods, or stroll through the display gardens out back. Leave enough time for a snack of German tacos or ice cream, or maybe a beer in the Brewbonnet Bier Garten.

INGRAM

Immerse yourself in the world of art or theater at the **Hill Country Arts Foundation** (830-367-5120), a cultural center on the Guadalupe River. At the Duncan-McAshan Visual Arts Center and Smith-Ritch Point Theatre complex, you can look, you can learn, and you can do. Two thousand square feet of galleries host shows continuously. Famous artists give lectures. Studios, including a ceramics lab, and workshops for learning or honing artistic skills of all kinds go on all year, taught by top professionals in the visual arts. The Art Library housed here offers volumes on art history, instruction, media and technique, as well as biographies of artists and various audio visual resources. It's at 507 W. Highway 39.

If you enjoy the livelier side of the arts, stay for a performance in the **Smith-Ritch Point Theatre** (830-367-5122), outdoors in the amphitheater in the summer or indoors in cooler months. You're as likely to find Shakespeare here as an operetta, musical revue, Broadway show, play or drama. Call ahead for a current schedule.

JOHNSON CITY

You can request information about current activities from the **Johnson City Visitor and Tourism Bureau** (830-868-7684). There is another Visitor Center at **Lyndon B. Johnson National Historical Park** (830-868-7128 ext. 244). It lies two blocks south of U.S. Highway 290, between Avenue F and Avenue G. Watch for the sign.

Cruise into this hamlet on a quiet weekday in fall or early spring before tourist season begins, and you will get a feel for what rural life was like in the early parts of the twentieth century. Electric power didn't come to this region until the 1930s, connection to national telephone service until even later, and then only because native son Lyndon Baines Johnson was beginning to accumulate some political clout. Today, this peaceful village retains much of the natural charm that brought the first settlers to it. The scenic Pedernales River runs nearby, and cattle graze on peaceful pastures.

The history of Lyndon Baines Johnson, the thirty-sixth president of the United States, is preserved in **Lyndon Baines Johnson National Historical Park and the Lyndon B. Johnson State Park and Historic Site**. It is actually three parks, one in Johnson City, with a Visitor Center and the house and grounds where the future president spent much of his boyhood. The others are in the area near Stonewall where he was born in 1908 and buried in 1973.

The park in Johnson City offers several pleasures, including tours of the modest Johnson home, exhibits in several restored buildings, and the chance to see Texas Longhorn cattle. Not to be passed up is the Johnson City Visitor Center gift shop, a one-stop shopping destination for the Book Lover in search of information about LBJ and other prominent Texas politicians.

KERRVILLE

Summer is big in Kerrville, and the celebrations of its beginning every year have made the small city a national destination. The **Kerrville Folk Festival** (830-257-3600) and Texas State Arts and Crafts Fair (830-896-5711), both on Memorial Day weekend, kick off the season, and a **Wine and Music Festival** (830-257-3600) on Labor Day weekend winds it down. But hunting (830-792-3535), camping, golfing, and birding, not to mention shopping, keep the area attractive year-round. Details will be available from the Convention and Visitors Bureau (800-221-7958 or 830-792-3535).

The spring **Folk Festival**, almost three weeks of musical activities, is headquartered at Quiet Valley Ranch, a fifty-acre camping and theater facility just south of Kerrville. More than one hundred singers and musicians perform on the outdoor stage, and workshops are conducted for such specialized interests as songwriting or learning musical techniques, like blues guitar.

The **Texas Arts and Crafts Fair** is staged in Kerrville, with some two hundred artisans displaying and selling their work, and food vendors filling the air with the aromas of tacos and chili. Wine tastings, musical entertainments, exhibits, demonstrations, and even classes in such arts as playing the fiddle or dulcimer keep all sixteen acres of this show hopping from Thursday through Monday on Memorial Day weekend.

Visiting Kerrville during any of these festivities is not a matter for last-minute decisions, at least not if you want to spend the night in the area. Accommodations will be full. To help you make your plans, see www.ktc.net/kerrcvb/accommod.htm.

The **National Center for American Western Art** (830-896-2553) features works by contemporary artists that preserve the cowboy tradition or interpret the American West. It sits on ten acres of prime Hill Country land in a building designed by architect O'Neill Ford.

KYLE

Pulitzer Prize–winning author **Katherine Anne Porter** lived in a little house at 508 Center Street for ten years of her childhood. It has now been designated a National Literary Landmark, the Porter Museum (512-268-5341).

As First Lady Laura Bush said at the dedication: "There is so much more to this house than its remains. This is a corner of Katherine Anne Porter's imagination, and we are in it. This was a lifelong scene in her mind's eye, and how lucky we are to be trespassers here."

MASON

See exhibits dedicated to another famous writer, Fred Gipson, author of *Old Yeller* and *Savage Sam*, at **M. Beven Eckert Memorial Library** (915-347-5446) in downtown Mason.

NEW BRAUNFELS

By all means, start your tour of New Braunfels at the friendly **Visitor Center** (800-572-2626). It's at I-35 and Post Road, north of the city. You will need to pick up a map and some brochures if you want to take in all the historic and scenic sights this community has to offer. Information is also available about local river outfitters, rafting and floating guides, and other commercial enterprises related to getting in the water and having fun.

New Braunfels is home to more water recreation facilities per square foot than any other Hill Country city, with the state's largest water amusement park, the biggest pumping springs in the state, and two rivers. See **On the Trail of the Perfect Water Experience** above.

The home of **Ferdinand Jakob Lindheiner** at 491 Comal will beckon gardeners and lovers of native plants. The pioneer botanist roamed the Texas countryside in the mid-nineteenth century, collecting and classifying plants no one else had ever turned much of a scientific eye on. His adventures are chronicled in letters he wrote to fellow botanist George Englemann, collected by Minetta Altgelt Goyne into a volume called *A Life among the Texas Flora*.

Among several interesting museums in town, two are of particular note. **The Museum of Texas Handmade Furniture** (830-629-6504) at 1370 Church Hill Drive lies at the heart of Heritage Village, a historic site preserving the pioneer lifestyle. There you may admire Texas Biedermeier furniture made between 1845 and 1880, as well as English ironstone, pewter, and other artifacts from the 1700s. Nearby you'll find a working display of antique woodworking tools and other rustic exhibits. The **Wagenfuehr Home and Buckhorn Barbershop Museum** (830-627-2859) at 521 W. San Antonio Street has to be seen to be believed. A barbershop from the 1900s, it contains hundreds of hand-carved miniature circus figures and a collection of pictures on stones.

SAN MARCOS

Take Exit 205 from I-35 if you want to stop by the Convention and Visitors Bureau (512-393-5930 or 888-200-5620).

Water and education set the themes. Texas State University sits atop a hill, one of the first you'll encounter when you enter the Hill Country from the east, its skyline unmistakably a university's. Its significance for Book Lovers lies in the treasures of its Albert B. Alkek Library, with the Southwestern Writers Collection and Witliff Gallery of Southwestern and Mexican Photography. (See **Libraries of Austin and the Hill Country** above).

The water comes from the 150-million gallons a day outpouring from San Marcos Springs, which fills the lake at **Aquarena Center** (512-245-7570) and spills on down the San Marcos River. For more information, see **On the Trail of the Perfect Water Experience** above.

For drier enterprises, visit **Wonder World** (512-392-3760), where you can tour a cavern formed by an earthquake, view the Balcones fault line from a tower, have fun in a house of anti-gravity, and pet some wildlife, all in the same park.

STONEWALL

LBJ State Park Visitor Center (830-644-2252) and **National Historical Park** (830-868-7128) are two different parks, but they work together to complete for us the story of the early life of the thirty-sixth president of the United States, Lyndon Baines Johnson. Both the site of his birth and his grave are accessible any time you choose to visit. At the **LBJ State Park Visitor Center** tours form to cover these landmarks, as well as the seven-hundred-acre Johnson ranch which now houses the **Sauer-Beckmann Farm**, a living history farmstead depicting rural life in the first two decades of the twentieth century.

LBJ State Park also conducts viewings of the bat colony in the **Old Tunnel Wildlife Management Area** in the park. For information about schedules, call 830-238-4487.

VANDERPOOL

A few miles north of Vanderpool lies **Lost Maples State Natural Area** (830-966-3413), famed for its stand of big-tooth maples that turn the forest into an explosion of color in the fall and for its winged inhabitants, especially the green kingfisher, which you can add to your bird list any month of the year here. The period between mid-October and mid-November, when the maples are putting on their show, brings lots of visitors to the area, especially on weekends. Plan your trip for a weekday, if you can, and go tree-watching early in the day. You'll see more birds at that time, too, with eleven miles of hiking trail to saunter down. In the warmer months, both golden-cheeked warbler and black-capped vireo are possible.

The Reading Tour

Albert, Susan Wittig. *A Dilly of a Death*. New York: Berkley Publishing, 2004.
———. *Indigo Dying*. New York: Berkley Publishing, 2003.
Albert, Susan Wittig, and Bill Albert. *Death at Dartmoor*. New York: Prime Crime, 2003.
———. *Death at Glamis Castle*. New York: Prime Crime, 2004.
Barrett, Neal. *Dead Dog Blues*. New York: Kensington Publishing Group, 1994.
———. *Interstate Dreams*. Austin: Mojo Press, 1999.
———. *The Treachery of Kings*. New York: Bantam, 2001.
Beal, Chandra. *Splash across Texas! The Definitive Guide to Swimming in Central Texas*. Austin: La Luna Publishing, 1999.

Broadrick, Annette. *Too Tough to Tame*. New York: Silhouette, 2003.
Caro, Robert A. *Master of the Senate*. New York: Knopf, 2002.
——. *Means of Ascent*. New York: Knopf, 1990.
——. *The Path to Power*. New York: Knopf, 1982.
Crider, Bill. *The Texas Capitol Murders*. New York: St. Martin's Press, 1992.
Friedman, Kinky. *Elvis, Jesus and Coca Cola*. New York: Simon & Schuster, 1993.
——. *God Bless John Wayne*. New York: Simon & Schuster, 1995.
——. *Meanwhile Back at the Ranch*. New York: Simon & Schuster, 2003.
Gipson, Fred. *Old Yeller*. New York: HarperCollins Juvenile Books, 1989 (reissue).
——. *Savage Sam*. New York: HarperCollins Juvenile Books, 1962.
Kahn, Sharon. *Never Nosh a Matzo Ball*. New York: Scribner, 2000.
Michener, James. *Texas*. New York: Random House Trade Paper, 2002 (reissue).
Moorcock, Michael. *Blood: A Southern Fantasy*. New York: William Morrow, 1995.
Moreland, Peggy. *Her Lone Star Protector*. New York: Silhouette, 2002.
Porter, Katherine Anne. *Collected Stories*. New York: Harvest Books, 1979.
——. *The Leaning Tower*. New York: Harcourt, 1944.
——. *Pale Horse, Pale Rider*. New York: Harcourt, 1990 (reissue).
——. *Ship of Fools*. New York: Back Bay Paperback, 2000 (reissue).
Porter, William Sydney. *The Complete Works of O'Henry*. New York: Doubleday, 1953.
Riordan, Rick. *The Devil Went Down to Austin*. New York: Bantam, 2001.
Saylor, Steven. *Have You Seen Dawn?* New York: Simon & Schuster, 2003.
——. *A Twist at the End*. New York: Simon & Schuster, 2000.
Shrake, Edwin. *The Borderland*. New York: Hyperion Press, 2000.
Spencer, William Browning. *Irrational Fears*. Stone Mountain, Ga.: White Wolf Publishing, 1998.
——. *Zod Wallop*. New York: St. Martin's Press, 1995.
Sterling, Bruce. *Distraction*. New York: Bantam, 1998.
——. *Heavy Weather*. New York: Bantam, 1994.
——. *Holy Fire*. New York: Bantam, 1996.
Walker, Mary Willis. *All the Dead Lie Down*. New York: Doubleday, 1998.
——. *The Red Scream*. New York: Doubleday, 1994.
——. *Under the Beetle's Cellar*. New York: Doubleday, 1995.

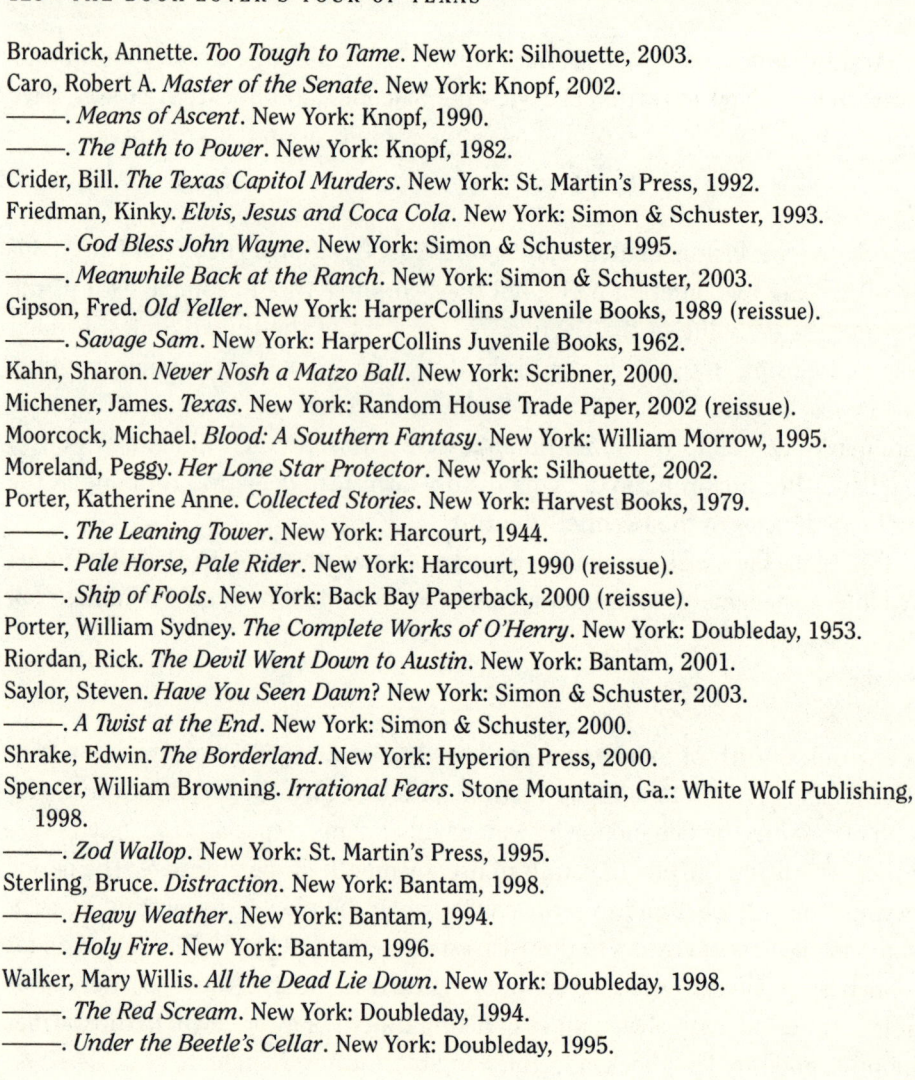

✴ 6 ✴

The Book Lover Tours San Antonio, the Brush Country, and the Rio Grande Valley

Alamo, Brackettville, Brownsville, Edinburgh, Goliad,
Laredo, McAllen, Mission, San Antonio

The sprawling city of San Antonio, which sits at the northern apex of the South Texas Plains, reigns over twenty million acres of flat brushland, prickly pear (nopal cactus) and mesquite, and oaks dwarfed by rainfall that barely tops twenty inches in a year.

Irrigation has created pockets of paradise in this unlikely scenery. Best known are the agricultural parts of the lower Rio Grande Valley, but wherever water can be drawn into fields, vegetables and fruit crops are grown. Atascosa County, for instance, immediately south of San Antonio, leads the state in commercial strawberry production and, with its eastern neighbor, Wilson County, produces more than a hundred million dollars in agricultural output each year, with beef and dairy cattle and other livestock making up a good portion of it.

Despite all those agricultural activities, the impression of vast emptiness is inescapable when you drive through this region. Even after Spanish conquest of the area had begun in the 1740s, no one lingered much between the Rio Grande and San Antonio. They blazed trails through the area, laid claims to it, later fought the Texas settlers over it, but took little profit from it. One of their most lasting legacies was the establishment of land-grant cattle ranches owned and run by Spanish-speaking cowboys, who enriched the English language with words like *vaquero, rodeo, bronco,* and *chaparral.*

In the 1820s, the governor of the Mexican state of Texas began allowing American emigrants into the area. It wasn't fifteen years before they were rattling arms, talking about wanting independence from Mexico. And the territory they laid claim to included the whole huge region south of San Antonio we call the brushlands today.

Eventually, disputes over the land between the Rio Grande and the Nueces River led to war between the Mexican government and the settlers. Mexico's president, General Santa Anna, marched an army into San Antonio, thinking to settle the matter once and for all, but he let himself get bogged down in the siege of a tiny fortification, an old mission called the Alamo. He remained there for thirteen days, held off by fewer than two hundred Texans led by William Barrett Travis and James Bowie.

Meanwhile, other Texans gathered at a small community east of there, called Washington-on-the-Brazos, and declared the independence of Texas from Mexico. At the Alamo, once Santa Anna attacked, his forces overran the little fortress and killed the defenders. Victorious, Santa Anna set out to rid the country of the troublemakers, and he collected and disarmed hundreds of prisoners of war along the way. At Goliad, he had some four hundred of them herded into a field and summarily executed.

That was Palm Sunday, March 27, 1836. Certain of ultimate victory, Santa Anna spent the next month chasing Sam Houston's ragged army. His overconfidence may have been Santa Anna's undoing. It apparently led him to split his forces, sending two thirds of them off on different errands, and, when he faced Houston at last, it led him to almost unbelievable carelessness. Houston lured him into an untenable position, burned the bridges at his back, and then surprised him in an attack that took place not at dawn, as the general had expected, but in the middle of the troops' afternoon siesta. The battle was a complete rout. Santa Anna was captured, along with seven hundred of his men, while more than six hundred Mexican soldiers were left dead on the field. Fewer than a dozen Texans died in the battle. The Republic of Texas was a fact.

In 1845, Texas gave up its independence to join the United States of America as its twenty-eighth state, but it took Mexico two more years and several bloody battles to relinquish the vast territory between the Nueces River and the Rio Grande.

San Antonio and the Alamo

When Santa Anna decided to begin marching his army toward San Antonio, Sam Houston decided that, rather than let the Mexican Army reoccupy the mission, he would send thirty-one volunteers led by James Bowie to destroy it. Once there, Bowie dug in and refused to carry out his orders. Houston sent William Barrett Travis to reason with him. Instead, Travis threw in with Bowie. They were determined to defend the Alamo. Within a couple of weeks, David Crockett joined them, bringing in some sixteen Tennessee Mounted Volunteers. When, less than two weeks later, Santa Anna entered San Antonio, about 170 Texans had gathered in the old mission and, led now by Travis, were sending out messengers pleading for reinforcements from fellow Texans. Only thirty-one men showed up, from the town of Gonzales. Apparently knowing he was doomed, Travis wrote to "the people of Texas and all Americans in the World."

I am besieged by a thousand or more Mexicans under Santa Anna. I have sustained a continual bombardment for 24 hours and have not lost a man. The enemy has demanded our surrender, otherwise the garrison will be put to the sword. I have answered the demand with a canon shot, and our flag still waves proudly from the walls. I shall not surrender nor retreat. I call upon you in the name of liberty, patriotism and everything dear to the American character, to come to our aid. The enemy is receiving reinforcements daily and will no doubt increase to three or four thousand within four or five days. I am determined to sustain myself as long as possible and die like a soldier. Victory or death.

It is said that Travis drew a line in the sand and told his men to step across it if they intended to stay until the end. One man chose to leave. Of those who stayed to defend the Alamo, all died in the final attack, except two who survived despite wounds.

That is the simple story of the Alamo. It's so simple, it has had to be told over and over again, reinterpreted by writers with different agendas. Was the battle of the Alamo a clash of giants? Were the men who fell heroes? Does it matter that they all had human flaws and that some perhaps did not die as "well" as the mythmakers had reported?

To many Texans, the battle of the Alamo is the defining moment of their history, a time when brave men deliberately chose to die rather than surrender so that a new Republic might be born. Could it be, as some now suggest, that they stayed only because they thought reinforcements would arrive in time to save them? Each new book about the events at the Alamo claims to lay bare the truth, to present a more accurate account, to dismantle the myths.

When John Myers tackled the subject in 1948 with his *The Alamo*, he summed up the attitudes of most of his contemporaries: "The Alamo isn't a structure now; it is a symbol of valor in the minds of men. It can never fall again." About a decade later, Lon Tinkle explored the key players' reasons for being in this place at this moment in time in *Thirteen Days to Glory*. The book won literary prizes and has remained popular, to some extent because it is suitable reading for young people. Another award winner that tells the story of the entire Texas Revolution is Stephen L. Hardin's *Texian Iliad: A Military History of the Texas Revolution*. "The story of the Alamo is our hagiography," he says. "Its heroes *are* our saints."

Three Roads to the Alamo, almost eight hundred pages with source notes and index, is William C. Davis's biography of Crockett, Bowie and Travis. It shows the men as they probably truly were, with all their faults and weaknesses, suggesting them as prototypes of the three kinds of men who won the West. Crockett was the explorer, the groundbreaker, always moving just ahead of civilization. Bowie was the type of man who moves into the vacuum created when the Crocketts move on, men who know how to profit from and even exploit the newly opened area, the entrepreneurs and gamblers, sometimes outlaws. Travis was the civilizer. Even though he fled Alabama under threat of debtor's prison, leaving behind a wife with one child and expecting another, he was educated, a lawyer who grew to be a builder of communities.

For all three, the frontier that was early Texas was an irresistible lure. Their joining in death at the Alamo has acquired mythical status. As Davis puts it, "Such a vacuum of information dominates the major portions of their histories that supposition, fabrication and myth have filled the empty spaces and are so oft-repeated that falsehood and legend stand side by side with fact in the canon of their biographies."

Davis takes considerable scholarly pain to make sure we know as much of the truth about these three heroes of the Alamo as history will yield up and to do it in a highly readable fashion.

Two other books among the many are notable for their usefulness. *Alamo Almanac and Book of Lists* by William R. Chemerka records the name of every person in any way connected to the Alamo. Beyond that, it endeavors to list every organization, book, movie, television production author, researcher, collectible, souvenir, painting, saying, song, toy, knickknack or other memorabilia associated with the Alamo. Besides being a treasure house of facts and trivia, this is a fun book to read. Open it at random in the alphabetical listing "The Alamo from A to Z" and find Fess Parker, Walt Disney's Davy Crockett, beside Alejo Perez, Jr., the eighteenth-month-old child who survived the battle.

Chemerka also provides a chronology that covers the Alamo from 1519, when Spain first staked its claim to the area, to 1997, when the Alamo was receiving some three million visitors a year. There are maps and action-filled illustrations by talented artists like Gary Zaboly, and a reproduction of Travis's last letter that clearly reflects the man of education he was.

Another book takes the idea of chronology even further, using hard facts to cut away the myth and performing a critical analysis of the source material to lay out what we actually know. *Blood of Noble Men: The Alamo Siege and Battle*, written by Alan C. Huffines and illustrated by Gary S. Zaboly, covers the siege day by day, showing where each major player was, including those in the Mexican Army, and what actions they were taking. Maps and detailed drawings make it easy to follow events despite the complexity resulting from covering the simultaneous movements of so many people. Huffines performs the historian's task admirably, without destroying our faith in the heroism of the men who died here.

For a more detailed study of the campaign of which the battle of the Alamo was only a part, see Stephen L. Hardin's excellent *The Alamo 1836: Santa Anna's Texas Campaign*. For an exciting novelization, *The Gates of the Alamo*, Stephen Harrigan's epic retelling, is a must. It captures in fiction more historical fact than some nonfiction accounts and humanizes the heroes without demolishing them. At least one reviewer in Texas has called it "the first great American novel of the twenty-first century," and its readability gained it a place on most prestigious bestseller lists.

Many citizens of the new republic were Hispanic. A look at their role is provided by *Defending Mexican Valor in Texas: The Historical Writings of*

Stephen Harrigan

José Antonio Navarro, 1853–1857. Navarro served this area in three different legislatures: those of Mexico, the Republic of Texas and the State of Texas. He signed the state's Declaration of Independence and helped write its constitution.

Writers at Home in San Antonio

Writers who call San Antonio home are many and varied. The scholarly end of the list is held down by world-renowned cultural historian Jacques Barzun, who as he closed in on ninety completed his masterpiece, *From Dawn to Decadence: 1500 to the Present: 500 Years of Western Cultural Life*. The New York Times Bestseller and finalist for the National Book Award for 2000 examines western culture from 1500 to the present, tracing the forces, the personalities and revolutions in social and political life that shaped the world we know today. "Dawn" was the Renaissance and Reformation that drew the west out of the Middle Ages. "Decadence" is the modern age of consumerism, poor education and empty and immoral art. Don't think this is a preachy book, though. No finer essayist has written in recent times than this witty, sharp observer of humankind.

T. R. Fehrenbach covers history, with works ranging from the signing of the Declaration of Independence to the history of the Korean War. To many Texans, his *Lone Star: A History of Texas and the Texans* is the definitive work on the subject.

A collection of sixty poems, some never published before, from Arab-American Naomi Shihab Nye, *19 Varieties of Gazelle: Poems of the Middle East* will open your eyes to the emotional lives of Arabs and Arab Americans. It was compiled after September 11, 2001. Wendy Barker's *Way of Whiteness* won the Writers League of Texas Violet Crown Award for Poetry in 2000 and was nominated for the National Book Critics Circle Award for Poetry. Also a poet (*My Wicked Wicked Ways*), Sandra Cisneros has received critical acclaim for her fiction, including novels *The House on Mango Street* and *Caramelo*, a multi-generational tale of a family that moves among Chicago, Mexico and San Antonio.

Sliver Moon, Jay Brandon's twelfth mystery novel, is the third about a young San Antonio District Attorney and his child-psychologist girlfriend. It tells the fascinating tale of a killing as witnessed by the two of them. He believes he saw the man shoot himself; she believes she saw someone else do it. The entanglements that ensue lead them both into what one reviewer called "the shark-infested waters of Texas politics." Brandon's experience in the DA's office of Bexar County infuses his stories with authenticity, but he depends on his characters and the relationships they develop to fuel the action.

Rick Riordan's *The Last King of Texas* is the third mystery novel in his series about private investigator Tres Navarre, whose talents extend from tracking down dangerous fugitives to teaching English at the University of Texas. For a mystery with a literary edge, one not afraid to examine the sometimes hazy border between good and evil, try Jim Sanderson's *La Mordida* or *Safe Delivery*, the one exploring corruption along the border, the other the moral ambiguities hiding in the byways of San Antonio. Alberto Ramon adds to both themes with *On Both Sides of the River*, about an attorney fighting corruption and murder in Eagle Pass.

From the heart of San Antonio to the tiny town of Saddle Gap, Carolyn Rogers leads us through a maze of drug dealing, murder and romance in *Home Is Where the Murder Is*, featuring San Antonio Police Lieutenant Rachel Grant.

A murder scatters the birdwatchers like a flock of gulls when J. S. Borthwick sends the heroine of her popular set-in-Maine series on an expedition into the heart of the birding paradise that is the south of Texas in *The Case of the Hook-Billed Kites*. Carolyn Hart's *Death on the River Walk* shows us the artsy side of one of San Antonio's most alluring attractions. Sandra Brown's New York Times Bestseller *Charade*, about the recipient of a transplanted heart who may be about to be murdered for it, is also set in the city. You will sometimes hear these kinds of action-adventure novels called "mainstream," but rest assured, the romance never gets lost in the plot, especially when it comes from the pen of Sandra Brown.

Whitley Strieber is such a gifted novelist in the horror genre that when he began writing what he called "true" accounts of being abducted by aliens, his command of the elements of fiction lent them an authority, and a downright creepiness, that had been lacking in the accounts of earlier abductees and made his books smash hits. *Communion* and *Transformation*, the two books that tell the tale of his continuing abductions since his earliest childhood in San Antonio, seem infused with a true horror, one actually experienced by the author himself. He has followed them up with several other books on the subject, though none has the power of the first two, and each succeeding foray into the world of UFO abductions dilutes the tale. Nonetheless, the subject has been the focus of most of his latest work.

Perhaps haunted throughout his life by sounds and visions that no one else can see, and owning an imagination that is wild and dark, Strieber converted the haunted shadows of New York's Central Park and the ruins of Harlem neighborhoods into some of the scariest settings ever invented in *Wolfen* and brought vampires ravening into the twentieth century with *The Hunger*.

Constance O'Banyon pens sensual romances, also writing as Micah Leigh and Tory Houston, but her action-filled plots and hot love stories are trademarks, no matter which pseudonym she uses. *San Antonio Rose* takes place during the Texas

Revolution and sees the heroine captured by Santa Anna, rescued by Indians, and finally settling in with her lover-turned-husband to build a family home.

Among children's writers who call San Antonio home, Diane Gonzales Bertrand has staked out territory with two age groups. Her juvenile novels, like *Alicia's Treasure* and *The Last Doll/La Ultima Muneca*, enchant children from nine to twelve. Once they are a bit older, they relish her young adult novels, especially *Trino's Time* and *Close to the Heart*. Many of Bertrand's characters are middle-class Latinos, a group not well represented in literature before she began writing. Wanting to reflect her own experience, she creates characters who share her cultural background.

Sarah Bird, who actually calls Austin home, has claimed the streets of San Antonio for a novel at once moving and hilarious. In *The Mommy Club,* a pregnant dreamer searches the city for a former lover, "a freelance mystic with a lot of enthusiasm for the carnal." Haunted by an abortion of earlier times, she's carrying a baby for another couple and learning along the way what real motherhood is all about. Bird uses food cravings, so much a part of pregnancy, in several roles, especially in capturing the essence of certain parts of San Antonio, as in this lament over the food vendors on San Fernando Plaza: "Fajitas, candy apples, agua frescas, caramel apples, nutty buddies, raspas, fudge, picadillo tacos, guacamole tacos, tripe tacos, beer, gorditas, cotton candy, popcorn, corn on the cob the Mexican way with sour cream and chili powder, exquisitos 'Hot Dogs,' calientos, but not a corn dog to be had on San Fernando Plaza."

The San Antonio Public Library serves readers well with lists of writers who call this area of Texas home. Particularly valuable for reading about the Latino experience is the bibliography maintained on the library's web site, www.sanantonio.gov/Library/collections.

By North American standards, San Antonio is an ancient city. The Spanish were exploring the area in the 1690s and the first missionaries appeared in 1718. A city with its roots sunk that deep is going to have ghosts. Hauntings, mysterious lights, strangers who appear in the night begging for help and then disappear—stories like these find a natural home among old adobe walls, picturesque missions, and other carefully restored remnants of the past. Stir a few urban myths into the mix, and tour some of San Antonio's famous ghost sites with tour director Docia Schultz Williams in *When Darkness Falls: Tales of San Antonio Ghosts and Hauntings* or *The Mystery and History of the Menger Hotel*. No one makes history more fascinating than this talented compiler, who salts it liberally with folklore and urban myth.

Perhaps even more useful is Williams's handbook for parents and grandparents, *Exploring San Antonio with Children: A Guide for Family Activities*. Pair it with *Insiders' Guide to San Antonio* by Paris Permenter and John Bigley, and prepare yourself to enjoy the city.

Once we leave the city and venture into the brush country south of San Antonio, we draw closer to the land described by Rolando Hinojosa in his group of short novels, "The Klail City Death Trip" series. Together they form a multigenerational record of life in an Anglo-Mexican community in the Rio Grande Valley much admired for its depiction of the two cultures. Another depiction is *150 Years of Valley Life: Nuestra Vida: A Pictorial History Commemorating Hidalgo County's 150th Anniversary*, a beautiful photographic essay told in black and white images, some dating from the 1800s.

Brownsville is the birthplace of Américo Paredes, a pioneer of Chicano literature whose most famous novel was *"With His Pistol in His Hand": A Border Ballad and Its Hero*. It is about Gregorio Cortez, the tenant farmer and vaquero who, accused of murder, fled a posse eventually made up of hundreds of men, including Texas Rangers, and eluded capture long enough to garner public sympathy and enter the outlaw folklore. When the book was published in 1958, it made a Ranger so mad he threatened to shoot the author. Today, it's a classic.

TREATS FOR BOOK LOVERS IN SAN ANTONIO

Rómulo Munguía Library
Universidad Nacional
Autonoma-San Antonio
P.O. Box 830426
600 Hemisfair Park
San Antonio 78283
210-222-8626

Holdings include the Henry Cisneros Archives and a large collection of books and other publications related to Mexico, Latin America, Canada and the United States; a collection of Spanish, English and bilingual books for children; Mexican books from the twentieth century; and videos of Mexican history and culture.

Latino Collection
San Antonio Central Library
600 Soledad
San Antonio 78205
210-207-2500
210-207-2534 TTY

Books, reference materials and journals about the Latino experience in Texas form the heart of this library, with biography, education, folklore, art, music, and religion among the subjects chronicled. A Texas Latino literature bibliography lists some fifty Latino authors of fiction and poetry who call San Antonio home and whose books may be found in the library.

(continued)

Special Collections and Archives
University of Texas at San Antonio
John Peace Library Building
1604 Campus
San Antonio 78205
210-458-5505

Special collections are books and manuscripts about San Antonio, the state of Texas, the American Southwest, Mexico during Spanish Colonial times and the Pacific Northwest. Vast holdings include some administrative records from Mexico from the sixteenth to the twentieth century; original documents from the days of the Republic and the Civil War; histories of San Antonio and of Texas counties; histories of Native Americans in the Southwest and Pacific Northwest; works by Texas authors, and much more.

Archives of the Institute of Texan Cultures
801 S. Bowie Street
San Antonio 78205
210-458-2381

Mexican American Archives Project collects primary source material relating to the history and culture of Mexican Americans in San Antonio and the Southwest. Papers include those of Albert Bustamante, Arcenio Garcia, Jose Gutierrez, Albert A. Pena, Jr., and Mexican American Democrats of Texas. The Archives also include manuscripts and other material on African-Americans, politicians, educators, musicians, and many San Antonio–related subjects.

Library Collections
McNay Art Museum
6000 New Braunfels
P.O. Box 6069
San Antonio 78209
210-805-1727

Holdings include material related to the history of art, the performing arts, and landscaping, with emphasis on scene design for opera, ballet and American musicals. Resources include reference works on gothic and medieval art and art of the American Southwest. Materials include catalogs, price guides, museum records, and vertical files on art-related subjects.

TREATS FOR BOOK LOVERS IN THE RIO GRANDE VALLEY

John Hunter Room Collection
Arnulfo L. Oliveira Library
University of Texas at Brownsville and Texas Southmost College
80 Fort Brown
Brownsville 78520
956-983-7410

Holdings include more than three thousand rare and local-history books on the development of Cameron and Willacy counties and northern Mexico, plus maps, microfilm, oral histories and photos. Also included are papers of Menton Murray, Bruce Underwood,

Brownsville Chamber of Commerce, and the archives of the university, which began in 1926. Special interests include books, manuscripts and war-related memorabilia of the U.S.–Mexico War. Hundreds of volumes from the collection of the Descendents of the Mexican War round out this collection, which is being developed in partnership with Palo Alto National Battlefield.

University Library

University of Texas–Pan American
1201 West University Drive
Edinburg 78541-2999
956-381-3306

Lower Rio Grande Historical Collection houses materials, both primary and secondary, related to the geographical area of Texas from Laredo to Corpus Christi to Brownsville and the Mexican states of Tamaulipas, Nuevo Leon, and Coahuila. In addition, as a Texas Regional Historical Resource Depository, it holds records for seven counties, phone books and city directories, periodicals, maps, photographs and other materials related to the South Texas/Northeast Mexico area, in both English and Spanish.

The Rio Grande Folklore Archive has more than ninety-nine thousand items of Mexican American folklore, collected and stored in a computer database. Folk beliefs, proverbs, tales and contemporary legends are some of the forms covered.

South Texas Archives

James C. Jernigan Libary
Texas A&M University–Kingsville
700 University Boulevard
Kingsville 78363-8202

Regional Historical Resource Depository holds microfilmed records of eleven neighboring counties. Other materials are four thousand rare books on the history of South Texas, university archives, microfilm of local government records, newspapers, ranch records, some ninety-five thousand photos or negatives and an extensive oral history collection.

Special Collections

Sue and Radcliffe Killam Library
Texas A&M International University
5201 University Boulevard
Laredo 78041-1900
956-326-2400

Holdings include papers, photographs and documents of Aldo Tatangelo, Ann Shanks, and other citizens, La Raza Unida of Laredo, Pan American Roundtable of Laredo, research materials of the Republic of the Rio Grande, and records of the university's history.

Luciano Guajardo
Historical Collection

Laredo Public Library
1120 E. Calton Road
Laredo 78041
956-795-2400

Holdings are materials relating to the history of Laredo, Texas, Webb County and northern states of Mexico in some 1,520 volumes and eleven thousand vertical files; works by local authors; City of Laredo government documents dating back to 1755; genealogical materials with Hispanic emphasis. Photos, maps, periodicals and other records are also held.

Attractions of the South Texas Plains and the Rio Grande Valley

San Antonio is a tourist magnet, thanks to its sunbelt climate, its close ties with the earliest and most dramatic Texas history, and the far-sightedness of the city fathers who understood the allure of the River Walk, the old missions, the parks and gardens and supported and marketed them aggressively. The city is the most popular tourist destination in the state.

But if ecotourism is your interest and you want to get close to nature, you will have plenty of opportunities outside the cities. Several wildlife refuges and management areas make it easy to enjoy wildlife up close, and public gardens celebrate the native plants.

As is true throughout Texas, even the smallest villages in this region often record local history in well-kept museums, and art collections are not unknown. Many communities host annual festivals, especially during the winter when they welcome folks fleeing the colder climes.

The major gateways into Mexico are Brownsville, Hidalgo, Laredo, Rio Grande City, and Eagle Pass.

Alamo

At **Santa Ana National Wildlife Refuge** (956-784-7500), you may not spot one of the resident jaguarundi or ocelot (they're pretty shy), but even the common birds are knock-your-socks-off showy. Flashy green jays and roseate spoonbills, tricolored heron and tropical kingbirds light up the 2,088 acres of brush, wetland and woodland along the bank of the Rio Grande. In the spring, warblers add to the color, and migrating raptors soar overhead, including the seldom-seen hook-billed kite and gray hawk. About half of all known species of butterflies find suitable habitat here. If you come during October, November or December, peak months for butterfly populations, you won't even have to leave the visitor center to enjoy them, thanks to the specialty garden planted there to attract them.

Self-guided nature trails ramble for miles. There's even one for wheelchairs. Between Thanksgiving Day and the end of April, you can take an hour and a half interpretive tram ride through the wilder areas. It's a good idea to call ahead to make sure the tram is operating.

Sunderland's Cactus Garden (210-787-2040) is a spectacular retail nursery with a display garden offering opportunities to learn about cactus and succulents, both native and exotic. About two thousand different species are represented here, some rare or endangered. Gardeners propagate many of them on site. The

WORLD BIRDING CENTER SITES

www.worldbirdingcenter.org
956-584-9156

Outstanding among the opportunities for observing wildlife, especially birds, is the 120-mile string of sites along the Lower Valley that together make up the **World Birding Center**. Nine separate locations offer up some five hundred species in mostly-easy-to-access parks, wetlands, and urban settings. Head-quartered in Mission at **Bentsen-Rio Grande Valley State Park** (956-519-6448), the Center encompasses a habitat from South Padre Island and Brownsville west and north to Roma. The sites share rare bird alerts, checklists, and news about birding trips and events, but each site posts its own hours of operation. Some are open only by appointment or reservation.

Bentsen-Rio Grande Valley State Park
Three miles south of Mission
on FM 2062
Open daily 8–5
956-585-0902

Edinburg Scenic Wetlands
714 S. Raul Longoria Road, Edinburg
Open 11–6 Tuesday through Saturday
956-381-9922

Estero Llano Grande State Park
FM 1015, Weslaco
Open by appointment only
956-585-1107

Harlingen Arroyo Colorado
Ramsey Nature Park
1000 Block South Loop 499, Harlingen
Open dawn till sunset
956-427-8873

Old Hidalgo Pumphouse
902 S. Second Street, Hidalgo
Open 10–5 Monday through Friday and
1–5 Sunday
956-843-8686

Quinta Mazatlan
600 Sunset Avenue, McAllen
Open by appointment only
956-682-1517

Resaca de la Palma State Park
4 miles west of Brownsville on Hwy 281
Open by appointment only
956-585-1107

Roma Bluffs
77 Convent Street, Roma
Open 8–4:30 Monday through Friday
956-849-4930

South Padre Island Birding and Nature Center
Laguna Madre Nature Trail
7355 Padre Boulevard
Open daily
956-761-3005

star of this awesome collection is a twenty-five-foot-tall specimen of *Packycereus pringlii*, supposedly the largest nursery-grown cactus in the state. Ironically, this monster is not a native Texan but an import from the Baja, California, area.

BRACKETTVILLE

When John Wayne got ready to shoot a movie about the Battle of the Alamo in the late 1950s, he couldn't very well use the Alamo itself as a setting, since by then it sat smack in the middle of a very modern-looking city. He needed to recreate the brushy, empty land as it had appeared in 1836, surrounding a Spanish mission with a distinctive roofline. He found the vast, empty space he was looking for on a ranch near Brackettville, and there he built **Alamo Village** (830-563-2580), one of the most realistic and complete sets ever constructed for a movie.

With its historic-looking adobe buildings and dirt streets, the huge set has since seen the shooting of parts of more than sixty productions. Today, the village welcomes visitors to an Old West experience that may include trail rides, gunfighter competitions, live music and mellerdramas and, always, lots of barbecue.

BROWNSVILLE

You can't get any further south in Texas than this bustling, colorful city right on the border with Mexico. An international flavor to shopping and eating, a devotion to history and the fine arts, and plenty of opportunities to interact with nature mark this unique destination.

Some fifteen hundred animals live in four major ecosystems within the **Gladys Porter Zoo** (956-546-7187) at 500 Ringgold Street. A Children's Zoo allows close up experiences with some small animals, and a nursery lets you check on newborns. The settings are very natural, an effect achieved with tropical and subtropical plants, flowing waterways, and natural building materials.

You can get your birding fix and see a highly unusual Sabal Palm forest at the same time at **Sabal Palm Audubon Sanctuary** (956-541-8034), several hundred acres of wildlife and native plants, like Texas indigo snakes and Texas ebony trees. A couple of miles of nature trails loop out from a nice little visitor center. Also of note in Brownsville are the **Museum of Fine Arts** at 230 Neale Drive (956-542-0941), the **Commemorative Air Force Rio Grande Valley Wing** at the airport (956-541-8585) and **Historic Brownsville Museum,** housed in a 1928 railroad depot at 641 E. Madison (956-548-1313). Matamoros, Mexico, is just across the Rio Grande. You can park your vehicle in downtown Brownsville and walk across the bridge.

GOLIAD

"Remember Goliad" became a rallying cry for Texans as they fought for independence. **Goliad State Park** (361-645-3405) comprises a restored mission and Spanish fort, Presidio La Bahia, where Fannin's troops were held before they were massacred, as well as a museum. Also on the grounds is **Zaragoza Birthplace State Historic Site**, commemorating a largely unsung hero. During the early days of the Civil War, Zaragoza prevented French troops from crossing into Texas from Mexico to join in the war.

LAREDO

With its population nearing 180,000, Laredo is the largest inland port in the country. It's worth stopping by the chamber of commerce at 2310 San Bernardo Street (956-722-9895) to pick up a guide to walking tours that will lead you through a wonderful maze of historic buildings, plazas, and neighborhoods. A science center, birding hot spots and several museums will fill a tourist's day.

Lamar Bruni Vergara Environmental Science Center (956-764-5701) showcases plants, fish and reptiles native to the Rio Grande watershed in indoor exhibits and an outdoor garden featuring ponds and wetlands, wildflowers and cactus. From here you can reach the **Paso del Indio Nature Trail** and the **River Road**, where you can pursue birds past woods, ponds and gravel pits. All three North American kingfishers hang out here, as do egret, heron, dove, ibis, various ducks and innumerable other species. **Lake Casa Blanca International State Park** (956-725-3826) is another birding hot spot.

MCALLEN

One of the country's largest Latin American folk art collections brightens the galleries at the **International Museum of Art & Science** (956-682-1564). Masks, textiles, pottery, paintings, prints and sculpture mix traditional and modern arts. Geology, paleontology and other natural science exhibits round out the collection. Look for it at 1900 Nolana.

MISSION

The **Texas Citrus Fiesta** in January, the **Texas Butterfly Festival** in October, and year-round opportunities for bird-watching and nature study make this city a popular destination. Mission has a special place in the hearts of many Texans as the birthplace and home of former Dallas Cowboy Head Coach **Tom Landry**. A **mural** downtown shows a record of his life and accomplishments at the corner of N. Conway and E. Tom Landry Avenue.

SAN ANTONIO

San Antonio is not a difficult city to drive in, as long as you stick to the freeways or explore no further than the downtown area. But the city and its suburbs spread out over most of the county's 1,256 square miles, and there is so much to do and see that good planning is essential. You will find help from the city's Visitor and Convention Bureau at 317 Alamo Plaza (210-207-6700 or 800-447-3372) or from their web site, www.visitsanantonio.com. Be sure to pick up a copy of the driving map for the Mission Trail.

Highlights of History, Art, Natural Science, Shopping and Family Fun

The San Antonio River and the rich farmland it flows through have been a lure to European explorers, missionaries and settlers since at least 1718, when the mission later known as the Alamo was established. Soon a whole string of missions sprang up for the purpose of educating local inhabitants in Catholicism. Game was plentiful, the river's water could be tamed and put to use through irrigation, and the soil yielded food throughout a long growing season. Franciscan friars attracted the local Indians to the missions, trained them in farming and religion, built granaries and a flour mill, chapels and churches, and laid the groundwork for the city that would grow around them.

Much of what the missionaries built can still be used today, including churches, at least one dam on the river and some of the irrigation system. Land they broke for the farming of grain and vegetables still yields food for humans and animals, and the livestock they brought in with them marked the beginning of ranching in the area.

Most folks will start their mission tour at the Alamo, but the other missions are well worth a visit, especially the beautifully-restored San Jose. All of them are open 9–5 every day, except Thanksgiving, Christmas and New Year's Day.

The chapel of **Mission San Antonio Valero** and the **Long Barrack** are the original buildings still standing on the east side of **Alamo Plaza** in downtown San Antonio. They seem small among the huge old trees and landscaped grounds, too small surely to be the heart of Texas history. But they are. All that's left of the **Alamo** (210-225-1391), they attract millions of visitors every year. And for Book Lovers, there's a special treat: the **Long Barrack Museum and Library** (210-225-1071), which houses not only mementos of the Republic of Texas era but also a collection of books and other documents about the period, with an intense focus on the Alamo and its defenders. For those who like their history writ large, there's the **IMAX Theater** (210-247-4629 or 800-354-4629) production *Alamo: The Price of Freedom* offered inside the River Center Mall at 849 East Commerce. The six-story-high screen will fill your eyes with the story of the 13 days of Texas glory told from a historian's viewpoint.

Mission San Jose (210-932-1001) was founded in 1720 and has been meticulously rebuilt and restored to allow visitors an unparalleled taste of life at this outpost of civilization in the eighteenth century. A granary and a flour mill reflect the importance of bread to the Europeans. A museum and bookstore offer insight into the mission's history, and a short film shows some of the problems overcome by early settlers. You will find a Visitor Center here, too. It's at 6701 San Jose Drive.

The other missions on the driving tour are **Mission Concepcion** (210-534-1540) at 807 Mission Road, **Mission San Juan Capistrano** (210-534-0749) at 9101 Graf Road, and **Mission San Francisco de la Espada** (210-627-2021) at 10040 Espada Road.

History is also well-served in several San Antonio museums, including the **Pioneer, Trail Drivers, and Texas Rangers Memorial Museum** (210-822-9011) at 3805 Broadway, preserving artifacts of the days of the cowboy. Homes of early residents are open for viewing, including **Guenther House** (210-227-1061) at 205 E. Guenther, the **Steves Homestead** (210-225-5924) at 509 King William Street, and **Casa Navarro State Historic Site** (210-226-4801) at 228 S. Laredo.

Casa Navarro is the historic site in San Antonio dedicated to showing the roles of Mexico and Mexicans in shaping the history of the area, and the **Mexican Cultural Institute** (210-227-0123) at 600 HemisFair Plaza Way presents art, film and performance featuring Mexican culture. African-American culture finds expression at the **Carver Community Cultural Center** (210-207-7211) at 226 N. Hackberry.

Ethnicity also plays a key role in the **Institute of Texan Cultures** (210-458-2300), a museum and educational forum that celebrates the contributions of 26 ethnic and cultural groups to Texas. Under the auspices of the University of Texas, it sits at 801 S. Bowie Street, 50,000 square feet of exhibits testifying to the state's diversity. It is also home to the **Institute of Texan Cultures Library**. During the second weekend in June, the **Texas Folklife Festival** (210-458-2390) lights up the area with arts and crafts, entertainment, and food representing the folkways of up to forty different cultures.

San Antonio's most famous landmark after the Alamo is the **Paseo del Rio**, or **River Walk**, a paved walkway that parallels the San Antonio River for about two and a half miles. It passes through an area of fine old homes, past lush plantings of tropicals and semitropicals providing color and fragrance year-round. Prostrate rosemary drapes over walls, while crape myrtle, lantana and hibiscus light up your passage past hotels, cafés, boutiques and gift shops. Boats offer rides on the river, live music swells from sidewalk musicians, and coffee shops or bistros beckon you in for a treat. Each December, twenty-five hundred luminarias light up the paseo. Other holiday times bring festivals, parades and arts and crafts fairs.

Once a year, in April, almost everyone in San Antonio gets involved in a huge ten-day festival, one that's been staged annually for two hundred years or so. Citizens and visitors alike celebrate the spirit of the city with **Fiesta San Antonio**, featuring parades on the river and the streets, fireworks, sports events, music and food, with up to 150 separate events in locations all around the city. You can get the details for the upcoming Fiesta at www.fiesta-sa.org or 210-227-5191.

San Antonio makes history fun. But a magnificent modern art museum, several military bases, and world-class family activities make sure the city keeps one foot firmly planted in the present. The **McNay Art Museum** (210-824-5368) at 6000 N. New Braunfels Street could see to that on its own. Despite its origins as an elegant estate, the McNay's focal point is a collection of the cream of modern American and European painting and sculpture. Cézanne and Picasso share the walls with O'Keeffe and Hopper. A strong collection called "Art after 1945" reveals the depth of art produced in modern America, especially from 1965 to 1990. An extensive collection of artworks associated with five hundred years of theatrical production and a group of prints, drawings and watercolors spanning artists from Mary Cassatt to Cy Twombly are also extraordinary.

At **San Antonio Museum of Art** (210-978-8100), collections range from antiquities and Islamic art to modern painting and sculpture. You will find it in the huge building that once housed Lone Star Brewery at 200 W. Jones Avenue, between Broadway and Saint Mary's Street.

Government in general, and the military in particular, is the largest employer in San Antonio. Three U.S. Air Force installations and one of the U.S. Army's key posts are based here. Access to the grounds of any of them may require a stop at the gate for a visitor's pass.

A museum at **Fort Sam Houston** (210-221-1886) recounts the Army's presence in the city since 1845. Exhibits feature past Fort Commanders, like Dwight D. Eisenhower, and important units, such as the Rough Riders and Buffalo Soldiers. Uniforms, firearms, vehicles, books, photographs and documents tell the story. In fact, a **reference library** that preserves military history is available to the public.

Located in Building 123 on Stanley Road, it's open 10–4 Wednesday through Sunday, closed on federal holidays except Memorial Day, Veterans Day and the Fourth of July.

Also on Stanley Road, the **U.S. Army Medical Department Museum** (210-221-6358) chronicles the development of military medicine since 1775.

If you've had enough of history and art, turn your attention to some of the kid-oriented activities San Antonio is famed for. Take the miniature train through shady **Brackenridge Park** on a hot summer day. While you're in that area, visit some of the thirty-five hundred denizens of the **San Antonio Zoo** (210-734-7184), one of the largest in the nation.

San Antonio Children's Museum (210-212-4453) uses giant toys to mesmerize smaller children into learning about the world and society. They can fly a kid-sized airplane, push a kid-sized cart through a grocery mart, use an ATM, drive a front-end loader and participate in hands-on science experiments. It's at 305 E. Houston Street downtown.

Not strictly for children but certainly appealing to the older ones, **Witte Museum** (210-357-1900) dominates the museum scene in San Antonio, with its dinosaur reproductions, live animals, two-thousand-year-old mummy and other natural and historic attractions. A permanent collection of over two hundred thousand items means meaty exhibits of history, science, natural science and anthropology year-round. The **H-E-B Science Treehouse** on the museum grounds is a fifteen-thousand-square-foot building that children adore, full of hands-on experiences with science, including meteorology.

SeaWorld (210-523-3611) is one of the largest family entertainment venues in the world. Four separate parks offer twenty-five shows, thrill-rides, and other experiences. Opportunities to get wet abound, including a raft ride down a churning stream and a flume ride that drops you through a five-story plunge a couple of times. If you prefer your adventure on the drier side and fancy the idea of being tossed head over heels at fifty miles an hour, you'll want to ride the Great White Rollercoaster. Or, if falling fast enough to experience weightlessness is your goal, the Steel Eel Hypercoaster is for you. For quieter adventures, feed the dolphins, watch Shamu the killer whale swim with humans, touch a shark, and visit the enormous behind-the-glass habitats where tropical fish, moray eels and other fantastic creatures of the deep live out their lives.

At two hundred acres, **Six Flags Fiesta Texas** (210-697-5050) is only a slightly smaller theme park than SeaWorld, and almost as wet. Among its famous rides are Bugs Bunny's White Water Rapids and a flume called the Twister. But there are also rides that will launch you from zero to sixty miles per hour in seconds, drop you into free fall, spin you, swing you, whip you, bump you and generally pummel you into having a great time. There are activities here for children of all ages, even those who don't "measure up" for some of the wilder rides. Live music and other shows and performances keep the grounds hopping.

The Reading Tour

150 Years of Valley Life: Nuestra Vida: A Pictorial History Commemorating Hidalgo County's 150th Anniversary. McAllen, Tex.: *Monitor of McAllen*, 2003.
Barker, Wendy. *Way of Whiteness*. San Antonio: Wings Press, 2000.
Barzun, Jacques, *From Dawn to Decadence: 1500 to the Present: 500 Years of Western Cultural Life*. New York: HarperCollins, 2000.
Bertrand, Diane Gonzales. *Alicia's Treasures*. Houston: Arte Publico Press, 1996.
———. *Close to the Heart*. Houston: Pinata Books, 2002.
———. *Trino's Time*. Houston: Pinata Books, 2001.
Bird, Sarah. *The Mommy Club*. New York: Doubleday, 1991.
Borthwick, J. S. *The Case of the Hook-Billed Kites*. New York: St. Martin's Press, 1982.
Brandon, Jay. *Sliver Moon*. New York: Forge, 2003.
Brown, Sandra. *Charade*. New York: Warner Books, 1994.
Chemerka, William R. *Alamo Almanac and Book of Lists*. Austin: Eakin Press, 1997.
Cisneros, Sandra. *Caramelo*. New York: Knopf, 2002.
———. *The House on Mango Street*. New York: Knopf, 1994.
———. *My Wicked Wicked Ways*. New York: Knopf, 1992 (reprint).
Davis, William C. *Three Roads to the Alamo*. New York: HarperCollins, 1998.
Hardin, Stephen L. *The Alamo 1836: Santa Anna's Texas Campaign*. Oxford, Eng.: Osprey Publishing, 2001.
———. *Texian Iliad: A Military History of the Texas Revolution*. Austin: University of Texas Press, 1994.
Harrigan, Stephen. *The Gates of the Alamo*. New York: Knopf, 2000.
Hart, Carolyn. *Death on the River Walk*. New York: Avon, 1999.
Hinojosa, Rolando. *Ask a Policeman*. Houston: Arte Publico, 1998.
———. *The Klail City Death Trip*. Houston: Arte Publico, 1987.
Huffines, Alan C., and Gary S. Zaboly. *Blood of Noble Men: The Alamo Siege and Battle*. Austin: Eakin Press, 1999.
McDonald, David R., ed. *Defending Mexican Valor in Texas: The Historical Writings of José Antonio Navarro, 1853–1857*. Austin: State House Press, 1995.
Myers, John. *The Alamo*. Lincoln: University of Nebraska Press, 1973.
Nye, Naomi Shihab. *19 Varieties of Gazelle: Poems of the Middle East*. New York: Greenwillow Books, 2002.
O'Banyon, Constance. *San Antonio Rose*. New York: Leisure Books, 1999.
Paredes, Américo. *"With His Pistol in His Hand": A Border Ballad and Its Hero*. Austin: University of Texas Press, 1986.

Parmenter, Paris, and John Bigley. *Insider's Guide to San Antonio*. Guilford, Conn.: Globe Pequot Press, 2002.
Ramon, Alberto. *On Both Sides of the River*. Carmel, Ind.: Guild Press, 1996.
Riordan, Rick. *The Last King of Texas*. New York: Bantam, 2001.
Rogers, Carolyn. *Home Is Where the Murder Is*. Johnson City, Tenn.: The Overmountain Press, 2002.
Sanderson, Jim. *La Mordida*. Albuquerque: University of New Mexico Press, 2002.
———. *Safe Delivery*. Albuquerque: University of New Mexico Press, 2000.
Speart, Jessica. *Border Prey*. New York: Avon, 2000.
———. *Coastal Disturbance*. New York: Avon, 2003.
———. *Gator Aide*. New York: Avon, 1997.
———. *Killing Season*. New York: Avon, 2002.
Strieber, Whitley. *Communion*. New York: William Morrow, 1987.
———. *Transformation*. New York: William Morrow, 1988.
———. *Wolfen*. New York: William Morrow, 1978.
Tinkle, Lon. *13 Days to Glory*. College Station: Texas A&M Press, 1996 (reprint).
Williams, Docia Schultz. *Exploring San Antonio with Children: A Guide for Family Activities*. Plano: Republic of Texas Press, 1998.
———. *When Darkness Falls: Tales of San Antonio Ghosts and Hauntings*. Plano: Republic of Texas Press, 1998.

★ 7 ★

The Book Lover Tours Houston and the Gulf Coast

Anahuac, Aransas Pass, Brazoria County, Brownsville, Clear Lake, Corpus Christi, Galveston, Houston, Kingsville, LaPorte, Pasadena, Port Aransas, Port Isabel, Richmond, Rio Hondo, Rockport-Fulton and Aransas NWR, Rosenberg, South Padre Island, Spring

History, natural science, including birds, reptiles, mammals and weather, beach activities, boating and fishing, and space exploration are the big themes in this region of Texas, which stretches from Galveston in the north to South Padre Island.

The big name in these parts is Sam Houston. The big city is his namesake. Sam led his ragtag army to victory over the Mexican Army in 1836, served as first President of the Republic, fiercely endorsed the entry of Texas into the Union, and just as fiercely opposed its secession. Reputed to have reached the height of six and a half feet, he lived large, marrying three times, representing his state in the U.S. Senate, earning a rep as a hard drinker, and never giving up his passion for Texas. When urged to join in the general enthusiasm for seceding from the Union, he said, "I love Texas too well to bring civil strife and bloodshed upon her." That sentiment lost him his job as governor.

His shrine is two-fold. On the battlefield near LaPorte, where his army decided the brief War for Texas Independence, rises a 570-foot monument to that victory, complete with a museum and a multi-image movie program that uses forty-two projectors. True Houston fans make the trek to Huntsville, the village in which he chose to build his home. His grave lies there.

As rich as this area is in history, the riches of natural history almost overshadow it. All along the coast, even within the cities, in natural sanctuaries and parks, bird life abounds, astonishing in both numbers of birds and numbers of species represented. Recognizing the value of making life easy on bird-watchers—not only do they bring tourist dollars, they are also committed to preserving natural resources—the state of Texas did a wonderful thing. It located the best sites for bird-watching along the whole coast, some of them on undeveloped land, some on private land, and some in areas already open to the public, and then did whatever needed doing to make each site more accessible, from grading pullouts for vehicles to building boardwalks and viewing platforms. To top off the effort, it created maps showing all the sites, some three hundred in all, and called the whole thing the Great Texas Coastal Birding Trail. The maps are available at visitor centers and chambers of commerce along the coast.

In many places, birds are not the only draw. Alligators sunning themselves beside a bayou, dolphins in the bay, and native and exotic plants in garden collections excite nature lovers, too. And weather, always a lively topic in any part of Texas, gets particular attention here, at least when talk of hurricanes fills the air. A huge storm killed more than six thousand people on Galveston Island not much more than a hundred years ago, the worst natural disaster in the history of the nation.

Time after time along this coast, from the sixteenth century on, ambition, investment, and speculation have been wiped out by flood, wind and wave. In the earliest years, the dark hand of disease clamped down on one human enterprise after another. A yellow fever outbreak in the village where Houston now stands forced the seat of government to relocate to Austin.

Today, improved weather forecasting means early warning, and everyone has ample chance to leave the coast should a hurricane threaten.

It is the beach, of course, that beckons many folks down to the sea—hundreds of miles of it, all open to the public. For others, it's the chance to throw a hook into a quiet bay or take a boat out where the big fish lurk. For still others, no mere earthly attraction can ever equal the appeal of space conquest and the place memorialized by radio exchanges between the control center in Houston and the astronauts in space, the Johnson Space Center.

The city that bears Sam Houston's name is a behemoth. It takes three counties to hold the city proper, and more for the communities that rim the suburbs.

According to the *Texas Almanac*, which tracks such things for every area of the state, the Houston metropolitan area's population hovers at 4.67 million. But Texans don't stack themselves on top of each other the way some others do. They spread out. In Houston, they string single-family dwellings across the flat plains and connect them with thousands of miles of freeways.

Until the advent of air conditioning in the 1930s, the population never grew past about one hundred thousand hardy souls. Once it became possible to shut up a house or an office and control the temperature and humidity behind closed doors, population soared. Today, if a building of any size remains in the city without that amenity, you will be hard pressed to find it. Museums, theaters and shops thrive on summer weather, because their cool interiors beckon visitors with welcome relief.

A City of Writers and Readers

Among those who find the atmosphere along the Gulf Coast perfectly amenable are a large number of writers of every ilk. The University of Houston lays claim to one of the very top creative writing programs in the country, fostering not only emerging writers but also an ambience of intellectualism that reaches beyond the campus into the interests of the community. Writers' conferences and workshops, readings by poets and authors, book signings, and competitions are ongoing. Libraries harbor collections of unique material and make them accessible to the public. Bookstores are numerous.

One of the key players in the literary stakes is a unique nonprofit organization called **Inprint, Inc.** Supporting the **University of Houston's Creative Writing Program**, it helps make many of its literary activities available to the public. Prime among those is the **Margarett Root Brown Houston Reading Series** (713-521-2026), which runs from fall to spring and brings leading writers to Houston to read from their work in public venues. The 2003–2004 series brought in a dozen authors, five Pulitzer Prize winners among them.

Poets gather once a month for **First Friday**, a free series of poetry readings held the first Friday of each month at 8:30 in the evening. The site is **Inprint House** (713-521-2026) at 1524 Sul Ross. An open reading follows the featured poet.

Then, once a year in October, poetry really takes center stage. The **Houston Poetry Fest** provides a week-long festival. If you love poetry, go fill your ears up with the real thing. There will even be workshops for learning something about writing. Find out details about the current year's festival at www.houstonpoetryfest.org or write to Houston Poetry Fest, P.O. Box 22595, Houston, TX 77227-2595.

If the first Friday in Houston is given over to poetry every month, hold the fourth Wednesday for the **Nuestra Palabra Showcase**. Staged in the **Talento Bilingue de Houston Theater** (713-222-1213), these readings and performances highlight the literary achievements of Latino and Latina writers. A nationally-known author headlines each event.

Among recent participants count Alisa Valdés-Rodrígues, whose novel *The Dirty Girls Social Club* not only was the first book by a Latina to debut on the New York Times Bestseller List but attracted the attention of no less a Latina star than Jennifer Lopez, who bought the film rights. In this charming story, six young women take turns as narrator to tell us about their lives, loves and careers in the modern world.

Between them, Inprint, Inc., and the University of Houston create a hotbed of serious literary activity. Faculty, students, and graduates contribute. Their pub-

---

NUESTRA PALABRA: LATINO/A WRITERS HAVING THEIR SAY

In 2002, Nuestra Palabra put together another premier literary event for the public, the first annual **Latino Book and Family Festival**. To find out how Nuestra Palabra promotes the literary work of Latino/a artists, visit their web site at www.nuestrapalabra.org or call 713-867-8943. For a taste of the outstanding work being produced by Latino/a writers, choose from this list, a brief sample of the authors and books being showcased monthly.

Almost a Woman by Esmeralda Santiago

Americanos: Latino Life in the United States by Edward James Olmos

The Aztec Love God by Tony Diaz

The Dirty Girls Social Club by Alisa Valdés-Rodrígues

Fast Red Road by Steven Graham Jones

I Used to Be a Chicana Superwoman by Gloria Velásquez

A Place to Stand and *Healing Earthquakes*, by Jimmy Santiago Baca, American Book Award and Pushcart Prize winner

Thirty an' Seen a Lot by Evangelina Vigil-Piñón, American Book Award winner

lishing credentials are too numerous to detail, but some of the poetry they have produced will give you a taste of the power of their work.

Whether you're a confirmed poetry lover or one of those who could never quite see what all the fuss was about, immerse yourself in Edward Hirsch's national bestseller, *How to Read a Poem and Fall in Love with Poetry,* for an enchanting exploration of the power and beauty of this most elusive of art forms. Hirsch is a multiple-award winning poet himself, as is Cynthia Macdonald, who founded the University of Houston Creative Writing Program and served as its first director. Her poetry collection *I Can't Remember* well illustrates her talents.

Robert Phillips has written or edited about thirty volumes in various literary forms, including poetry. To hear his unique voice, open one of his critically-acclaimed poetry collections, such as *Spinach Days* or *News about People You Know*. Adam Zagajewski lends an international note with his "poet in exile" experiences. See *Without End: New and Selected Poems*. To enjoy the works of a master short story writer, see Daniel Stern's collection *In the Country of the Young*.

Outside the UH zone, Venise Berry recreates a vivid part of Houston in her novel *Colored Sugar Water*, about the roles of both love and religious faith in the lives of African American women. Essentially nice people, her characters struggle with jobs and men and discover the strengths of their own spiritual gifts. Smart, sexy, funny and wise, it's about people you enjoy spending time with.

The three Houston-born Barthelme brothers have all left their mark on the literature of America. Steve Barthelme is probably known best for his collection of short stories, *And He Tells the Little Horse the Whole Story*. Frederick Barthelme's *Elroy Nights* captures his themes of mid-life angst among the middle class in the Deep South. For a taste of what the literary style called "postmodernism" is all about, read either *The Dead Father* or *Snow White* by the third Barthelme, Donald. They are prime examples of this challenging mode.

Such serious literature is strong in Houston, but Houston is home to Romance Writers of America, too, the eighty-six-hundred-strong writers organization whose members produce among them the bulk of the paperback fiction sold in this country each year. That's of *all* paperback fiction. Romance novels account for more than half of it. And lest you think that paperback and romance are synonymous, consider the fact that they scarf up a third of the sales of *all* popular fiction published in this country, in whatever size or format.

Romance Writers of America studies these things. They know that the number of people who read at least one romance novel a year is over fifty million and growing. They know those people pour well over a billion and a half dollars into the economy every year to feed their yen for romance. They know lots of other things about those people, too, like where they buy novels (mostly in the mall), and what they admire in male characters (muscles) and in female characters (intelligence), and lots of other details.

No matter where in the United States you live, if you read romance fiction at all, you've probably felt the guiding hand of Romance Writers of America. They help writers write for you and booksellers sell to you, and they hand out awards called RITAs, which make sure-fire lures for readers.

Houston-based writer Jan Freed regularly takes home laurels, including reviewers' choice and readers' awards. Especially popular are *One Tough Texan*, which appears in a special double volume with a story by romance pioneer LaVyrle Spencer called *Sweet Memories*, and *The Wallflower*, a Harlequin Super Romance. Freed chooses the hoariest of themes—widower with small child hires lovely young nanny—and infuses them with bright dialogue, lively action and solid secondary characters to create pleasers for a modern audience.

Perhaps Houston's most successful romance novelist is Judith McNaught, whose latest works seem to have evolved into romantic suspense. With both historical and contemporary romances in the traditional forms in her past, McNaught broke onto the New York Times Bestseller List in 1988 with *Something Wonderful* and has made yearly appearances since.

Thrillers of a somewhat tougher kind come from the pen of internationally-known novelist David Lindsey. Although he makes his home in Austin, Lindsey sets novels throughout Texas and other regions of the world, and Houston is the setting for several. Five of them feature Houston homicide detective Stuart Haydon. One, *Mercy*, focuses on a female counterpart, Carmen Palma. It became a New York Times Bestseller and was filmed by HBO.

Lives of Famous Citizens

Biographies of Houston's famous citizens, both historical and contemporary, make fascinating reading. And apparently, they are pleasing to write, too, since there are so many of them. Sam Houston's life has been endlessly dissected and reconstructed. James Michener had a go at it in his novels *Texas* and *The Eagle and the Raven*. Houston's correspondence has been published in several volumes, edited by Madge Thornall Roberts. His life among the Cherokees has been singled out in Jack Gregory's *Sam Houston with the Cherokees: 1829–1833*.

His marriages are detailed in various books. *Sam Houston's Wife: A Biography of Margaret Lea Houston* by William Seale and Madge Roberts's *Star of Destiny*

WHERE TO MEET A FAMOUS WRITER IN HOUSTON

Murder by the Book

2342 Bissonnet
Houston 77005
713-524-8597
888-4-AGATHA

www.murderbooks.com

So, if Houston is so full of famous writers, what's your best chance of stumbling across one? Maybe at one of the sixty yearly events featuring authors that are sponsored by the nation's oldest and largest specialty bookstore devoted to mysteries, Murder by the Book. Anne Perry has been known to put in an appearance here, as well as suspense-meisters like David Baldacci, Janet Evanovich, and Michael Connelly.

Here awaits not only an enormous selection of your favorite genres, including imports from England that may not be available elsewhere, but also many books signed by their authors, Gregory McDonald, maybe, or James Lee Burke. Selection varies, of course, so come in and browse. You can at least stop by the gift shop and pick up a memento of your favorite writer, like a t-shirt sporting "Robicheaux's Dock & Bait Shop."

Another thing you can get here is tips about what to read. When it comes

Murder by the Book

(continued)

to Texas and Texans and murder and mystery, the staff says you can't go wrong with these listed below. Or stop by the store and get even more up-to-date advice.

The Red Scream by Mary Willis Walker

Meanwhile Back at the Ranch by Kinky Friedman

Sunset and Sawdust by Joe R. Lansdale

A Kiss Gone Bad by Jeff Abbott

Dead on the Island by Bill Crider

The Big Red Tequila by Rick Riordan

Mercy by David Lindsey

Heartwood by James Lee Burke

Austin City Blue by Jan Grape

Death by Dissertation by Dean James

Bitch Factor by Chris Rogers

Fade the Heat by Jay Brandon

Buck Fever by Ben Rehder

are about the marriage to Margaret Lea, and the novel *The Raven's Bride* by Elizabeth Crook speculates about the details of his marriage to Eliza Allen.

Sam Houston is seen as the ideal hero for children's books, and many have centered on his life and exploits, including *An American in Texas: The Story of Sam Houston* by Peggy Caravantes for ages four to eight, and *Sam Houston Is My Hero* by Judy Alter for ages nine to twelve.

Modern biographies include *Sam Houston and the American Southwest* by Randolph B. Campbell and *Sam Houston* by James L. Haley. Both capture the essence of the man who would lead Texas to independence.

On the question of the state's secession from the Union, Haley quotes one of Houston's saddest speeches: "Once I dreamed of empire, vast and expansive for a united people.... The dream is over. The golden charm is broken.... From one nation we have become two ... to attest how vain were the dreams of those who believed that the Union was a thing of forever."

On a more modern note, reading *Barbara Bush: A Memoir* is like sitting down with a warm, wise and witty woman and letting her tell you her life's story at her own pace and in her own voice. It just so happens that this particular woman has been wife to one U.S. president and mother to another, a distinction she shares only with Abigail Adams, from the early days of the nation. Mrs. Bush traveled the world and consorted with the powerful through the several decades of her husband's public service as U.S. Congressman from Texas, as Ambassador to the United Nations, Envoy to China, Director of the CIA, Vice President and President of the United States. And she kept a diary through it all.

Thanks to that and a remarkable memory for names and people, Mrs. Bush recreates her experiences for us in a fascinating autobiography. It's full of revealing snap shots, like that of the boorish side of Raisa Gorbachev, who insisted to Mrs. Bush that society was falling apart in the West because she had seen it on CNN, and who refused an invitation to visit an art gallery in Paris, saying "she had seen a Picasso show before." And China was a world of its own. The Bushes knew their hotel rooms were bugged by their hosts, because every time they privately expressed a wish for something, it would soon mysteriously appear.

The man with whom Mrs. Bush shares her life, the forty-first president of the United States, has been written about often. Like any other politician, he made his share of enemies throughout his career. But he is usually honored by all for the contributions he made to defending his country during World War II. War correspondent Joe Hyams tells the story of George Herbert Bush's experiences as a bomber pilot on the front lines in *Flight of the Avenger*. It includes a harrowing account of the event in which he almost lost his life: with an engine shot out, he had to bail out of his bomber into the sea. He carried those experiences—of being shot at, of watching buddies go down in flames and disappear forever—into the White House. Hyams quotes him as saying, "Those memories were constantly in my mind when we were discussing committing troops and estimating expected combat losses. . . . That experience is not essential for a president, however. We have generations of kids who may one day become president, and I hope that they will never have to fight or be in a war."

George Bush was commissioned at eighteen, the youngest pilot in the Navy. No matter where his life took him after that, he always maintained ties with family and friends. He wrote letters, often long, expansive letters, detailing the facts of his life. Today, those letters make a formidable record of the life of a devoted husband, friend and citizen, collected in *All the Best, George Bush: My Life in Letters and Other Writings*.

Barbara Jordan was the first black woman from the south to serve in the U.S. House of Representatives. She grew up in Houston's Fifth Ward, attended segregated schools, fought for voting rights for all people, and inspired more than one generation of women, white and black. Her remarkable story is told in *Barbara Jordan: American Hero* by Mary Beth Rogers, a loving biography of an extraordinary woman whose voice still echoes in the memories of all who ever heard it.

No one who heard Barbara Jordan speak ever forgot that voice. She could have been addressing the U.S. House of Representatives or she could have been reciting nursery rhymes. The voice of this child of a Baptist minister was strong and beautiful enough to stop listeners in their tracks. Its mesmerizing qualities seemed almost to force the most reluctant audience to hear, and when she raised it on the people's behalf, she became an orator of extraordinary power, an American hero. She devoted her life to working within the political systems of both Texas and the United States to combat racism and sexism.

Beyond the City

Once you leave Houston behind and venture into the flat, open coastal plains, your mind may turn again to history, natural history, and weather.

The history of Europeans in Texas begins with the first book ever written about Texas, Cabeza de Vaca's *La Relación*. First published about 1542, it is still in print today and is accessible for readers of English in many translations. An excellent choice is *The Narrative of Cabeza de Vaca* by Rolena Adorno and Patrick Charles Pautz. The same two also produced a book about the famous explorer called *Álvar Núñez Cabeza de Vaca: His Account, His Life, and the Expedition of Pánfilo de Narváez*, which won three prestigious prizes in the field of historical literature.

Shipwrecked on Galveston Island in 1528, de Vaca and several other Spaniards lived among the native tribesmen until they could escape in 1534. The last four of them left alive struck out west, crossed Texas into New Mexico, living off the land and the largess of other tribes they encountered, until they finally turned south and stumbled into a Spanish camp in 1536. Historians figure they had walked more than two thousand miles in all. De Vaca's tales of adventure, hardship, and exotic peoples helped fuel other men's belief in riches lying undiscovered in the desolate area north of the Rio Grande, eventually motivating Coronado to launch an expedition in search of cities made of gold.

A biography, *Álvar Núñez Cabeza de Vaca* by Valerie Menard, is suitable for reading by ages nine to twelve. The journey itself is compellingly told in *We Asked for Nothing: The Remarkable Journey of Cabeza de Vaca* by Stuart Waldman and illustrated by Tom McNeely, for the same age group.

Galveston Island, Pirates, and Storm

In the first two decades of the nineteenth century, Galveston Island was a haven for pirates and privateers, of whom Jean Lafitte is best known today for supporting the United States in its War of 1812 against the British. Despite that noble action, Lafitte was actually an unregenerate pirate, and the U.S. Navy eventually ran him off the island.

SPECIAL TREATS FOR BOOK LOVERS IN THE HOUSTON AREA

Houston Metropolitan Research Center

Houston Public Library
500 McKinney
Houston 77002
832-393-1313

The purpose of the Center is to preserve and make available records of business, religious, and civic organizations; private papers and records of important citizens; and maps, audiovisuals and architectural drawings that document the history of Houston. Special components include records of African American citizens, families, churches, newspapers and other institutions; Mexican-American heritage and culture; an architectural collection of some 125,000 drawings, engineering plans and photographs, plus the papers of prominent architects of Houston; photographs of historical Houston; an oral history collection; the Texas Jazz Archive; and Regional Historical Resource Depository records of the governments of Harris and Galveston counties.

Texas and Local History Department collects Texana and material pertinent to Houston. Holdings include books of state and local interest, some rare; periodicals from the nineteenth century to the present; documents relating to state and regional governing agencies; thousands of biographical and subject files; maps beginning with the Spanish colonial period; newspaper clippings; and miscellaneous resources, such as telephone books and school and college yearbooks.

Clayton Library Center for Genealogical Research is one of the best such public research libraries in the country. It makes available family and county histories, state and local records, lineages of patriotic societies, books, census records, passenger records, military records and more.

Woodson Research Center

Rice University
6100 Main
Houston 77251-1892
713-348-2586

This research center houses records of the university, collections of rare books amounting to some twenty-seven thousand volumes, and four hundred collections of manuscripts in subjects ranging from the historical to the literary, from politics to business. Special collections include personal and professional papers of biologist Julian S. Huxley and of Oveta Culp Hobby, communications pioneer and public servant. Stars of the rare book collections include Allen H. Stevenson Collection on the history of paper and watermarks; Benjamin Monroe Anderson Collection on the History of Aeronautics; Carroll and Harris Masterson Texana Collection on the history of Texas, including histories of some modern corporations.

(continued)

Robert James Terry Library, Special Collections

Texas Southern University
3100 Cleburne Street
Houston 77004
713-313-7011

Holdings include the following records: Houston League of Business and Professional Women; Texas Southern University Archives; Barbara Jordan Papers; Curtis Graves Papers; and Thomas Freeman Papers.

Heartman Collection

This is the largest collection of African-Americana in the Southwest, with twenty-two thousand books, slave narratives, journals and musical scores. It is supplemented by the African Art Gallery, which preserves and exhibits traditional art from Africa.

Special Collections and Archives

M. D. Anderson Library
University of Houston
114 University Libraries
Houston 77204-2000

Extensive holdings include books from medieval and Reformation periods; several collections of Houstoniana, Texana and American West material; a feminist and lesbian collection; several collections of literature and drama; and others featuring both science and the occult sciences. You will also find the collected works of science fiction writer Fritz Leiber.

John B. Coleman Library Special Collections/Archives

Prairie View A&M University
FM 1098
Prairie View 77446
936-857-2612

The papers of two individuals form the heart of this research center. The Hyman Collection holds the research material collected by educator, historian, and author Dr. Harold M. Hyman in such subjects as police powers and Constitutional law. The Delco Collection gathers the official and personal papers of Wilhelmina Ruth Fitzgerald Delco, the first African-American elected at large from Travis County, who was sent to the Texas House of Representatives in 1975.

A story of privateers like Jean Lafitte is told engagingly in a historical romance novel by Marti Phillips called *The Last Pirate*. Set in New Orleans and the Gulf with the War of 1812 as the backdrop, it introduces characters like the famous pirate and general Andrew Jackson to further the action and romance.

During the War for Texas Independence, ships from the Texas Navy prevented supplies from reaching Santa Anna by sea, and once the war ended in 1836, settlement began of what would become the city of Galveston. In time, huge Victorian mansions grew along fancy boulevards, reflecting the fortunes being made in railroads, banking, cotton, and fishing. By 1900, Galveston was a city of vast riches. That was the year of the storm that changed everything.

The turn-of-the-century event that put Galveston on the world's weather map, the Great Storm, killed some six thousand people. Afterwards, the U.S. Corps of Engineers spent eight years raising the grade of the whole island by ten to twelve feet. They also built a seventeen-foot sea wall that now stretches across about a third of the island's beach, all in hopes of preventing the tragedy from ever happening again.

Many books tell the tale, some based on firsthand accounts by survivors. One is the story of Isaac Monroe Cline. He was the man the U.S. Government had put in charge of meteorological matters in the city, head of the newly-created Texas Section of the U.S. Weather Bureau. Meteorologist, citizen and family man, he saw himself as a scientist, experienced in the ways of strange phenomena of the atmosphere, confident in his ability to predict the weather.

In Erik Larsen's dramatic *Isaac's Storm*, we see this self-assured man ensconce his wife and three young daughters in a home just three blocks from the sea. We hear him, even as the storm approaches, tell the editor of the local newspaper that the idea that Galveston could be seriously damaged by the oncoming storm is "simply an absurd delusion." With such details, Larsen turns this story from a simple account of a natural catastrophe into a story of human weakness and hubris, and thus into tragedy. He filters the horrors of that deadly night through the true experiences of Isaac Cline himself, who paid a terrible price for his arrogance.

Meanwhile, elsewhere along the coast, Texas was turning into a shipping, oil and industrial giant. The Battle of San Jacinto, fought in 1836, freed Texas from Mexican rule. It took place about where the Houston suburbs of Pasadena and Deer Creek sit today. Just before that, several hundred Texas soldiers, led by Captain James Fannin, were captured and then shot by the Mexican Army in what became known as the Goliad Massacre, thus adding "Remember Goliad" to the battle cry of "Remember the Alamo" that rang out at the Battle of San Jacinto. The treaty that officially ended the war was signed at Velasco on May 14, 1836. Master storyteller Elmer Kelton used this unique point in history for the focus of his novel *Massacre at Goliad*.

Not long after that, ship channels were being dug, railroads brought in, factories built. Sugar was planted in what is now Sugarland, home to Imperial Sugar Company. Cattle ranching hit the big time. Eventually, modern highways traced the coastline and shrimping fleets proliferated. Petrochemical processing became key to the area's prosperity. And tourists discovered Padre Island and South Padre Island.

Of Whooping Cranes and Sea Turtles

Other tourists discovered a birder's paradise. Hundreds of species of birds make their homes along the coastline. Hundreds more migrate twice a year along pathways that cross over the coast. And there are plenty of birder-friendly places from which to view them all.

If you'd really like to enjoy some of the avian pleasures of this region but feel overwhelmed by the choices available for bird-watching, your best resource is a guidebook called *Exploring the Great Texas Coastal Birding Trail: Highlights of a Birding Mecca*, by Mel White. A veteran birder, White guides you expertly to the choice spots along the four-hundred-mile Birding Trail that tracks the coastline, steering you down birdy country roads and through parks and refuges. Take along your best field guide, but trust White to tell you what to expect to see in each location and at what season. Of course, if you will be on the central coast between November and March, you will want to know about whooping cranes.

At a height of five feet, with a wingspan of more than seven feet, whooping cranes are the largest native North American birds. They are also among the most endangered. Their numbers vary from year to year, but the Texas coast flock numbers around 150. They spend the summers nesting and rearing young in Canada. In the fall, they fly some twenty-five hundred miles to spend the winter on the Texas shore. A whole wildlife refuge has been put aside for them near Port Aransas. As the weather warms in the spring, the flock will once again take flight for their northern nesting sites.

Although recommended for reading by ages nine to twelve, *Whooping Cranes* by Janice Parker and Karen Dudley can serve a much wider audience. Both clear and comprehensive, with photos and drawings, it tells the story of the whooping crane, from what it eats to how its feathers are arranged, and fleshes out the tale with an enchanting bit of folklore plus instructions on folding a paper crane. Educational and entertaining, it's a great introduction to whoopers for the whole family.

The Turtle Lady: Ila Fox Loetscher of South Padre by Evelyn Sizemore recounts the story of a woman whose efforts to save the Kemp's ridley sea turtle from extinction made her a leading conservationist in Texas. The cover photo on this book, showing the aged Loetscher (she lived to ninety-seven) embracing one of the endangered animals like the valued creature it is, makes this one irresistible.

Texas wildflowers range far beyond the bluebonnet and paintbrush. Some two hundred native flowering plants flourish in this region. *Wildflowers of Houston and Southeast Texas* by John and Gloria Tveten helps you identify them with color photos and provides a bit of native plant lore where appropriate. If you stroll the beaches, you may appreciate some help in identifying the beautiful shells you're collecting. A mainstay reference is *Texas Monthly Field Guide to Shells of the Texas Coast* by Jean Andrews.

Attractions of Houston and the Gulf Coast

The Gulf Coast is where you come if fishing is what it's all about for you. You can find an opportunity to fish from a pier, from the shore, from a kayak, from your own boat or a chartered boat. You can drift fish, lure fish or fly fish. You can fish saltwater flats or coral formations or the depths of the deep blue sea. You can hire a guide, buy a boat or bait, and eat seafood three times a day.

For information about fishing, boating, and beach sports, contact the chamber of commerce or visitor center in each area or visit the area's web site. All boating, as well as hunting and fishing, is regulated by the state. See the web site maintained by Texas Parks and Wildlife for information about licensing, regulations and other requirements for fishing, hunting and boating, www.tpwd.state.tx.us, or call 512-389-4800 or 800-792-1112 during business hours.

ANAHUAC

This city wasn't designated Alligator Capital of Texas by the state legislature for nothing. In the fall, the folks celebrate their scaly neighbors with a two-day festival, **Texas Gatorfest (409-267-4190)**. Of course, they're also celebrating the opening of hunting season with the **Great Texas Alligator Roundup**.

The treasure of Anahuac is **Anahuac National Wildlife Refuge (409-267-3337)** about eighteen miles southeast of town. There can be alligators here, too, by the way, as there can be in almost any undeveloped (and some quite highly developed) areas near the coast.

In the spring, thousands of songbirds, too heat-loving to spend the winter in North America, return to the continent when the weather warms. They arrive on the coast exhausted from a nonstop trip across the Gulf from the Yucatan Peninsula and drop into the first tree they spot. If you happen to be standing around here with binoculars and a bird book, you can add a lot of species to your life list. More than 250 species have been spotted here. Most of them will move on to their summering grounds to breed, but some forty species do nest here during the summer. In winter, you'll have the spectacle of thousands of vacationing water fowl who thought the Texas coast quite far enough south to travel for the winter. What to look for among them? White-face ibis, roseate spoonbill, and yellow rail, for starters, as well as thousands upon thousands of snow geese.

Aransas Pass

In June, you can attend the biggest shrimp cooking and eating orgy in the world, the annual **Shrimporee** (361-758-2750 or 800-633-3028), complete with first-class musical entertainments and plenty for the kids to do.

You can also do a bit of bird-watching here, with three spots from the **Great Coastal Birding Trail** nearby and **Newbury Park Hummingbird Garden** on Lamont Street, just off Business 35. Designed to lure hummingbirds from far and away, this little garden offers the chance to see hummingbirds aplenty. Most will be ruby-throated, but buff-bellied, black-chinned and the super-aggressive rufous are also possible, especially during migrations in September.

Baytown

The Great Texas Coastal Birding Trail spot here is **Baytown Nature Preserve** on the west side of town.

Brazoria County

Water recreation and beach sports define the attractions throughout Brazoria County. Many miles of beaches run along both ocean and rivers, and fishing opportunities range from casting in the surf to hauling in a sailfish. Three wildlife refuges, **Brazoria, Big Boggy and San Bernard**, offer opportunities to interact with nature. And museums remind us of the area's heritage.

This is the region settled by the first colonists brought into Texas by Stephen F. Austin in the early 1820s. It's also the site of many important developments in the Texas road to independence. **Brazoria County Historical Museum** (979-864-1208) in Angleton depicts those vital moments in history. Just west of there, **Columbia Historical Museum** (979-345-6125) in West Columbia at 247 E. Brazos stands on the site of the first capitol of the Republic of Texas, established there for a few months in 1836. Sam Houston was sworn in as first President of the Republic near here, too.

While in West Columbia, make a point of visiting the **Varner-Hogg State Historic Site** (979-345-4656), which preserves a plantation house from the 1830s and makes it accessible for tours. There are sixty-six acres of nature in the welcome shade of big old pecan trees to enjoy, and every year, festivals are held to celebrate Black History Month, Texas Independence Day, San Jacinto Day and Christmas.

For a close-up look (eye to eye in some cases) at the wildlife that lives below the surface of the bay, plan a visit to **Sea Center Texas** (979-292-0100) at 300 Medical Drive in Lake Jackson. It's like Texas Parks and Wildlife meets

Disneyland. A modern Visitor Center houses several aquaria with big glass walls, behind which dwell some champion specimens of Gulf Coast waters, including those found in bays, coastal marshes and estuaries. Meet Gordon, the three-hundred-pound grouper. He doesn't do much except stare back at those staring at him, which might be you or one of the sharks he shares his fifty-thousand-gallon home with.

Most popular with the young and curious is the twenty-foot Touch Pool which allows them to reach into an open tank and stroke the objects of their affection, such as snails, clams, crabs, and such. Wander outside the Visitor Center to find an elevated boardwalk and ramble around five acres of coastal marsh and enjoy the butterfly-hummingbird garden, while admiring the many species of birds and animals that frequent the area.

CLEAR LAKE

Space Center Houston (281-244-2100) is the Official Visitors Center of **NASA's Johnson Space Center**, the organization to which Neil Armstrong was speaking when, having just set his lander on the surface of the moon, he reported, "Houston, the Eagle has landed." Exciting exhibits recreate historical moments in space and show how modern space systems are developed and controlled, as well as how astronauts are trained. Computer displays, movies, and an IMAX theater help you experience the thrills. You can also take a guided tour of the Johnson Space Center itself, by tram, and see how it all works in the real world.

CORPUS CHRISTI

A **Botanical Garden and Nature Center** (361-852-2100) at 8545 S. Staples offers a civilized way to bird-watch, as you stroll the level paths of this stop on the **Great Texas Coastal Birding Trail** and pause to smell the roses or admire the plumeria, hibiscus, oleander and bougainvillea that color the place up almost year-round. Step inside the Exhibit House where you'll find bromeliads, cycads, cacti and succulents, or spend an hour or two in the Orchid House admiring one of the largest collections of these exotic flowers to be found in the Southwest. Outside again, enjoy the shade along the Bird and Butterfly Trail, and watch for pelicans and spoonbills near Gator Lake.

You can see the treasures of Corpus Christi Bay from the water side via a narrated tour aboard a four-hundred-passenger paddle-wheel boat. **Captain Clark's Flagship** (361-884-8306 or 361-884-1693) departs from Slip #49, Peoples Street T-Head, several times a day.

Texas State Aquarium (361-881-1200 or 800-477-GULF) at 2710 N. Shoreline Boulevard lets you interact with the most glamorous creatures of the sea. If you think you've seen a big aquarium before, wait until you stand beside the four hundred thousand gallons of seawater that make up Dolphin Bay, a protective home and display area for dolphins that can't be released into the wild for various reasons. Diving shows, feeding demonstrations, and even hands-on-the-fish programs educate while they entertain. Popular programs like otter training, bird rehabilitation, or reptile identification make for a full schedule.

USS Lexington **Museum on the Bay** (361-888-4873) is moored in Corpus Christi Bay at 2914 North Shoreline Boulevard, just off State Highway 181. For anyone reared on World War II movies or who remembers the real thing, this beautiful old ship will set your heart aflutter. She's a floating museum now. You can visit crew areas and the bridge, see a historical film, and clamber all over this national treasure.

Corpus Christi Museums
For the art lover in you, there's **Art Center of Corpus Christi** (361-884-6406) at 100 N. Shoreline Boulevard, where you can often catch an artist at work in one of the open studios. **The South Texas Institute for the Arts** (361-825-3500), housed in a striking white building at 1902 N. Shoreline, overlooks the bay and offers an Art Museum with almost two thousand items in its permanent collection, focusing on modern art and work by Texas artists. **The Asian Cultures Museum and Educational Center** (361-882-2641) at 1809 N. Chaparral exposes visitors to Asian culture. And the **Corpus Christi Museum of Science and History** (361-826-4650) houses historically accurate replicas of two of the ships that sailed with Columbus on his first voyage to the New World. October is the big month at this facility. They devote two whole weeks to Columbus Day.

Padre Island National Seashore
Padre Island lies about twenty miles south of Corpus Christi. South Padre Island is altogether different. You can't drive from one to the other.

In fact, driving opportunities are pretty restricted on Padre Island. There is only one paved road and the area where standard vehicles are permitted is limited. Unless you're equipped for primitive camping and have a four-wheel drive vehicle, you will probably find the pleasures offered near the Visitor Center quite enchanting enough to hold your attention. There's a three-quarter-mile looping trail through the grasslands for birding and a beach for swimming and sunbathing. If you plan to foray into the interior of the park, the National Park

Service strongly advises you to stop at the Visitor Center (361-949-8068) for safety and orientation materials.

Of special interest to visitors here is the opportunity to witness one of the hatchling releases, in which the Park Service releases newly-hatched Kemp's ridley sea turtles into the sea. To find out when the next such event is scheduled, call the **Hatchling Hotline** (361-949-7163).

GALVESTON

You can't miss **Moody Gardens** (800-582-4673), whose three spectacular pyramids dominate the landscape as you approach the island. Don't stop there if you have only an hour or two to spend. Plan a whole day around a visit to this kid-friendly place.

One pyramid houses a rainforest with its attendant flora and fauna: orchids and violets growing from rock crevices, tropical birds flying about, bats hanging in their caves, piranhas grinning in the gurgling streams. Another holds an aquarium—a million-and-a-half-gallons-of-water aquarium—featuring fish of every bright hue, as well as sharks, penguins and other denizens of watery places. The third pyramid's exhibits of scientific experiments and phenomena make the air buzz with the excitement of learning about nature. An IMAX 3-D Theater will keep the blood pumping, and the IMAX Ridefilm Theater offers a "high-impact, immersive simulation" that will make you believe you're riding through the skies at warp speed.

The Strand Historic Landmark District maintains a Visitor Center (409-765-7834) at 2016 Strand. The Strand is the shop-by-day, party-by-night heart of the city of Galveston, but it is also a place of trolleys and horse-drawn carriages, museums and theaters and impressive historic architecture. And it's the homeplace of the **1877 Tall Ship Elissa** (409-763-1877), a two-hundred-foot-long square rigger rescued from the junk heap by the Galveston Historical Foundation and restored to its original beauty and majesty. The romance of the high seas lives again as you stand at her wheel, gaze up her one-hundred-foot-tall mast, and imagine yourself hundreds of miles from shore, soaring across the open sea toward Calcutta or other ports of call. You'll find her moored at Pier 21, a block off the Strand.

Near the Tall Ship, **Texas Seaport Museum** (409-763-1877) offers a look into the role of seafaring vessels in the nineteenth century. At one time, Galveston was called "Ellis Island of the West" for the number of immigrants who arrived at her port in such vessels. The names of more than 130,000 of those newcomers are collected into a computerized database, which is available for public access. It includes many people whose first point of embarkation in America was Texas, from 1846 to 1948.

> **NOTABLE MUSEUMS AT THE STRAND NATIONAL HISTORIC LANDMARK DISTRICT**
>
> The 1877 Tall Ship Elissa (409-763-1877) at Pier 21
>
> The Mardi Gras Museum (409-763-1133) at 2211 Strand
>
> The Railroad Museum (409-765-5700) at 25th and Strand Streets
>
> The Galveston County Historical Museum (409-766-2340) at 2219 Market Street
>
> David Taylor's Classic Car Museum at 1918 Mechanic Street (409-765-6590)
>
> The Ocean Star Museum at Pier 19 (713-975-6442)

Once a year, early in December, the Strand National Historic Landmark District turns itself into Victorian London. During the weekend of **Dickens on the Square**, characters from the stories and novels of Charles Dickens roam the streets. Queen Victoria herself may lead a parade, and Ebenezer Scrooge will almost certainly put in an appearance at this festival honoring the author of "A Christmas Carol," *Oliver Twist*, *A Tale of Two Cities*, and *David Copperfield*. Galveston goes all out for **Mardi Gras**, too, the season beginning with Epiphany each year and continuing through Fat Tuesday. Parades, balls, pageants, charity events, contests, parties and processions headline the largest Mardi Gras celebration in Texas.

Two other historical districts deserve a look while you're in Galveston.

A TREAT FOR BOOK LOVERS

Galveston and Texas History Center
Rosenberg Library
2310 Sealy Avenue
Galveston 77550
409-763-8854 ext. 127

The oldest continuously-operating library in the state, the Rosenberg is the proud depository of maps, photographs, rare books and manuscripts detailing the history of Galveston and Texas, as well as of artworks depicting local history and other subjects. Manuscript collections include papers from such prominent early Texans as Samuel May Williams, Gail Borden, John Grant Tod, Jr., James Morgan, and others, as well as records of business, civic and religious organizations.

A photo collection documents the city's history from before the Great Storm through the devastation of the storm of 1919 and shows the building of the sea wall and causeway and the raising of the island's grade. Some of the most interesting papers include letters written during and after the storms by ordinary citizens, describing survivors' experiences.

Ride a horse-drawn carriage through the **Silk Stocking Historical District**, 24th and 25th Streets between Avenue L and Avenue O. Or take a self-guided tour through the **East End Historical District**, 11th to 19th Streets between Market and Broadway, for a taste of the lifestyle of the wealthy from another era. You can get maps and directions at the Galveston Historic Foundation (409-765-7834) or pick up brochures at any local Visitor Center.

Several nineteenth-century homes are open for tours. **Ashton Villa** at 2328 Broadway (409-762-3933) was built in 1859, survived the Civil War and the Great Storm, and became a symbol of the late-Victorian Gilded Age. Fully furnished with heirlooms and antiques, it will transport you to another time.

Bishop's Palace at 1402 Broadway (409-762-2475) is the place to tour if opulence excites you; if you enjoy magnificent hand-carved interiors of mahogany, oak and maple, even rosewood and satinwood; if chandeliers of Venetian crystal stir your blood and you dream of fireplace mantels lined in silver. Don't miss this example of Victorian sumptuousness.

Other historic homes worth visiting include **Moody Mansion** (409-762-7668) at 2618 Broadway, decorated elegantly in eighteenth-century French style; a wonderful example of Greek Revival, the **Powhatan House** at 3427 Avenue (409-763-0077); the oldest home in Galveston, the **Menard House** built in 1838 at 1605 33rd Street (409-765-7834); and the **Williams House** (409-765-7834), built by Samuel May Williams, "The Father of the Texas Navy," at 3601 Avenue P in 1839.

Several opportunities exist to get out of your car and experience this area by alternate means of transportation. **The Colonel** (409-740-7797), a replica of a nineteenth-century triple-decker paddleboat, will cruise you around the bay, departing from Moody Gardens. To tour the Port of Galveston, board the **Harbor Tour** boat departing from Pier 22 or take a ride on both land and water in an amphibious vessel with **Galveston Island Duck Tours** (409-621-4771). Catch a trolley for a four-and-a-half-mile ride from the Seawall to the Strand. To see even more, hop a **Treasure Island Tour** (409-765-9564) train at Seawall Boulevard and 21st Street and cruise at a breathtaking fifteen miles per hour through historic districts, past famous homes, past the shrimp fleet, and so on for seventeen miles of some of the best sights available.

For information about beach sports, camping and fishing opportunities on Galveston Island, contact the Visitor Information Center (888-425-4753).

HOUSTON

This city's **Visitor Center** (713-437-5556 or 800-4-HOUSTON) at City Hall, 901 Bagby Street, is reportedly the largest in the country, boasting more than ten thousand maps, brochures, flyers and other tourist-friendly documents, along with a cordial staff who can help you figure out what to make of it all. Since you're downtown, start your day of sightseeing at 410 Bagby Street at the **Downtown Aquarium** (713-223-3474) and let the kids take a ride on a train, a carousel or a Ferris wheel, all the while learning about underwater life.

Houston may not be the first venue you think of when cows and horses come to mind, but the fact is that the largest exposition of working and show stock in the state takes place right here in early spring each year. As does about three weeks of rodeoing, barbecuing, and almost nonstop professional entertaining, with the biggest names in the music business putting in appearances. Not just one or two headliners but a score or more light up the stages during the **Houston Livestock Show and Rodeo** (832-667-1000). Daily performances begin with a grand entry, followed by kick-up-the-dust rodeo events and a calf scramble, and end with a concert entertainer. It all happens in Houston's showpiece Reliant Park at 8334 Fannin Street. Check out this year's schedule at www.rodeohouston.com.

If your tastes turn to quieter pursuits, take advantage of the year-round performing arts offerings in Houston's celebrated **Theater District**. Resident companies in theater, ballet, symphony, and opera, along with a host of smaller repertory and performance-artist venues, are up to the challenge of the most demanding works, from grand opera to dance, chamber music to jazz. For information about current performances, call 713-223-4544 or see the web site at www.houstontheaterdistrict.org.

When it comes to preserving and displaying the best of human endeavor, Houston takes a backseat to no city. More than sixteen museums lie within blocks of each other in the **Museum District** alone. You can find out what's going on at each of them by visiting the web site at www.houstonmuseumdistrict.org. Many other museums are found outside the district.

Perhaps most often cited as the best of the best, the **Children's Museum of Houston** (713-522-1138) at 1500 Binz keeps winning awards for its success at interesting children in learning about the way the world works and making it easy for them to do so. Hands-on exhibits are the key, and children's experiences range from learning how a television studio operates to collecting insects and testing water quality.

Equally impressive is the **Museum of Fine Arts, Houston** (713-639-7300, 1001 Bissonnet Street and 5601 Main Street), with its complex of museums, art schools, decorative arts centers, and sculpture garden. It hosts internationally acclaimed exhibits and holds a world-class collection of its own. Two off-campus sites include **Bayou Bend Collection and Gardens** (713-639-7750, at 1 Westcott

Street) and **Rienzi** (713-639-7800, at 1406 Kirby Drive), housing significant collections of American and European furniture and decorative arts respectively. Tours are available at both. These fabulous historic homes are not to be missed if you love expressions of elegance, grace, luxury and beauty.

Private art collectors John and Dominique de Menil left a similarly impressive legacy to the world, available for all to see at the **Menil Collection Museum** (713-525-9400, at 1515 Sul Ross), where some fifteen thousand paintings, sculptures, prints, drawings, photographs, and rare books reside. They include one of the best-regarded surrealist collections in existence, along with masterpieces from around the globe.

Houston Museum of Natural Science (713-639-4629) at One Hermann Circle Drive attracts children with its Cockrell Butterfly Center, where they get to interact with the fluttering beauties; its IMAX theater; and exhibits of such kid

HOUSTON: DIVERSITY IN THE ARTS

Houston celebrates diverse cultural experiences with a wide selection of both museums and performing arts.

Buffalo Soldiers National Museum (713-942-8920, at 1834 Southmore) preserves and honors the history of African-Americans in their roles as protectors of the United States of America, from frontier times to the present. "Buffalo Soldiers" is the proud nickname earned by the Tenth U.S. Cavalry in their conflict with the Cheyenne on the Texas Plains. It has come to signify all of African descent who serve their country in the military. Live re-enactments of historical events and other special programs bring the past to life.

The Ensemble Theater (713-520-0055), a distinguished professional theater company, presents performances focused on the African-American experience.

MECA (Multicultural Education and Counseling through the Arts) (713-802-9370) offers a wide range of performances, highlighting various cultures, both American and international.

Talento Bilingue de Houston (713-222-1213) is a Latin-American cultural center that hosts entertainment events and art exhibits showcasing Latino talent.

Kuumba House Dance Theater (713-524-1079), an educational as well as a performing entity, captures the beauty and excitement of African culture through various forms, including dance, theater, music and art.

Project Row Houses (713-526-7662) is a group of twenty-two renovated inner-city homes from the past that now serve as public galleries for exhibiting art commemorating neighborhood revitalization and celebrating themes of the African-American experience.

Tien Hou Temple (713-236-1015, at 1507 Delano) is Houston's Chinatown treasure, a showcase for the dramatic art associated with Eastern philosophies.

pleasers as dinosaur remains. Combine it with a few hours at the nearby **Houston Zoo** (713-533-6500), at 1513 N. MacGregor in Hermann Park, if you really want to wear them out.

Ways to get wet in Houston rank high on most summer travelers' list of must-knows. Choose from **Adventure Bay** (281-498-7946) at the corner of Beechnut and Eldridge; **Lake Houston State Park** (281-354-6881), for swimming, camping and nature watching; **The Reef** (713-991-3483), with 20 acres of spring-fed lake; **Six Flags WaterWorld** (713-799-12340), a park that lives up to its reputation; or **SplashTown Waterpark** at 21300 I-45 North in Spring (281-355-3300).

LaPorte

At 3523 Battleground Road (Texas Highway 134) lies some of the most historic real estate in Texas: the **San Jacinto Battleground** (281-479-2431), which is both a State Historic Site and a National Historic Landmark. This is where the army of Texans led by Sam Houston took the Mexican Army by surprise, captured their leader, General Antonio Lopez de Santa Anna, and put an end to the War for Texas Independence. A tower of concrete faced with dazzling Texas limestone rears 567 feet above the plain, memorializing those dramatic moments. An observation platform at 489 feet provides a breathtaking view over the city. In the base of the monument, you'll find **The San Jacinto Museum of History** (281-479-2421), a comprehensive compilation of human history in Texas.

Another attraction here is the opportunity to board and explore the **Battleship Texas** (281-479-2431), which played active roles in both World Wars, serving as the flagship on D-Day, when Texan Dwight David Eisenhower commanded the invasion of Europe to free it from occupying armies.

Kingsville

The **King Ranch** is the stuff of legend. Currently at about 825,000 acres spread over four counties, it has grown from a nineteenth-century Texas Longhorn operation to a world leader in ranching, having developed the Santa Gertrudis breed and introduced several other breeds to Texas cowboys. Farming of every crop suitable to the area—from sugar cane to citrus fruit, retailing, and tourism have expanded operations for the twenty-first century.

The ranch operates its own **Visitor Center** (361-592-8055) on Highway 141 West just west of Kingsville, offering guided tours in ranching, history, agri-

TREATS FOR BOOK LOVERS

The Albert and Ethel Hertzstein Library

San Jacinto Museum of History
One Monument Circle
LaPorte (Houston) 77571
281-479-2421
Open by appointment.

Hidden within the recesses of the San Jacinto Museum of History lies a rich treasure trove of rare books, documents and manuscripts relating to the history of Texas, ranging from Orders of the Spanish Inquisition to the latest biographies of veterans of the Battle of San Jacinto, and featuring military history and developments in art and culture in between.

Some of Sam Houston's personal belongings are housed here, along with maps, blueprints, journals, Bibles, deed records and other records. It was descendants of Sam Houston, Stephen F. Austin and other Texas heroes whose gifts began the library in 1939.

South Texas Archives and Special Collections

James C. Jernigan Library
Texas A&M University–Kingsville
361-593-2776

Books, manuscripts and audio-visuals about the history and natural history of South Texas, along with official university archives and rare books, are housed here. The library is also Regional Historical Resource Depository for the Texas State Library and Archives System, housing local government records from the eleven surrounding counties.

Special Collections and Archives

The Mary and Jeff Bell Library
Texas A&M University–Corpus Christi
6300 Ocean Drive
361-825-2301

The focus of this library is the history of Corpus Christi, South Texas and Mexico. It contains printed, oral and visual collections that include the papers of public servants, pioneers of the historical Chicano movement, and other key historical figures, as well as material relating to writers, collectors, scientists, and civic and business leaders. Family photo collections and works on genealogy, history, surveying, birding, and other aspects of culture round out the collection.

The library also participates in both the Federal Depository Library Program and the Texas State Publications Depository Program, archiving many government publications.

---

culture, wildlife watching and birding. You'll need reservations for some tours. The **King Ranch Museum** displays artifacts from ranching history, and the **Saddle Shop** offers goods from boots to luggage and gift items from books to office chairs. For an up-to-date list of scheduled events, see www.kingranch.com.

Pasadena

Right in the heart of one of the largest urban areas in the nation, you will find a place where the deer and the buffalo roam. Along with swamp rabbits, bobcats, coyotes, alligators, turtles, snakes and birds—about 370 species in all, living in a wilderness preserve of native trees, grasses and animals. In **Armand Bayou Nature Center** (281-474-2551) at 8500 Bay Area Boulevard, a six-hundred-foot boardwalk lets you stroll across a pond and observe the wildlife living there. An observation deck offers a view of grazing bison, and there's a full schedule of educational and family-oriented activities, such as guided tours and natural history exhibits.

Port Aransas

Fishing tournaments and bird-watching, sailboating and dolphin spotting, scuba diving and waterfront dining: if you can't find entertainment to suit your temperament, you're just not looking. At the **Port Aransas Birding Center**, look for white tailed hawk in winter, maybe groove billed ani in summer, and magnificent frigate bird in fall. This is the heart of the Great Texas Coastal Birding Trail and is appropriately rife with birds all year long. And this is the home of the annual Whooping Crane Festival. The Tourist Bureau is ready to hand out details. Call 361-749-5919 or 800-452-6278.

Port Isabel

The **Historic Lighthouse** built in 1853 offers a chance to spiral up the stairs, if you have the energy, and peer out over the bay. And the **Port Isabel Historical Museum** preserves artifacts and documents dating from the area's first settlement. Shrimp cook-offs, boat parades, and wildlife watching round out your stay in this friendly town. The chamber of commerce has the details at 800-527-6102.

Richmond

To get a real feel for what it was like to be among the first few hundred Anglos to accompany Stephen F. Austin into Texas in 1821 and start turning the wilderness into a home, treat yourself to the **Fort Bend Museum** (281-342-6478) at 500 Houston Street. It takes you through the War for Texas Independence, the days of great sugar and cotton plantations, the Civil War and subsequent events, into the twentieth century. The **Research Library** is of value in the study of Austin and his colony, as well as in research on the history of the Fort Bend area in general. The museum also offers tours of two historic homes.

Rio Hondo

Nowhere in the world will you find a mix of plant and animal life just like the one at **Laguna Atascosa National Wildlife Refuge** (210-748-3607), where plants, birds, and animals that have stretched their habitat as far north as they can mix with those who have reached their southernmost outpost. The mix of freshwater and saltwater areas with marshy land is ideal for diversity, making this a nationally-known hot spot for birders.

Rockport-Fulton and Aransas NWR

For such modest-sized towns (about ten thousand folks altogether), Rockport and Fulton offer spectacular experiences for lovers of nature and history, from the Hummingbird Festival in September to **Zachary Taylor Park**, where that general camped in 1845. Or if fishing is your pursuit, you'll love the great fishing opportunities provided by the state at Copano Bay Fishing Pier. The Rockport-Fulton Area Chamber of Commerce (800-242-0071) is at 404 Broadway.

Aransas National Wildlife Refuge (361-286-3559) is the center of whooping-crane watching activities during the winter, and some three hundred other species of birds are up for sighting throughout the whole year. You can see the whoopers with binoculars from a viewing deck at the refuge, or you can catch one of the numerous charter boats that will take you out into the shallow waters to get a closer view. For hummingbirds, visit the native-plant garden in the Texas Department of Transportation rest area. And don't miss seeing the biggest live oak tree in Texas at **Goose Island State Park** (361-729-2858). Experts say it's about a thousand years old.

Rosenberg

Three silvery domes housing working telescopes strike a note of real contrast with the surrounding woods and marshlands at **Brazos Bend State Park** (979-553-5101). **George Observatory** (979-553-3400) offers the public an opportunity to peer through the professional optics on Saturday nights. Daytime activities at the park include wildlife-spotting, camping, fishing and hiking.

South Padre Island

This is a community wholly devoted to tourism. Fun in the sun is the only business here. The Visitor Center (956-761-6433) welcomes you at 600 Padre Blvd. You can surf or sunbathe, fish or golf, ride horses or go boating, windsurf or hunt shells, build sand castles or eat yourself silly on seafood. Nor do you have to get sandy and salty to get wet in this water-loving community, thanks to **Schlitterbahn Beach Waterpark** (956-772-SURF). Water coasters, slides and chutes galore make it all possible, along with the largest manmade surfing wave you're ever likely to see and tubing adventures aplenty.

If you feel the need to balance such experiences with a bit of education, visit the **Pan-American Coastal Studies Laboratory** (Isla Blanca Park) to learn about the area's marine life, or take in one of the shows about endangered sea turtles at **Sea Turtle, Inc.** (956-761-4511), founded by conservationist Ila Loetscher to rescue Kemp's ridley sea turtles from extinction and operated today to protect sea turtles of all kinds.

The Reading Tour

Abbott, Jeff. *A Kiss Gone Bad*. New York: Onyx Books, 2001.

Adorno, Rolena, and Patrick Charles Pautz. *The Narrative of Cabeza de Vaca*. Lincoln: University of Nebraska Press, 2003.

Alter, Judy. *Houston Is My Hero*. Fort Worth: Texas Christian University Press, 2003.

Andrews, Jean. *Texas Monthly Field Guide to Shells of the Texas Coast*. Austin: Texas Monthly Press, 1992.

Baca, Jimmy Santiago. *A Place to Stand*. New York: Grove Press, 2002.

Barthelme, Donald. *The Dead Father*. New York: Pocket Books, 1976.

Barthelme, Frederick. *Elroy Nights*. New York: Counterpoint Press, 2003.

Barthelme, Steve. *And He Tells the Little Horse the Whole Story*. Baltimore: Johns Hopkins University Press, 1987.

Berry, Venise. *Colored Sugar Water*. New York: Dutton, 2002.

Brandon. Jay. *Fade the Heat*. New York: Pocket Books, 1991 (reprint).

Burke, James Lee. *Heartwood*. New York: Island Books, 1999.

Bush, Barbara. *Barbara Bush: A Memoir*. New York: Scribner, 1994.

Bush, George. *All the Best, George Bush: My Life in Letters and Other Writings*. New York: Scribner, 1999.

Caravantes, Peggy. *An American in Texas: The Story of Sam Houston*. Greensboro, N.C.: Morgan Reynolds, 2003.

Campbell, Randolph B. *Sam Houston and the American Southwest*. 2nd ed. New York: Pearson Longman, 2001.

Crider, Bill. *Dead on the Island*. New York: Walker & Company, 1991.

Diaz, Tony. *The Aztec Love God*. Tallahasee, Fla.: FC2, 1998.

Friedman, Kinky. *Meanwhile Back at the Ranch*. New York: Simon & Schuster, 2002.

Grape, Jan. *Austin City Blue*. New York: Five Star Books, 2001.

Haley, James L. *Sam Houston*. Norman: University of Oklahoma Press, 2002.

Hirsch, Edward. *How to Read a Poem and Fall in Love with Poetry*. New York: Harcourt, 1999.

Hyams, Joe. *Flight of the Avenger*. New York: Harcourt, 1991.
Jones, Steven Graham. *Fast Red Road*. Tallahasee, Fla.: FC2, 2000.
Kelton, Elmer. *Massacre at Goliad*. New York: Forge Books, 1965.
Lansdale, Joe R. *Sunset and Sawdust*. New York: Knopf, 2004.
Larsen, Erik. *Isaac's Storm*. New York: Vintage Books, 2000.
Lindsey, David. *Mercy*. Rev. ed. New York: Bantam, 1991.
Macdonald, Cynthia. *I Can't Remember*. New York: Knopf, 1997.
Menard, Valerie. *Álvar Núñez Cabeza de Vaca*. Hockessin, Del.: Mitchell Lane Publications, 2003.
Michener, James. *Texas*. Austin: University of Texas Press, 1989.
Olmos, Edward James. *Americanos: Latino Life in the United States*. New York: Little, Brown & Company, 1999.
Parker, Janice, and Karen Dudley. *Whooping Cranes*. Austin: Raintree/Steck Vaughn, 1997.
Phillips, Marti. *The Last Pirate*. Ormond Beach, Fl.: Southern Star Books, 1999.
Phillips, Robert. *About People You Know*. Huntsville, Tex.: Sam Houston University, 2002.
Rehder, Ben. *Buck Fever*. New York: St. Martin's Press, 2003.
Riordan, Rick. *The Big Red Tequila*. New York: Bantam, 1997.
Roberts, Madge Thornall. *The Personal Correspondence of Sam Houston: 1852–1863*. Denton: University of North Texas Press, 2001.
———. *Star of Destiny*. Denton: University of North Texas Press, 1993.
Rogers, Chris. *Bitch Factor*. New York: Bantam, 1998.
Rogers, Mary Beth. *Barbara Jordan: American Hero*. New York: Bantam, 2000 (reprint).
Santiago, Esmeralda. *Almost a Woman*. New York: Perseus Books Group, 1998.
Seale, William. *Sam Houston's Wife: A Biography of Margaret Lea Houston*. Norman: University of Oklahoma Press, 1977.
Stern, Daniel. *In the Country of the Young*. Dallas: Southern Methodist University, 2001.
Valdés-Rodrígues, Alisa. *The Dirty Girls Social Club*. New York: St. Martin's Press, 2003.
Velásquez, Gloria. *I Used to Be a Chicana Superwoman*. Houston: Arte Publico Press, 1997.
Vigil, Evangelina. *Thirty an' Seen a Lot*. Houston: Arte Publico Press, 1987.
Walker, Mary Willis. *The Red Scream*. New York: Crime Line, 1995 (reprint).
Waldman, Stuart, and Tom McNeely. *We Asked for Nothing: The Remarkable Journey of Cabeza de Vaca*. New York: Mikaya Press, 2003.
White, Mel. *Exploring the Great Texas Coastal Birding Trail: Highlights of a Birding Mecca*. Guilford, Conn.: Globe Pequot Press, 2003.
Zagajewski, Adam. *Without End: New and Selected Poems*. New York: Farrar Straus & Giroux, 2003.

The Book Lover Tours East Texas

Beaumont, Bonham, Center, Clarksville, Coldspring, Conroe,
Hemphill, Honey Grove, Huntsville, Jasper, Jefferson, Kilgore,
Kountze, Nacogdoches, Texarkana, Tyler, Uncertain

To anyone whose impressions of Texas have been formed by experiences in other parts of the state, East Texas will come as a surprise. It is not flat, not dry, not wind scoured. It's green. The horizon is usually obscured by towering trees, and the air is often so still, you can hear the mosquitoes buzz. People who grow up in East Texas tend to speak with a drawl, eat catfish and okra, and appreciate a really good ghost story. So close your eyes, take a deep breath, and imagine you are deep in the heart of the Old South, because you are.

From the beginning, Texas was a slave-holding state. The stories that slaves brought with them, like the foods and the songs, infused the culture developing in Texas, enriching the heritage of all. African American writers are letting their voices be heard from this region today, and black characters appear in most of the fiction that is set in East Texas.

That setting, full of the mysteries of forest and swamp, often assumes the stature of a character, too, as it does in the works of William Humphrey, who lived in Clarksville during the 1930s. *Home from the Hill,* his first novel, made Humphrey famous. *The Ordways* followed. He left a proud string of short stories ranging over decades of literary magazines. But his masterpiece was the autobiographical *Farther Off from Heaven,* which tells how, at thirteen, he witnessed the disintegration of his parents' marriage and his father's death. This work captures and preserves perfectly the small East Texas town of the 1930s, as well as the swamps and marshes infested with alligators and cottonmouth moccasins around it.

The gothic overtones of Humphrey's work are echoed today in the best work of Joe Lansdale, whose settings are full of forest and swamp and old, gray tales of murder and madness. *The Bottoms* is the sort of literary horror novel that defies the reader to put it down after the first couple of pages. *A Fine Dark Line* makes coming of age in the 1950s the scariest experience imaginable. Lansdale's works range from such finely wrought accomplishments to raunchy thrillers like *Mucho Mojo*, whose adolescent humor seems to have enormous appeal and a large readership.

Memoirist Mary Karr makes some of Lansdale's characters look tame in the story she tells of her own upbringing in far southeast Texas. *The Liar's Club: A Memoir* and *Cherry* depict a family shaped by alcohol and insanity, with plenty of violence thrown in. Intense, vividly detailed, and, against all bets, funny, these books paint a true human portrait and never lose your interest doing it. And Kathy Hepinstall takes the gothic into the downright bizarre with *The Absence of Nectar*, in which two children are convinced their wicked stepfather intends to do them in. So is the reader.

The lovely stories of J. California Cooper reveal a gentler side of East Texans, especially in the collection called *Some Love, Some Pain, Sometime*. Her narrators sound like women you'd overhear telling their love troubles to a best friend; she catches the cadence and expressions of the East Texas vocal style to perfection. Cooper's works, particularly novels like *Family* and *The Wake of the Wind*, touch on enormous issues—the legacy of slavery, interracial relationships, escaping racism and sexism, how to live a moral life—but her voice is simplicity itself, a pleasure in your mind's ear.

Traditional "women's fiction" of this region includes Elizabeth Forsyth Hailey's *A Woman of Independent Means*, whose heroine is a native of Honey Grove. Most of the novel's actions take place in Dallas, New York, and abroad, but the title character, lively Bess Garner Steed, always reflects the civility of her upbringing among the gentry of Honey Grove. Told in the form of letters written by Bess, this popular novel spans decades of the twentieth century, ending in the 1960s.

Often mislabeled "romance" because of its name, *Love Is a Wild Assault* by Elithe Hamilton Kirkland is actually historical fiction based closely on the life of real Texas pioneer Harriet Potter. Abandoned by a husband who couldn't stay out of gambling salons and left with two children to face starvation in the wilderness, Harriet struggles against obstacles almost unthinkable today, working her way through several husbands and finding adventure and romance among the hardships.

History is a rich resource for the writers of this area. Tribesmen lived in the forests as long as twelve thousand years ago. By AD 1450, the Caddo Indians were building villages, growing maize, and trading with other tribes. Among the many books about the Caddo peoples, one comes from Cecile Elkins Carter, Cultural Liaison for the Caddo Tribe of Oklahoma. Her book draws on archeology, oral history and the writings of early explorers to recreate the history of the author's people and bring it into the modern age in *Caddo Indians: Where We Came From*. F. Todd Smith's *The Caddo Indians: Tribes at the Convergence of Empires, 1542–1854* provides more detail for a crucial period. The story of the tribes that still live as tribes in East Texas is told for readers aged nine to twelve in *The Winding Trail: The Story of the Alabama-Coushatta Indians* by Vivian Fox.

The French explorer LaSalle found an Indian settlement when he arrived in 1685 at Nacogdoches, which is today called "the oldest town in Texas." The Spanish later built a string of missions, including one at Nacogdoches, and by 1779 streets had been laid out for the town. In the next century key events of the War for Texas Independence played out nearby, earning the town another nickname, "The Cradle of Texas Liberty." Nacogdoches has known nine flags during historical times, three of them for republics that never got off the ground. A biography of a city, *The Nacogdoches Texas Story: An Informal History* by Joe Ellis Ericson tells the whole story entertainingly and accurately. The same author offers a more extensive view with *Early East Texas: A History from Indian Settlements to Statehood*.

Sadly, it was in this area near Nacogdoches that in 2003 the shuttle *Columbia* broke apart, sending seven astronauts to their deaths and strewing debris over hundreds of square miles. The full story is told in *Comm Check . . . : The Final Flight of Shuttle Columbia* by Michael Cabbage and William Harwood.

Two books are important to an understanding of the role slavery played in early Texas history. For a close look into the daily lives of people, black and white, when plantation life was flourishing in East Texas, consult Elizabeth Silverthorne's *Plantation Life in Texas*. This author's tone is dispassionate, but her descriptions of the everyday trafficking in human beings will chill any modern reader. Illustrator Charles Shaw adds much visual detail to the account.

Randolph B. Campbell's *An Empire for Slavery: The Peculiar Institution in Texas, 1821–1865* delves into the historical roots of the practice and documents its effects upon the state's political and economic development, including those that led to secession from the Union and the War between the States. *Civil War Texas: A History and a Guide* by Ralph A. Wooster provides an easily absorbed overview of the part Texas played.

Rising from Poverty: Two East Texas Biographies

Both Sam Rayburn and Helen Green were born to poor families, one white, one black, and both rose to prominence in service to others. Helen Green's *East Texas Daughter* tells of her rise from poverty in Tyler to pioneer African American leadership in health and health education administration in Texas. The first black woman admitted into a Dallas school of professional nursing, she worked her way to the top of her profession, constantly breaking ground for the thousands of women who came after her.

In an interview published in *U.S. News and World Report* less than a month before his death, Sam Rayburn, who was born in Bonham in 1882 and served as Speaker of the U.S. House of Representatives longer than any other person, recounted a story. He told how he asked his father for permission to leave home to attend East Texas Normal College in Commerce. It didn't occur to him to ask for money. He counted on figuring out how to get by. As they parted at the train station, his father handed him $25, a year's hard-scraped savings. Understanding the sacrifices his parents had made to raise that money toward his education, he vowed to himself to make sure his family would always have "a place to sleep," as long as they lived. As soon as he had the money, he built a home in Bonham for the family.

You will find this touching account in a most unusual book compiled, edited and published by three remarkable men: H. G. Dulaney, Director of the Rayburn Library; Edward Hake Phillips, Professor of History at Austin College; and MacPhelan Reese, writer-in-residence at the Library. Their 489-page book, *Speak, Mister Speaker*, is an autobiography, the story of Sam Rayburn's life and works, told entirely in his own words as they were selected, ordered and edited by this

A TREAT FOR BOOK LOVERS

The Sam Rayburn Library and Museum

Located on U.S. Highway 56 west of downtown Bonham
903-583-2455

This beautiful columned building preserves artifacts from Sam Rayburn's public and political life, as well as personal memorabilia. The formal office of the Speaker of the House in Washington is replicated splendidly, and artifacts from the White House and Capitol lend an air of authenticity and weight to the exhibit.

To step into the library is to enter the presence of the shapers of not just Texas but the United States. Here is housed a complete congressional record, from the first Congress of 1785 into the sessions of the 1980s. Mr. Sam's personal library is here, the books he used as working tools, as well as his official papers. The University of Texas maintains a presence here. Its **Research and Collections division of the Center for American History** facilitates research.

---

dedicated team. Another standard is *Rayburn: A Biography* by D. C. Bacon and D. B. Hardeman.

The East Texas Oil Patch

In 1901 something happened that would change the State of Texas dramatically. An oil driller who had left a string of dry holes behind him struck oil south of Beaumont. By the 1950s, oil was being produced in 80 percent of the 254 counties of the state. *Giant under the Hill: A History of the Spindletop Oil Discovery at Beaumont, Texas, in 1901* captures the excitement of that first strike and of "the gusher" age that followed it. The book is researched and entertainingly written by three local historians: Jo Ann Stiles, Judith Linsley, and Ellen Rienstra.

Spindletop Boom Days by Paul N. Spellman tells the story through the voices of many who were there, drawing on accounts they left behind.

In 1930, another chapter of the oil saga opened when strikes near Henderson and Kilgore tapped into the East Texas Oil Field, a lake of oil underlying some 140,000 acres of woods, fields, towns, and forests. A fascinating account of the impact of that event is found in James M. Day's *The Black Giant: A History of the East Texas Oil Field and Oil Industry Skulduggery and Trivia*.

HOT SPOTS FOR BOOK LOVERS

East Texas Research Center

R. W. Steen Library
Stephen F. Austin State
University campus
Nacogdoches 75962
936-468-4100
www.lib.sfasu.edu/etrc

Historical, cultural and economic development of East Texas is the major concern of this research library. Holdings reach from collections of rare books to records of the local lumber industry, from forest history to maps, newspapers, photographs, and oral histories of the region. Material includes corporate and family archives and Nacogdoches obituary notices from 1882 to the present. The center also serves as a County Records Regional Historical Depository and holds the university archives and records.

Archives and Special Collections

James G. Gee Library, Texas A&M
University–Commerce
PO Box 3011,
Commerce, Texas 75429
903-886-5720
www.tamu-commerce.edu/library

Unique Material on African Americans, and More

The Special Collections housed here are relatively small but unique. They include the letters and other papers of local figures, including a scrapbook kept by a serviceman during World War I, rare photographs of African Americans from the nineteenth and twentieth centuries, a collection on Texas wildflowers, documents and photographs from the Buckner Children's Home, documents relating to the use of the bateau on Lake Caddo, and more. Records of the university are supplemented by faculty publications. You can access descriptions of the archives directly at the web site.

Beauty and the Book

Kathy L. Patrick, Owner and Stylist
690 FM 728
Jefferson 75657
Take Highway 49 two miles west to
FM 728, and turn right.
903-665-7520

This is surely the only place in Texas where you can buy a signed first edition of a first-class novel and get your hair done while you sit down to read it. Kathy Patrick has just the pizzazz to pull that act off. A long history in the book industry and a keen eye for literary quality don't hurt, either, and Patrick is fast becoming known as a "mover" in the national fiction market. She is the founder of Pulpwood Queens, a grassroots book club that started in her living room and has grown into more than thirty chapters, spreading rapidly from coast to coast, gaining national attention on such shows as Oprah Winfrey's Oxygen Network and *Good Morning America*, and influencing the choices a lot of readers are making about fiction.

Beauty and the Book Salon and Bookstore

A tireless promoter of her business and of reading and literacy, Patrick hosts book signings and author speeches for her customers, takes writers into local schools, and even organizes literary tours, all with the kind of humor that leads club members to wear tiaras and hot-pink t-shirts. Her Beauty and the Book experience is not to be missed.

When asked to name the best books about her part of the world, here are the titles the head Pulpwood Queen listed:

Love Is a Wild Assault by E. H. Kirkland

Jefferson: Riverport to the Southwest by Dr. Fred Tarpley

Dancing in Cadillac Light by National Book Award Winner Kimberly Willis Holt

The Absence of Nectar by Kathy Hepinstall

Screen Door Jesus and Other Stories by Christopher Cook

Life Is So Good by George Dawson

A Piece of Mine by J. California Cooper

The Last of the Honky-Tonk Angels by Marsha Moyer

Roseborough by Jane Roberts Wood

If Nights Could Talk by Marsha Recknagel

The Second Coming of Lucy Hatch by Marsha Moyer

(*continued*)

Scarlett O'Hardy's Gone with the Wind Museum and Gift Shop

Scarlett O'Hardy's Gone with the Wind Museum and Gift Shop

> ### Scarlett O'Hardy's Gone with the Wind Museum
>
> Bobbie Hardy, Owner
>
> 408 Taylor Street
> Jefferson 75657
> 903-665-1939
> www.scarlettohardy.com
>
> Another treasure unique to the town of Jefferson, this small museum and gift shop collects and exhibits memorabilia connected with Margaret Mitchell's 1936 Pulitzer Prize–winning bestseller, *Gone with the Wind*, and the movie that premiered three years later, starring Clark Gable and Vivian Leigh. Any item of any sort associated in any way with these two classics is fair game for inclusion. You will find a replica of the dress Scarlett made from the drapes, a pair of seats from the theater in Atlanta that premiered the film, a signed first edition of the novel, character dolls from the Franklin Mint, and copies of a hundred editions of the novel, plus correspondence, biographies, photographs and books about the author and actors.
>
> *Gone with the Wind* collectors visit the gift shop in search of memorabilia the Hardys are willing to sell: out-of-print copies of the novel, for instance, or books about the *GWTW* phenomenon. While there, visitors can pick up a souvenir spoon featuring Scarlett and Rhett, or maybe a mug, pencil or magnet.
>
> You will find no more knowledgeable a *GWTW* collector than Bobbie Hardy. She loves her subject and loves sharing it with other fans.

Attractions

East Texas is one of the areas where cotton really was king, and antebellum fortunes were made from it. Pastureland full of grazing cows has largely replaced the cotton, but the pace of life around here still hints of southern gentility. Fine old homes and public buildings from the nineteenth century still stand in almost every town, and history seems to be draped in Spanish moss. In the fall, native pecan, oak and gum set the pine forests ablaze with color. In spring, redbud and dogwood decorate the woods.

This is a region of small towns. Beaumont is the largest city, with a population of about 114,000. Folks are proud of their heritage and celebrate it with museums and memorials throughout the region, and many communities host annual festivals. Nature, in the form of forests and lakes and the creatures they harbor, offers opportunities to explore, observe, learn and enjoy the outdoors, from fishing on the Gulf to birding in the Red River Valley.

BEAUMONT

This thriving city by the sea has so many museums you will hear it called the "museum capital of Texas." One of the most charming is the **McFaddin-Ward House**

(409-832-2134) at 1906 McFaddin Avenue, the epitome of early-twentieth-century elegance. Built in the opulent Beaux Arts style, it will transport you to the Gilded Age with its grand staircases and elaborate ornamentation, swags, scrolls, urns and all. The estate's gardens feature forty thousand square feet of lawn and twenty thousand square feet of garden beds.

If that's not enough floral gratification for you, head for the **Beaumont Botanical Gardens** (409-842-3135) and enjoy its old-fashioned roses, camellias and herbs under giant trees draped with Spanish moss. You will find the gardens in Tyrell Park, which also holds **Warren Loose Conservatory** (409-842-3145) and **Cattail Marsh** (409-866-0023), a wetlands area with paths for hiking, biking, and bird-watching. The park lies at the end of Babe Zaharias Drive.

Other museums depicting the lives of prominent people are the **Babe Didrikson Zaharias Museum** (409-833-4622), **John J. French Historic House and Museum** (409-898-3267) at 2985 French Road, and **Edison Plaza Museum** (409-981-3089) at 350 Pine Street.

The history of oil exploration and development sparks the exhibits at **Spindletop/Gladys City Boomtown** (409-835-0823) at Highway 69 and University Drive, a re-creation of the 1901 town that sprang up at the site of the first oil strike, and **Texas Energy Museum** (409-833-5100) at 600 Main Street.

Two nature sanctuaries turn into birding hot spots during spring and fall migrations, since they serve as rest stops for thousands of birds: **High Island Boy Scout Wood and Smith Oaks Nature Sanctuaries** (713-932-1639).

BONHAM, HOME TO MR. SAM

The home at **Sam Rayburn House Historic Site** (903-583-5558) was erected in 1916. In 1934 Rayburn had it remodeled. This place deserves the description its curators have given it—"an authentic time capsule." Fellow Texans Lyndon and Lady Bird Johnson were frequent guests here. The guide will tell you "stories" ranging from the poignant to the quaint about the house and grounds.

CENTER

You can enter **Sabine National Forest** from Texas Highway 87, about eleven miles southeast of town.

COLDSPRING

Enter **Sam Houston National Forest** on its eastern edge from here. Nearby Lake Livingston offers outstanding water recreation and camping sites at Wolf Creek Park (936-653-4312).

CONROE
Lake Conroe Park and Pavilion (936-788-8302) lies about seven miles west of I-45 on Highway 105 West. Swim, fish, hit a volleyball, toss a horseshoe, or have a picnic. If you want to play golf, just look around. Several challenging courses are available to the public. **Jones State Forest** (936-273-2261) has nature trails to explore. It's a popular spot to look for red cockaded woodpecker. Take FM 1375 from I-40 to reach **Sam Houston National Forest**. Several campgrounds and recreational areas provide a full spectrum of activities for the outdoor-minded. You can get on the 128-mile **Lone Star Hiking Trail** here, too. Full details are available from Lake Conroe Area Convention and Visitors Bureau (936-538-7112) at 505 West Davis Street.

CROCKETT
East of town on Texas Highway 7 you can enter **Davy Crockett National Forest**, more than 160,000 acres for camping, picnicking, boating, hiking, and nature watching. Equestrian trails are available, and in early spring, the forest looks as though a snowstorm has hit it along the spectacular Dogwood Trail.

HEMPHILL
Toledo Bend Reservoir, which lies along the eastern edge of **Sabine National Forest**, is the fifth largest man-made reservoir in the country, and it offers water sports, camping, hiking and plenty of wildlife habitat to explore. And it's only part of this huge national resource. Miles of roads are open in the forest for hiking, biking or horseback riding. Watch for that elusive red cockaded woodpecker in here, too.

HUNTSVILLE
Sam Houston's home town has maintained the property and many of the buildings that belonged to the first President of the Republic of Texas and made them available to visitors at **Sam Houston Memorial Museum Complex** (936-294-1832), 1836 Sam Houston Avenue. A charming park offers respite from the Texas sun or a place to picnic in the shade. On the south side of town, you can't miss the **statue** of Sam. The top of his head reaches to almost eighty feet above the ground (936-291-9726). Nearby you'll find the **National Forest** that bears his name.

JASPER
Access to **Angelina National Forest** lies thirteen miles northwest on Highway 63.

JEFFERSON

Antiques and unusual craft and gift shops attract enough people to the village of Jefferson every year to keep more than sixty bed and breakfast accommodations in business, not to mention a couple of historic hotels, assorted cottages and lodges, inns, motels, RV parks and private "vacation homes." This is such a lovely place to spend a couple of days, deep in the piney woods and close to the eerily beautiful Caddo Lake State Park, that it draws people in year-round. Tours of historic homes, a chance to ride in a river boat or a mule-drawn wagon, Scarlett O'Hardy's Gone with the Wind Museum, and the unique Beauty and the Book Salon and Bookstore are other attractions.

KILGORE

At the height of the "gusher age," twelve hundred oil wells were operating here. Some of them still are. **East Texas Oil Museum** (903-983-8295) on the campus of Kilgore College tells the story of oil, how it was discovered, produced, and how it affected the lives of East Texans.

KOUNTZE

This tiny town is the gateway into the Big Thicket, the three-hundred-thousand-acre remnant of forests that were once ten times that size and today attracts canoers, hikers and bird-watchers into the swampy woods. The Alabama-Coushatta Indians make their home in the Big Thicket on a reservation near Livingston.

NACOGDOCHES

The **Mast Arboretum** (936-468-4343) on the Stephen F. Austin State University campus will delight the garden lover in you. It blooms most of the year, with azaleas and camellias in cooler weather and native wildflowers, colorful perennials and roses when the weather warms up. A Shade Garden provides a haven for exotic gingers and ferns, and pileated woodpeckers nest in the area.

Since this is the oldest town in the state, take time to visit the **Old Stone Fort** (936-468-2408), also on the campus. It was built in 1936 as a replica of the 1779 home of the city's founder, made of stones salvaged from the original.

TYLER

Flowers are the trademark of this part of the state and especially of Tyler, "The Rose Capital of the World," where the twenty-two-acre **Municipal Rose Garden** (903-531-1212) at 1900 W. Front Street vies for the title of the world's largest public planting of roses. In the spring, an **Azalea and Flower Trail** (800-235-5712) gets all the attention as homeowners open their gardens for tours, showing off not only their azaleas but dogwood, tulip, and wisteria, too.

UNCERTAIN

Any of the 150 folks in Uncertain can point you to **Caddo Lake State Park** for camping, fishing, hiking and nature watching, show you where to rent a canoe for plying the calm waters under moss-draped cypress trees, or tell you how to get a ride on the steamboat *Graceful Ghost*.

The Reading Tour

Bacon, D. C., and D. B. Hardeman. *Rayburn: A Biography*. Austin: Texas Monthly Press, 1987.
Cabbage, Michael, and William Harwood. *Comm Check . . . : The Final Flight of Shuttle Columbia*. New York: Free Press, 2004
Campbell, Randolph B. *An Empire for Slavery: The Peculiar Institution in Texas, 1821–1865*. Baton Rouge: Louisiana State University Press, 1991 (reprint).
Carter, Cecile Elkins. *Caddo Indians: Where We Came From*. Norman: University of Oklahoma Press, 2001.
Cook, Christopher. *Screen Door Jesus and Other Stories*. 2nd ed. Austin: Host Publications, 2001.
Cooper, J. California. *Family*. Garden City, N.Y.: Anchor Press, 1991.
———. *A Piece of Mine: Stories*. Garden City, N.Y.: Anchor Press, 1991.
———. *Some Love, Some Pain, Sometime*. Garden City, N.Y.: Anchor Press, 1996.
———. *The Wake of the Wind*. Garden City, N.Y.: Anchor Press, 1999.
Dawson, George. *Life Is So Good*. Minneapolis: Econo-Clad Books, 2001.
Day, James M. *The Black Giant: A History of the East Texas Oil Field and Oil Industry Skulduggery and Trivia*: Austin: Eakin Publications, 2003.
Dulaney, H. G., Edward Hake Phillips, and MacPhelan Reese. *Speak, Mister Speaker*. Bonham, Tex.: Sam Rayburn Foundation, 1978.
Ericson, Ellis. *The Nacogdoches Texas Story: An Informal History*. Bowie, Md.: Heritage Books, 2003.
Green, Helen. *East Texas Daughter*. Fort Worth: Texas Christian University Press, 2003.
Fox, Vivian. *The Winding Trail: The Story of the Alabama-Coushatta Indians*. Austin: Eakin Publications, 1995.
Hailey, Elizabeth Forsyth. *A Woman of Independent Means*. New York: Viking Press, 1987.
Hepinstall, Kathy. *The Absence of Nectar*: New York: Putnam Publishing Group, 2001.
Holt, Kimberly Willis. *Dancing in Cadillac Light*. New York: Putnam Publishing Group Juvenile, 2001.
Humphrey, William. *Farther Off from Heaven*. New York: Random House, 1977.
———. *Home from the Hill*. New York: Random House, 1960.

———. *The Ordways*. New York: Random House, 2000.
Karr, Mary. *Cherry*. New York: Viking Press, 2000.
———. *The Liar's Club: A Memoir*. New York: Viking Press, 1999.
Kirkland, Elithe Hamilton. *Love Is a Wild Assault*. New York: Doubleday, 2000 (reprint).
Lansdale, Joe. *The Bottoms*. New York: Mysterious Press, 2000.
———. *A Fine, Dark Line*. New York: Mysterious Press, 2003.
———. *Mucho Mojo*. New York: Mysterious Press, 1994.
Linsley, Judith Walker, Ellen Walker Rienstra, and Jo Ann Stiles. *Giant under the Hill: A History of the Spindletop Oil Discovery at Beaumont, Texas, in 1901*. Austin: Texas State Historical Association, 2002.
Mitchell, Margaret. *Gone with the Wind*. New York: Scribner, 1936.
Moyer, Marsha. *The Last of the Honky-Tonk Angels*. New York: William Morrow, 2003.
———. *The Second Coming of Lucy Hatch*. New York: Avon, 2003.
Recknagel, Marsha. *If Nights Could Talk*. New York: Thomas Dunne, 2001.
Smith, F. Todd. *The Caddo Indians: Tribes at the Convergence of Empires, 1542–1854*. College Station: Texas A&M Press, 1995.
Spellman, Paul N. *Spindletop Boom Days*. College Station: Texas A&M Press, 2001.
Tarpley, Fred. *Jefferson: Riverport to the Southwest*. Austin: Eakin Press, 1983.

✶PHOTO CREDITS✶

Listed in order of appearance:

Photo of Jane Roberts Wood courtesy of Dub Wood
Photo of Elmer Kelton courtesy of Elmer Kelton
Photo of Lucia St. Clair Robson courtesy of Doug Coulson
Photos of the Robert E. Howard Home courtesy of Cross Plains Project Pride. Artwork by Mark Schultz and Manuel Carrasco, reproduced with permission
Photo of Leon C. Metz courtesy of Leon C. Metz
Photo of Front Street Books storefront and logo artwork courtesy of Jean Hardy
Photo of The History Merchant courtesy of Richard Hazlett
Photo of Sherrie McLeroy courtesy of Bill McLeRoy
Photo of the Armstrong Browning Library in Waco copyright by the Waco Convention and Visitor Bureau, used by permission
Photo of Books & Java Bookstore in Lake Canyon courtesy of Michael Doyle
Photo of Stephen Harrigan by Shannon McIntyre, used by permission
Photo of Murder by the Book by Walter Bistline, courtesy of David Thompson
Photo of Beauty and the Book Salon and Bookstore courtesy of Kathy Patrick
Photos of Scarlett O'Hardy's Museum and Gift Shop by Robert Miller, courtesy of Bobbie L. Hardy

INDEX

Abell Library Center at Austin College, 70
Abilene attractions, 28–30
Adorno, Rolena, 152
Ajilvsgi, Geyata, xii
Alamo, 122–26, 134, 136
Albert, Susan Wittig, and Bill, 98
Albert and Ethel Hertzstein Library, 167
Allender, Michael, 39
alligators, 157
Alpine, 48
Alter, Judy, 68, 150
Amarillo attractions, 9–10
Amarillo Slim, x, 6–7
Ambrose, Stephen E., 69
Anahuac, 157
Anderson, Christopher, 42
Andrews, Jean, 157
Apaches, 46
Aransas Pass, 158
Archer City, 19, 31
Archive of the Vietnam Conflict, 8
Archives of the Big Bend, 48
Arlington, 80
Armstrong Browning Library, 73–74
Arnulfo L. Oliveira Library, Brownsville, 130
assassination of John F. Kennedy, 67
Austin: attractions, 107–10; reading and writing, 102–07; Treats for Book Lovers, 103
Autry, Gene, 72, 79

Bacon, D. C., 177
Ball, Eva, 46

Barker, Wendy, 126
Barr, Nevada, 43–44
Barrett, Neal, Jr., 100
Barthelme brothers, 147
Barzun, Jacques, 126
batwatching sites, 112–13, 132, 133
Beal, Chandra, 101
Bean, Judge Roy, 46, 55
Beaumont, 181–82
Beaumont attractions, 181
Beauty and the Book Salon and Bookstore, 178–79
Bedichek, Roy, 41, 102
Bemelmans, Ludwig, 41
Berry, Betsey, 102
Berry, Venise, 147
Bertrand, Diane Gonzales, 128
Biderman, Rose G., 67
Biffle, Kent, x
Big Bend: attractions, 37–41, 48; fiction, 42–45; history, 37–38; natural history, 39–41; nonfiction, 45–49; Treats for Book Lovers, 47–49
Big Bend National Park, 45, 48, 49–50
Bigley, John, 129
Bird, Sarah, 128
birdwatching, 12, 38, 40–41, 50–51, 78, 109, 110, 132, 133, 144, 156, 158, 167, 168
Bishop, Jim, 67
Blagg-Huey Library at Texas Woman's University, 75
Bonham, 177, 182

Booked Up, Inc., 31
Books & Java, 107
Border Heritage Center, 47
Borthwick, J. S., 127
Bowie, James, 123–24
Boyd, Paula, 24
Bracketville, 134
Brakefield, J. F., 67
Brandon, Jay, 126
Brazoria County attractions, 158–59
Broadrick, Annette, 100
Brown, Sandra, 63–64, 102, 127
Brownsville attractions, 134
Brownwood, 30
Buck, Frank, 69–70, 79
buffalo (bison), 16, 22
Buffalo Gap Historic Village, 29
Buffalo Soldiers, 18, 46, 53, 165
Burks, Brian, 46
Burnet, 114
Bush, Barbara, 57, 150
Bush, George H. W., 41–42, 57, 106
Bush, George W., 41–42, 57, 150–51

Cabbage, Michael, 175
cactus, 40
Campbell, Randolph B., 150, 176
Caprock Canyons State Park and Trailway, 11
Caravantes, Peggy, 150
Caro, Robert A., 100–101
Carter, Cecile Elkins, 175
Castel, Albert E., 71
Castillo, Rafael, 102
caves of the Hill Country, 113
Central Library at University of Texas at Arlington, 77
Chappell, Henry, 5
Charles, Patrick, 152
Chemerka, William R., 124–25
Chillicothe, 19, 32
Cisneros, Sandra, 126
Civil War, 17–20, 62, 71
C. L. Sonnichsen Special Collections, 47
Comanches, 15–16, 21–24, 31, 95
Conan the Barbarian, 26
Connally, Nellie, 67
Conroe, 183
Cook, Elizabeth, 150
Cooper, J. California, 174
Corpus Christi attractions, 159–60
cowboy poetry, 11, 26
Cox, Mike, 45
Crider, Bill, 99
Crockett, city of, 183

Crockett, Davy, 123–24
Cross Plains, 30
Cynthia McDonald, 147

Dallas-Fort Worth Metroplex (DFW): attractions, 79–83, 84–88; fiction, 63–65; history, 62–68; Kennedy assassination, 67
Davis, William C., 124
Day, James M., 177
DeGolyer Library at Southern Methodist University, 76
Denison, 61, 68, 77–78
Denton, 75, 83
Dobie, J. Frank, 102
Douglas MacArthur Academy of Freedom, 30
Dubose, Lou, 42
Dudley, Karen, 156
Duke, Cordia Sloan, 3–4
Dulaney, H. G., 176
Dyess Air Force Base, 29

East Texas: attractions,181–85; background, 173; biographies, 176; fiction, 174; history, 175, 177; Hot Spots for Book Lovers, 178–81
East Texas Research Center, 178
Eisenhower, Dwight David, 68
Eisenhower, John S. D., 69
El Paso: attractions, 51–52; Bush family, 41–42; fiction, 42–43; natural history, 40–41; nonfiction, 45–46; overview, 37–39; Treats for Book Lovers, 47
Erickson, John R., 4–5
Ericson, Joe Ellis, 175
Eugene McDermott Library at University of Dallas, 75
Evans, Douglas B., 40
Evans, James, 39

Fehrenbach, T. R., 22–23, 126
Ferber, Edna, 43
Fitzgerald, Ken, 65
Fleming, Carl M., 40
Flores, Dan, 9
Flynn, Robert, 16, 19
Fort Concho National Historic Landmark, 32
Fort Davis attractions, 53–54
Fort Parker, 21, 22
Fort Richardson, 23, 28
Fort Worth attractions, 84–88
forts. *See* Texas Forts Trail
Fox, Vivian, 175
Frantz, Joe B., 3–4
Fredericksburg attractions, 114

Freed, Jan, 148
Friedman, Kinky, 99
Frontier Texas, 28
Front Street Books, 48, 49
Frum, David, 42

Gainesville, 69, 79
Galveston: attractions, 161–63; history, 152, 154–55; Treats for Book Lovers, 162
Gerhart, Ann, 42
Gilb, Dagoberto, 44
Gipson, Fred, 97, 106, 117
Globe of the Great Southwest, 56
Goliad, 135
Gonzales, Ray, 44,
Goodnight, Charles, ix, 2–3, 8
Gordon, Alex, 72
Govenar, Alan B., 67
Graham, Don, xii, 102
Gray, A. W., 64
Great Texas Coastal Birding Trail, 144, 156, 158
Great Storm of Galveston, 154–55
Green, Chloe, 64
Green, Helen, 176
Gregory, John, 148
Gregory, Sarah, 64
Grey, Zane, 24, 45
Guadalupe Mountains National Park, 43, 54–55
Gulf Coast Treats for Book Lovers, 167

Hacker, Margaret Schmidt, 21
Hagan, William T., 21
Hailey, Elizabeth Forsyth, 174
Haley, J. Evetts, ix, 2–3, 47
Haley, James L., 150
Haley Memorial Library, 47
Hank the Cowdog, 4–5
Hardeman, D. B., 177
Hardin, Stephen L., 124, 125
Harrington, Stephens, 125
Hart, Carolyn, 127
Harwood, William, 175
Haseloff, Cynthia, 23
Hemphill, 183
Henderson, Arleen Kilgore, 44
Hepinstall, Kathy, 174
Highland Lakes, 110–11
Hill Country: attractions of town and village, 114–19; biographies, 100–101; caves, 112–14; lakes and parks, 110–12; overview, 95–96; writers and books, 96–100
Hillsboro, 88
Hinojosa, Rolando, 129
Hirsch, Edward, 147

History Merchant, The, 66
Houston, city of: attractions, 163–66; biographies, 148–52; history, 144–45; literary events, 145–46, 165; Special Treats for Book Lovers, 153–54, 167
Houston, Sam, 98, 143, 148, 150, 183
Houston literary events, 145
Howard, Robert E., xi, 26–27, 30
Huffaker, Bob, et al., 67
Huffines, Alan C., 125
hummingbirds, 41, 50, 158
Humphrey, William, 173–74
Huntsville, 144, 183
Hyams, Joe, 151
Hylton, Hilary, 101

Ingram, 115
Institute of Texan Cultures, 130
Irving, 88
Ivins, Molly, 42

James, Frank and Jessie, 45–46, 70–71
Jefferson, 178–81, 184
John B. Coleman Library, 154
Johnson, Lyndon Baines, 100–101
Johnson, Terry C., 5
Johnson City attractions, 116
Jordan, Barbara, 151–52

Kahn, Sharon, 99
Kaplan, John, 67
Karr, Mary, 174
Kelton, Elmer, 16–18, 28, 102, 155
Kemp's ridley sea turtle. *See* sea turtles
Kerrville attractions, 116–17
King Ranch, 166
Kiowas, 23, 31
Kirkland, Elithe Hamilton, 174
Kissinger, Rosemary, 22
Koresh, David, 73

Lafitte, Jean, 152, 154
Laguna Atascosa, 169
Langtry-Del Rio attractions, 55
Lansdale, Joe, 174
Laredo attractions, 135
Larsen, Eric, 155
Lea, Tom, 42
League of Texas Writers (Texas Writers League), 102–3, 126
Leckie, William H., 46
Lee, Jim, 68
Le May, Alan, 23–24
Lightfoot, D. J., 20

Lindsey, David, 148, 150
Linsley, Judith, 177
Long Barrack Museum and Library, 136
Lost Maples Natural Area, 96, 119
Loving, Oliver, 3
Lubbock attractions, 11
Luciano Guajardo Collection in Laredo, 131
Lyndon B. Johnson State Park, 119

Marathon, 49
Marfa, 37, 44, 55–56
Martin, Allana, 44
Mary and Jeff Bell Library, 167
Mary Coutts Burnett Library at Texas Christian University, 76
McAllen, 135
McCarthy, Cormac, 42–43
McCathern, Gerald, 6
McDonald, Walt, 26
McDowell, Robert, 26
McKinney, 89
McLeRoy, Sherrie S., 68, 71
McMurtry, Larry, xii, 16, 19, 22, 28, 31, 42, 75
McNaught, Judith, 148
McNay Art Museum Library, 130
McNeely, Tom, 152
Meinzer, Wyman, 4, 39
Menard, Valerie, 152
Meredith, D. R., ix, 6–7
Mesquite, 89
Metz, Leon C., xii, 45–46
Michener, James, 96, 97–98, 101, 148
Midland-Odessa: attractions, 56–58; Bush family, 41–42; Treat for Book Lovers, 58
Mission, 135
Moffett Library at Midwestern University, 33
Moorcock, Michael, 99
Moore, Laurie, 64
Moreland, Peggy, 100
Murder by the Book, 149
Museum of the Big Bend, 48
mustangs, 15–16
Myers, John, 124

Nacogdoches, 175
National Cowboy Symposium, 11
native plants, 9, 40, 55, 109, 115, 132, 134, 144, 156
Navarro, Jose Antonio, 126
Neeley, Bill, 21
Nelson, Barney, 41
New Braunfels attractions, 118
New York Times Bestseller List, 25, 63, 97, 126, 127, 148

Nocona, Peta, 20
Nuestra Palabra, 146
Nye, Naomi Shihab, 126

O'Banyon, Constance, 127
O'Henry. *See* Porter, William Sydney
Oñate, Don Juan de, 15

Padre Island, 155
Padre Island National Seashore, 160–61
Palo Duro Canyon, 2, 7, 12
Panhandle and Plains: attractions, 9–12; fiction, 4–7; history, 1–4; natural history, 7–8, 11–12
Paredes, Américo, 129
Parent, Laurence, 39
Parker, Cynthia Ann, 3, 20–21
Parker, Janice, 156
Parker, Quanah, 15, 20–22
Parmenter, Paris, 129
Pasadena, 168
Patoski, Joe Nick, 39
Peterson, Jim, 40
Peterson, Paul R., 71
Phillips, Edward Hake, 176
Phillips, Marti, 154
Phillips, Robert, 147
Port Aransas, 168
Porter, Katherine Anne, xi, 30, 96–97, 117
Porter, William Sydney, 97, 98, 103, 108
Porter Henderson Library, 33
Port Isabel, 168
Powell, A. Michael, 40
Preston, Amarillo Slim. *See* Amarillo Slim
Pulitzer Prize, 18, 42, 43, 97, 98, 101, 145–47

Quanah, 30
Quantrill, William Clarke, 70–71

Rafferty, Robert, 79
Ramon, Alberto, 127
Rathjen, Frederick W., 4
Rau, Margaret, 72
Rayburn, Sam, 176–77
Reavis, Dick J., 73
Red River Valley, 24
Reese, MacPhelan, 176
Reynolds, Loys, 79
Richmond, 168
Rienstra, Ellen, 177
Rio Grande Valley: attractions, 132–36; Treats for Book Lovers, 130–32
Rio Hondo, 169
Riordan, Rick, 127
Roberts, Madge Thornall, 148

Robson, Lucia St. Clair, 21, 22
Rockport-Fulton, 169
Rodrígues, Alisa Valdés. *See* Valdés-Rodrígues, Alisa
Rogers, Carolyn, 127
Rogers, Mary Beth, 151
Romance Writers of America, 25, 147–48
Romulo Munguia Library, Universidad Nacional, 129
Rose, Francis L., 9
Rosenberg, 169
Rosenberg Library, 162
Rossie, Cam, 101

San Angelo attractions, 32
San Antonio: attractions, 136–40; history, 121–26; missions, 136–37; Treats for Book Lovers, 129–31; writers, 123–29
Sanders, Leonard, 68
Sanders, Marc, 65
Sanderson, Jim, 127
San Jacinto Battleground, 144, 166
San Marcos attractions, 118–19
Santa Anna, 122–23, 128, 154
Santanta, 23
Saunders, George, 20
Saylor, Steven, 98
Scarlett O'Hardy's Gone with the Wind Museum, xi, 180–81
Seale, William, 148
sea turtles, 155, 156, 161
Shakespeare on the Plains, 56
Sherman, 61, 70–71, 77–78
Shrake, Edwin, 98
Silverthorne, Elizabeth, 175
Sizemore, Evelyn, 156
Skiles, Jack, 46
Smith, F. Todd, 24, 175
Sonnichsen Special Collections (C. L.), 47
South Padre Island, 169
South Texas Archives at Texas A&M University, Kingsville, 131
South Texas Plains, 121–22
Space Center Houston, 159
Spearing, Darwin, 32
Special Collections, James G. Gee Library, 178
Special Collections at M. D. Anderson Library, 154
Special Collections at Texas Southern University, 154
Special Collections at University of Texas at San Antonio, 130
specialty libraries, using, xii
Spellman, Paul N., 177

Spencer, William Browning, 99
Spur Award, 18, 21, 23
Sterling, Bruce, 100
Stern, Daniel, 147
Stiles, Jo Ann, 177
Stokes, Donald and Lillian, 40
Strandtmann, Russell W., 9
Strieber, Whitley, 127
Sue and Radcliffe Killam Library, Laredo, 131
Swanson, Doug, 65
Swindle, Howard, 64

Tennant, Alan, 39
Texas Almanac, xii
Texas Book Festival, 102
Texas Forts Trail, 28
Texas Rangers, 15–16, 17, 19, 45, 90–91
Texas Tech University Southwest Collection, 8
Thibodeau, David, 73
Thomas, Jodi, x, 6, 25
Thompson, Ronda, x, 6
Tinkle, Lon, 124
Tioga, 72, 79
Travis, William Barrett, 122–26
Troncoso, Sergio, 44
Turkey, x, 12
Tveten, John and Gloria, 156
Tveten, John L., xii, 156
12th Armored Division Memorial Museum, 29

University of Texas–Pan American, 131
Utley, Robert M., 45
Utopia Rescue Ranch, 99

Vaca, Cabeza de, 152
Valdés-Rodrígues, Alisa, 146
Victorio, 46

Waco, 72–73, 89–91
Waldman, Stuart, 152
Walker, Mary Willis, 98–99
Waltz, Jon R., 67
water experiences, 110–12
Wauer, Roland H., 40, 41
Weatherford, 92
Webb, Walter Prescott, 4, 41, 45
Western Writers of America, 18, 21
Whatley, Bruce, 72
White, Mel, 156
whooping crane, 155–56
Wichita Falls, 19, 25, 33–34
William A. Blakley Library at University of Dallas, 76

Williams, Docia Schultz, 128–29
Willis Library at University of North Texas, 75
Wills, Bob, x, 12
Winegarten, Ruth, 65
Wood, Jane Roberts, ix, 5–6
Woodson Research Center, 153

Wooster, Ralph A., 176
World Birding Center Sites, 133
Wright, Stuart A., 73

Zaboly, Gary S.,125
Zagajewski, Adam, 147
Zimmer, Barry R., 40